RHYMING WORD FUN

Write one-syllable words that rhyme with "dip." Remembe

end with the "ip" sound. How many words can you make?

THAT'S LOGICAL

Here are two logic puzzles for you to try. Use the charts to help as you think.

The tennis team drew names to see who would be partners in a doubles game. Can you find the partners?

Morgan drew the name of a boy who is called by his nickname, Bill. Brenda's partner has a name that starts with the same letter as hers. Lindsey's partner is not Logan.

Doubles Partners				
	Ellsworth	William	Logan	Brian
Brenda				
Karina				
Lindsey				
Morgan				

Who is each player's partner?

__________ Brenda

__________ Karina

__________ Lindsey

__________ Morgan

The Davis children are comparing their ages. Margie is 9 years old. Susan is older than Margie. Hannah is younger than Susan. Joe is the oldest. No two children are the same age. Can you find their ages?

	Names			
Ages	Margie	Susan	Joe	Hannah
8 years old				
9 years old				
10 years old				
11 years old				

What is each child's age?

__________ Margie

__________ Susan

__________ Joe

__________ Hannah

RHYMING RIDDLES

Hink-pinks are one-syllable words that rhyme. Read each riddle.
Think of words that rhyme with the boldfaced words and answer the riddles.
Write the words on the lines to make hink-pinks! The first one has been done for you.

Where does a dandelion come from?

It grows from a **weed** seed.

Where does water from the clouds go?

It goes down a **rain** ________________.

What do you need if your shorts get wet?

You need a **spare** ________________.

What do you call a gloomy Monday?

It is a **gray** ________________.

What is another name for a sunny place?

It is called a **hot** ________________.

What do you get if you put ice in the lake?

You get a **cool** ________________.

What do you call a covering for a hurt knee?

It is a **scratch** ________________.

What do you get if you dam up a river?

You get a **fake** ________________.

VACATION DAY

Can you find at least 10 things that are not right in this picture?
Circle the things you find.

RHYME TIME

Write the correct rhyming word pair to answer each riddle.

LOUD DUCKY TUB DAMP TUNE CROWD FUNNY LAMP SICK BUNNY CUB LUCKY CHICK JUNE

Where does a baby bear take a bath? ____________________

What is a summer song? ____________________

What is a light left out in the rain? ____________________

What is a rabbit that tells jokes? ____________________

What is a baby bird with the flu? ____________________

What is a noisy group of people? ____________________

What is a bird that wins a prize? ____________________

THE ROCK STARS

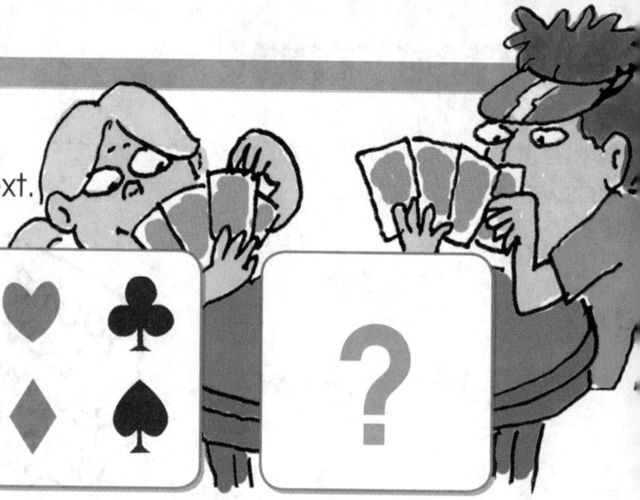

Look at the first row of symbols.
Circle A, B, C, or D to show what comes next.

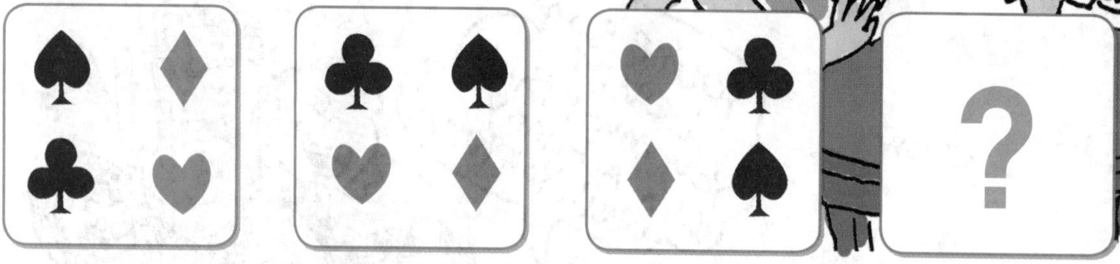

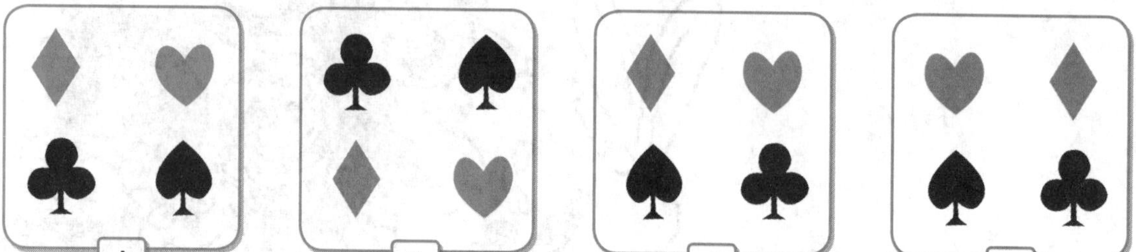

?

A

B

C

D

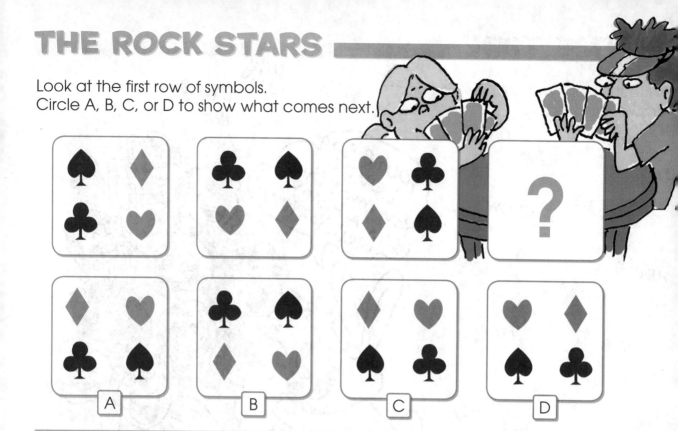

Which number in each line is the odd one out? Circle each one.

18 20 24 30 36 38

125 129 133 137 151

FIELD TRIP TO WASHINGTON, D.C.

Washington, D.C., is the capital of the United States. Here are some of the sights visitors see in Washington, D.C. How many can you identify? Write each letter in the correct box.

Something Extra

Washington, D.C., is the only U.S. city that is not part of a state. D.C. stands for "District of Columbia."

A. United States Capitol Building
B. Supreme Court Building
C. Vietnam Veterans Memorial
D. National Air and Space Museum
E. White House
F. Jefferson Memorial
G. Lincoln Memorial
H. Washington Monument and Reflecting Pool
I. Original Smithsonian Institution Building

KNOWLEDGE TEST

Do you know your facts? Read each sentence. Circle true or false.

Pablo Picasso was a famous baseball player.

true **false**

To play croquet, you need mallets, balls, and wickets.

true **false**

A portrait is a painting, drawing, or photograph of scenery.

true **false**

Origami is the Japanese art of paper cutting.

true **false**

A goal in a soccer game counts as one point.

true **false**

An opera is a play with words that are sung.

true **false**

Mars is closer to the Sun than Earth is.

true **false**

ADDING UP THE FACTS

Read the question and guess the best answer. Then solve the problem. The sum gives you the correct answer to the questions.

What mammal can eat 250–500 pounds of plants in a day?

giraffe	214	246
elephant	314	+ 68
alligator	304	______

______

What animal can lay 400 eggs at a time?

dolphin	765	478
cobra	745	+ 367
leaf-cutter ant	845	______

______

The world's fastest animal can travel over 200 miles per hour. What is it?

peregrine falcon	777	179
bald eagle	677	+ 598
cheetah	667	______

______

The world's largest animal can weigh over 150 tons and be 110 feet long. What is it?

gray whale	1,054	1,456
blue whale	2,064	+ 608
killer whale	2,054	______

______

What fish can swim 68 miles per hour?

blue shark	5,298	2,769
swordfish	6,208	+ 3,539
sailfish	6,308	______

______

What type of bird can fly backwards?

hummingbird	12,031	9,782
robin	11,921	+ 2,249
blue jay	12,931	______

______

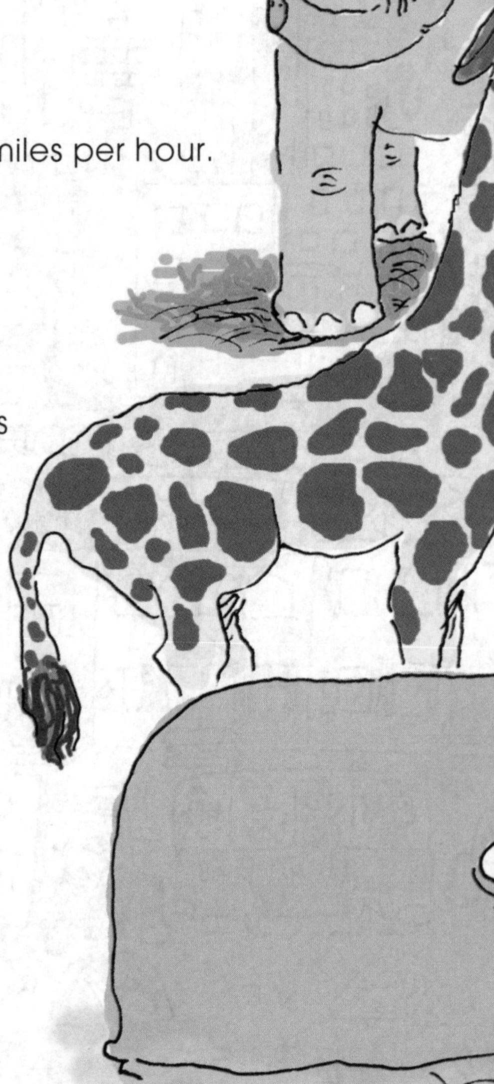

DOWNTOWN

These two downtown scenes are almost alike.
Can you find at least 10 things that make the two cities different?
Circle the things you find.

THE COUNTY FAIR

Find and circle the hidden pictures.

3 pizza slices

4 apples

5 birds

5 bananas

9 tickets

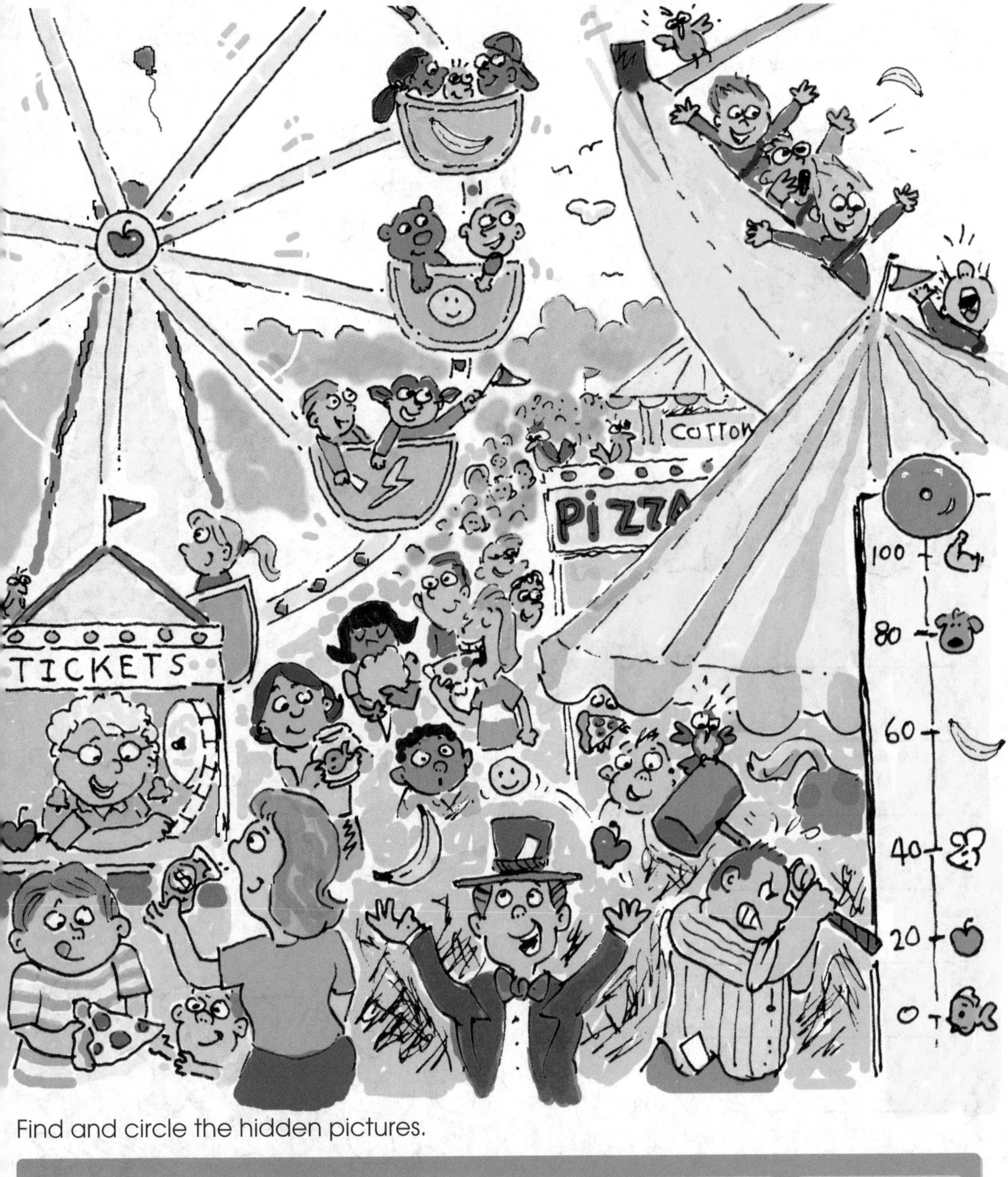

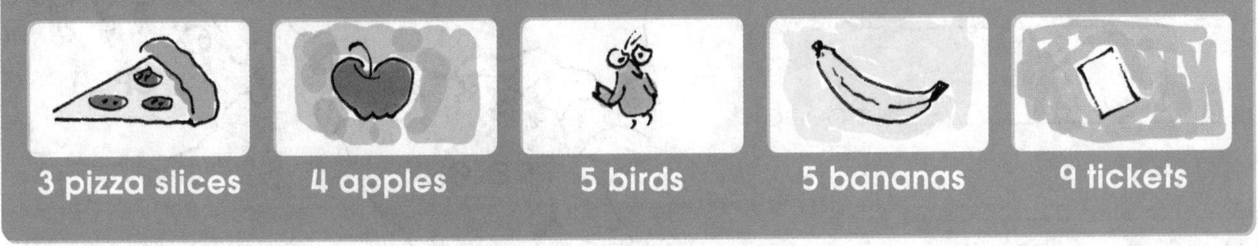

BOUND TOGETHER

A group of dolphins is called a pod, and a group of lions is called a pride. On the lines below, write the group words that go with the animals, people, or objects.

HERD

FLOCK

TEAM

FLEET

CROWD

a ____________________ of birds

a ____________________ of ball players

a ____________________ of drawers

a ____________________ of cards

a ____________________ of ants

a ____________________ of flowers

a ____________________ of ships

a ____________________ of cows

a ____________________ of people

a ____________________ of fish

DECK

BED

SCHOOL

CHEST

COLONY

PERFECT PATTERNS

Draw the missing pictures to complete the patterns.

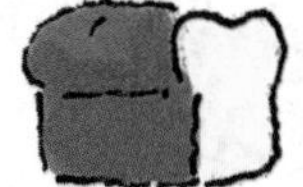
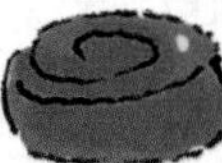

PICK A PRIZE

You have 225 tickets to spend on prizes.
Can you spend the exact number of tickets you have?
Circle the items you'll get.

THEY SOUND THE SAME!

Homophones are words that sound alike, but have different meanings and spellings. To solve this puzzle, write the correct homophone for each clue word. The first one has been done for you.

2. POOR

Across

2. pour
3. paws
5. pedal
8. passed
9. seas
10. plain
11. stake
13. ant
14. deer
15. meet
16. cellar

Down

1. poor
2. peddle
3. past
4. sees
5. pause
6. dear
7. seller
10. plane
11. steak
12. meat
13. aunt

NUMBERS & NAMING WORDS

Read the poem. Write the numbers on the lines.

Totally True
Part of Hong Kong borders China. Hong Kong also has more than 200 islands.

One man on his way to Hong Kong ________
Took three hundred good friends along.
He went with six dancing bears ________
And two hundred new chairs. ________
He brought one hundred tan dogs ________
Along with five hundred green frogs. ________
His twelve sons wore forty-eight shirts. ________________
Three daughters had thirty-three skirts. ________________

Write each naming word from the poem under the correct heading.

PEOPLE	PLACES	ANIMALS	THINGS

BAKING DILEMMA

Chef Dexter has a recipe for a fantastic new cake. After mixing all the ingredients just right, he discovered that the oven won't work! Follow the directions in each box until you reach the finish. Then you can tell Chef Dexter why the oven isn't working.

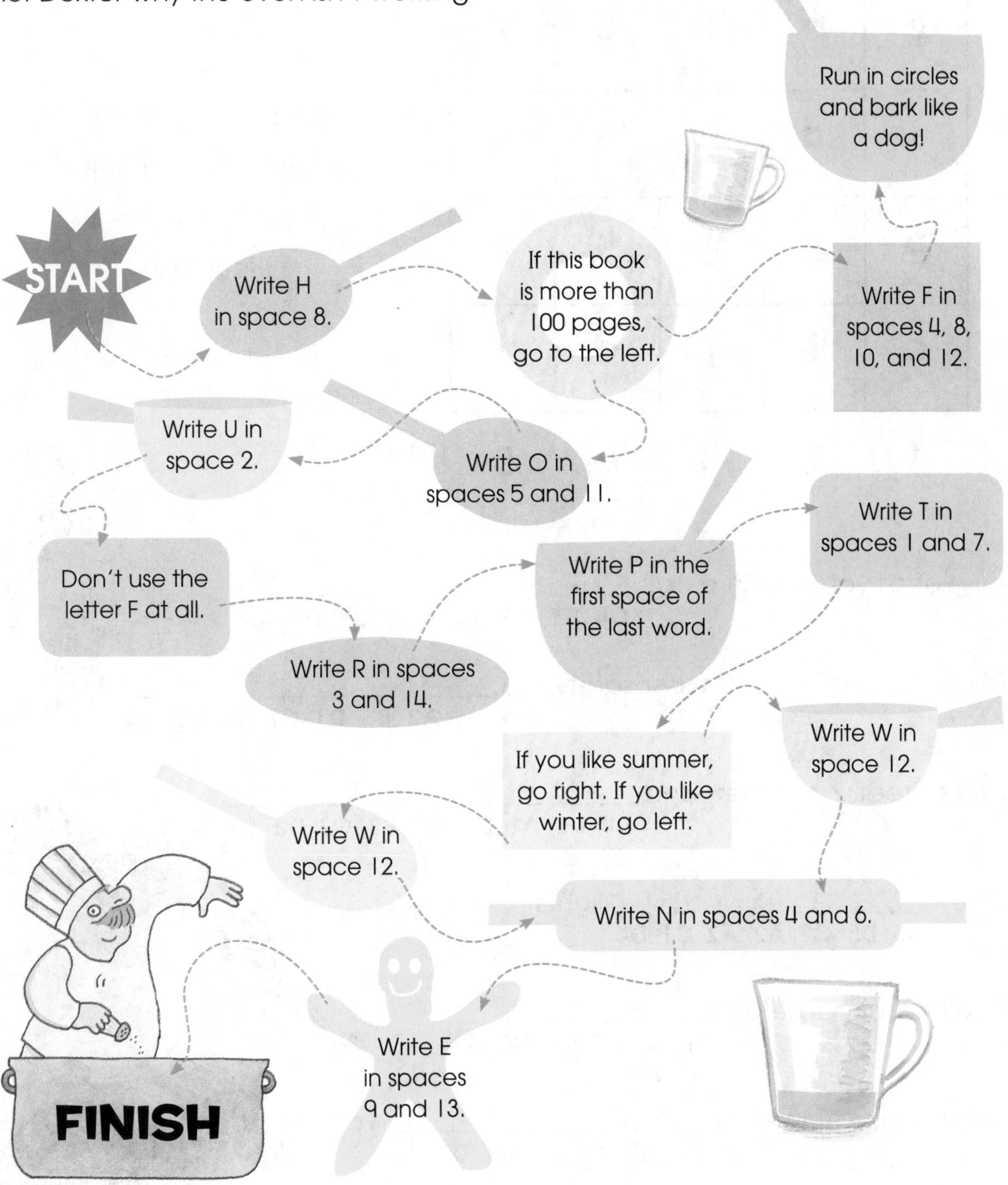

START
Write H in space 8.
If this book is more than 100 pages, go to the left.
Write F in spaces 4, 8, 10, and 12.
Run in circles and bark like a dog!
Write O in spaces 5 and 11.
Write U in space 2.
Don't use the letter F at all.
Write R in spaces 3 and 14.
Write P in the first space of the last word.
Write T in spaces 1 and 7.
If you like summer, go right. If you like winter, go left.
Write W in space 12.
Write W in space 12.
Write N in spaces 4 and 6.
Write E in spaces 9 and 13.
FINISH

What does Chef Dexter need to do to get the oven to work?

1	2	3	4	5	6	7	8	9	10	11	12	13	14

SAFETY DOUBLE-CHECK

Use the grid to solve each clue.

D	g	p	l	c	r
C	i	a	n	s	u
B	b	y	w	k	e
A	o	f	j	d	t
	1	2	3	4	5

traffic protect
injury seat belt
safety crosswalks
lifeguard

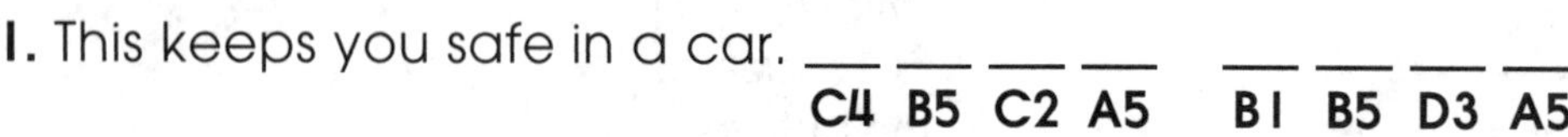

1. This keeps you safe in a car. __ __ __ __ __ __ __ __
C4 B5 C2 A5 B1 B5 D3 A5

2. This person helps with water safety. __ __ __ __ __ __ __ __ __
D3 C1 A2 B5 D1 C5 C2 D5 A4

3. Cross streets at corners and __ __ __ __ __ __ __ __ __ __.
D4 D5 A1 C4 C4 B3 C2 D3 B4 C4

4. Obey __ __ __ __ __ __ __ lights.
A5 D5 C2 A2 A2 C1 D4

5. A fall might cause an __ __ __ __ __ __.
C1 C3 A3 C5 D5 B2

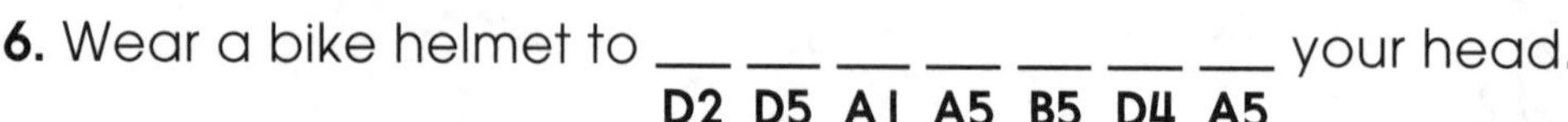

6. Wear a bike helmet to __ __ __ __ __ __ __ your head.
D2 D5 A1 A5 B5 D4 A5

7. "Do not pet strange animals" is a __ __ __ __ __ __ rule.
C4 C2 A2 B5 A5 B2

WEATHER OR NOT

Color the weather words in the puzzle yellow.
Color the outer space words blue.

Totally True
The energy in one lightning flash could light a 100-watt light bulb for more than three months!

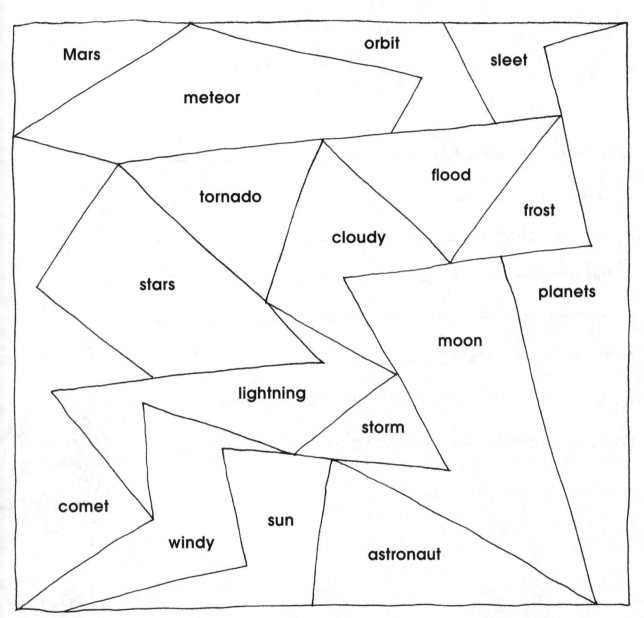

Mars
orbit
sleet
meteor
flood
tornado
frost
cloudy
stars
planets
moon
lightning
storm
comet
sun
windy
astronaut

What word names the yellow shape you colored?

____

DINOSAUR RIDDLE

Pick one word from the box to fit each clue, and write the answer on the line. Then write the first letter of each word in order in the boxes below. Write the last letter of each word in the remaining boxes to solve the riddle.

next teach dash
warm IOU once
no

1. a very small amount of something ____________
2. one time ____________
3. not hot, not cold ____________
4. the opposite of "yes" ____________
5. a written promise to pay back a debt ____________
6. immediately following ____________
7. to show someone how to do something ____________

How did the dinosaur feel after eating a pillow?

BIG, BIG NUMBERS

Have you ever said, "I would never do that in a million years"? You're going to have to live a long time to make that true. A million (1,000,000) has 6 zeros. A trillion (1,000,000,000,000) has 12 zeros.

Answer each question by writing the word for each number, one letter per box. When you're finished, read down at the arrow to learn the word for the number with 100 zeros.

			↓						
1. How many legs do spiders have?			g						
2. Two weeks equals how many days?		f							
3. The names of how many continents contain the word America?	t								
4. At what age do you become a legal adult?	e								
5. How many seasons are in a year?		f							
6. What time is one hour before midnight?		e							

THE SHAPE OF THINGS

How many shapes can you find in the picture?
Count them and write the total.

Cubes ______

Pyramids ______

Circles ______

Rectangles ______

Ovals ______

Triangles ______

Cylinders ______

Spheres ______

Squares ______

Cones ______

Total number of shapes ______

A MOUSE & MORE

Find and circle the words in the word search.
Look across and down.

```
    K F       G H
    S F H B K N
    G R A Y C O         E J A X T F
  G H M D O Q S G Y C A T M J C U F T
  H W H I S K E R S Q R Q P O D R R A P
  W B A M E L V E F K S M A L L R E I E
    H H A N     C H E E S E H W Y H L J
                B R O W N G B F E K F
                         H E T R A P
```

whiskers
ears
tail
nose
furry
trap
small
gray
brown
cheese
cat

mammal
insect
tuna
reptile
eagle
frog

Answer each clue to solve the riddle.

1. This bird is a U.S. symbol.

2. A rabbit is this class of animal.

3. an amphibian

4. a fish

5. A bee is this class of animal.

6. An alligator is this class of animal.

If dessert comes after dinner,
what comes after dessert? ______________________

TREE SEARCH

Find and circle the words in the word search.
Look across and down.

- ash
- apple
- aspen
- beech
- birch
- cedar
- cherry
- chestnut
- cypress
- elm
- fir
- maple
- pine
- spruce
- sycamore
- willow

```
B D O P D
T A S H M X Y
P D X E D S C I R K R P R
Q B F J Q P Q R G T A I O
S R E G O R E P O A J N M E X
U O B K E U U N F Q S V E H L N
R N A V I T C C J M A P L E W M L
W U P P G B E E C H W E U G S E
P K R J D W A V E N K W Q V B A
G L H O R A P S Y C A M O R E U T
X E V F I R U O N A C Y P R E S S
W I L L O W X U I V S X J O
M A B I R C H S R I S K U
P O X S   A H C   B T
A H C
G E H
M S E
C T R
I N R
O U Y
P T Q
```

Answer each clue to solve the riddle.

1. This tropical fruit has yellow skin.
2. This fruit is usually round and can be red, yellow, or green.
3. This citrus fruit is round and orange.
4. This citrus fruit has a greenish skin.
5. This citrus fruit is yellow.

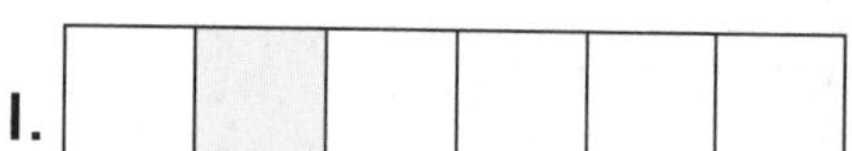

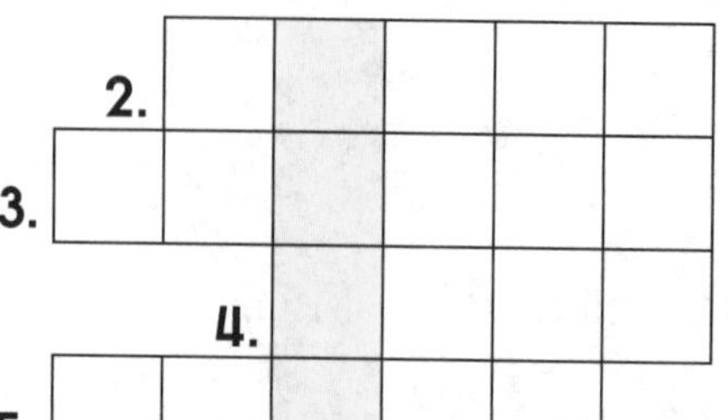

- orange
- lime
- apple
- banana
- lemon

Which kind of tree claps? ____________________

DOUBLE-CROSS

Cross out the items listed.
The remaining words will be a riddle and its answer.

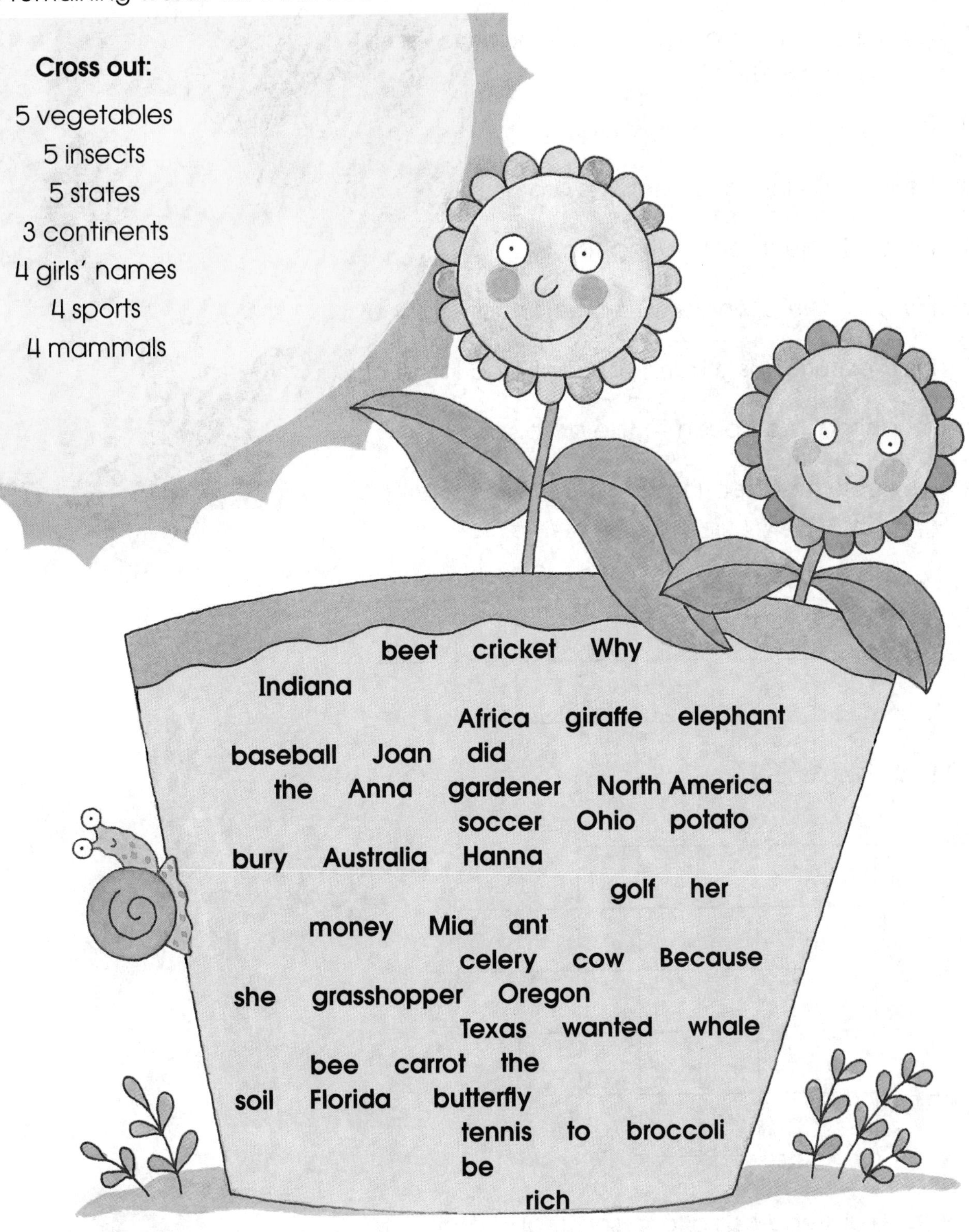

Write the riddle. ____?

Write the answer. ____.

UNDERWATER RIDDLE

Answer each clue to solve the riddle.

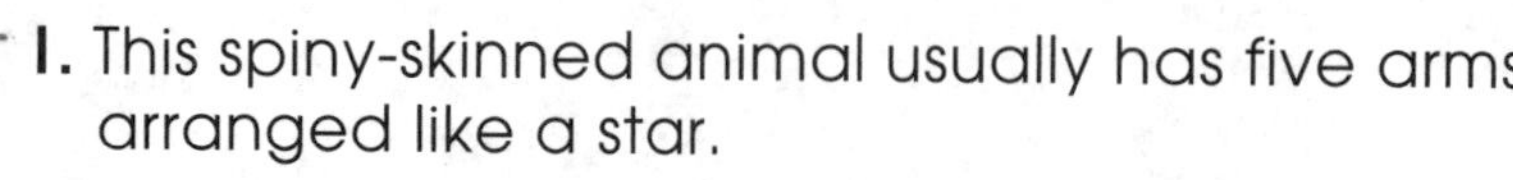

1. This spiny-skinned animal usually has five arms arranged like a star.

2. These plants grow underwater.

3. The largest animal on earth is a blue ________.
4. This is a large, meat-eating fish.
5. This looks like a whale with an elongated snout.
6. This creature has a hard, flat shell and large claws.
7. This animal is a cousin to the octopus.
8. This sleek, meat-eating creature lives on land and in the sea.

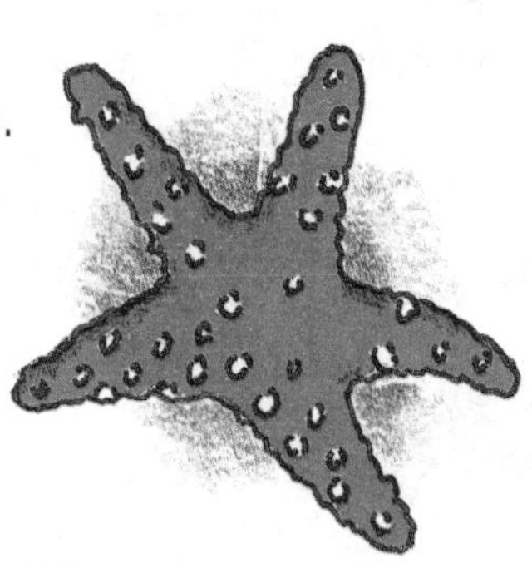

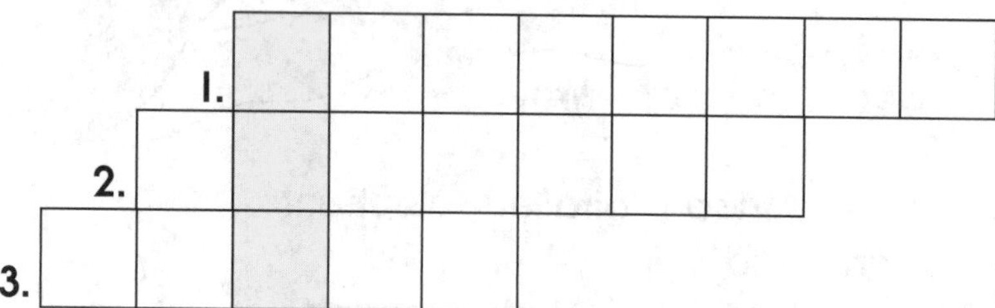

4.
5.
6.
7.
8.

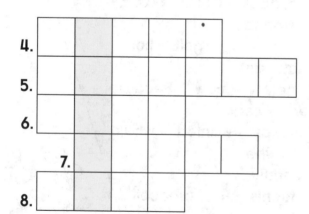

whale
shark
starfish
dolphin
seaweed
seal
squid
crab

This special steed has a long snout and a curly tail.
If you try to ride it, you will surely fail.

What is it? ______________________________

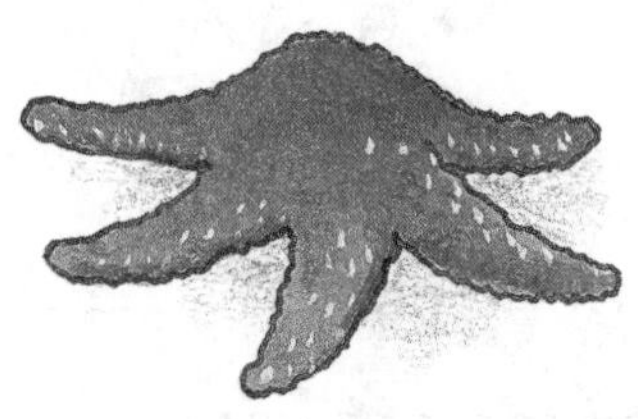

TIC-TAC-TOE VARIATION

Choose which player will be X and which player will be O. Take turns drawing an X or an O at each intersection. Play until there are four Xs or four Os in a row horizontally, vertically, or diagonally or until the grid is filled. Whoever gets four in a row first wins!

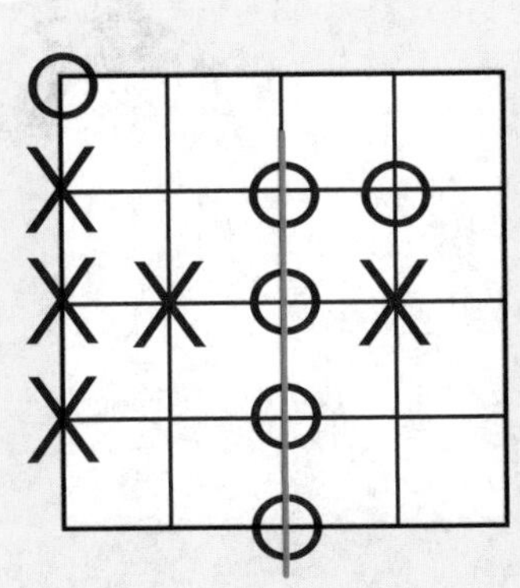

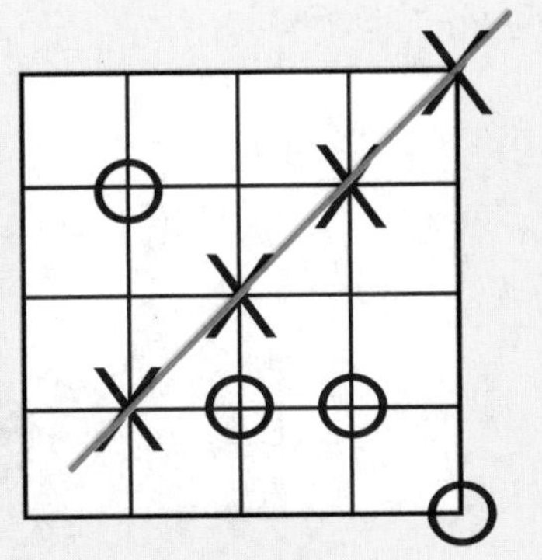

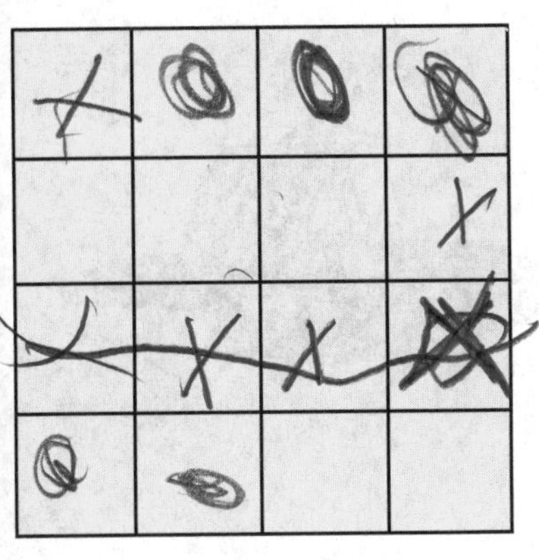

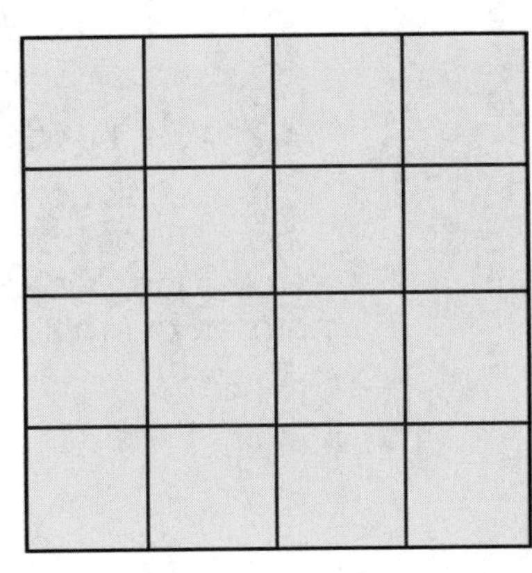

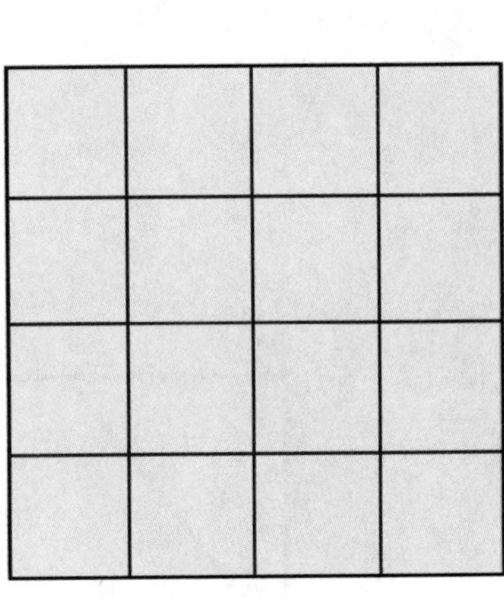

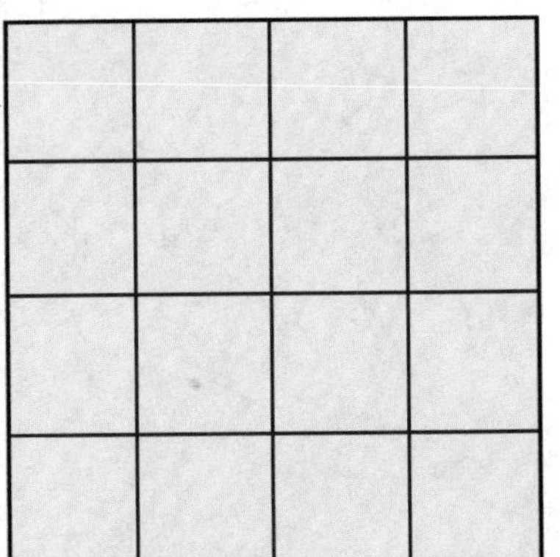

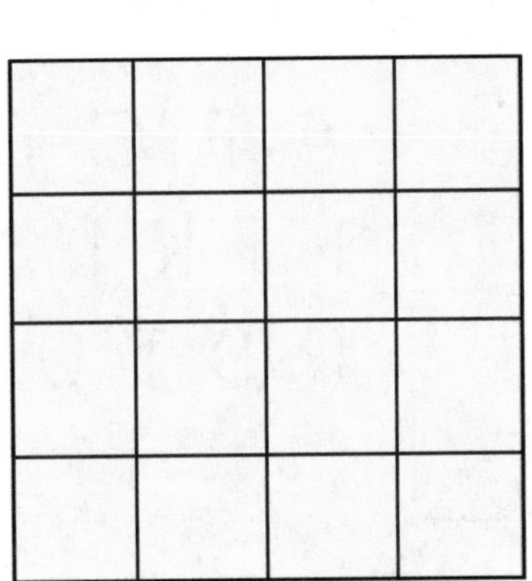

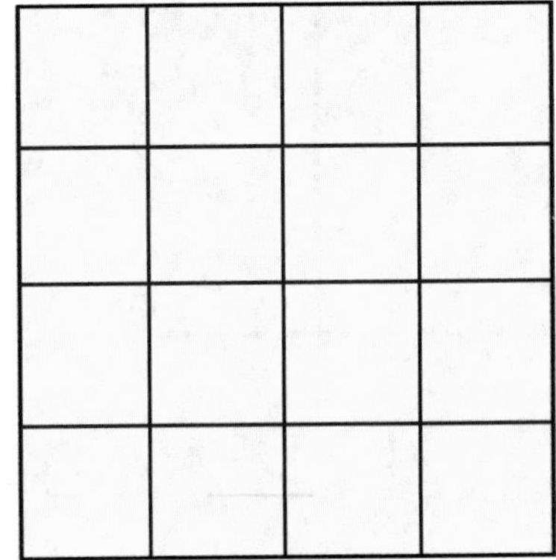

HANGMAN

One person thinks of a word and draws the same number of dashes as letters in the word. The other player guesses the letters. If a guess is right, the letter is written on the correct dash or dashes. If the guess is wrong, a body is drawn one part at a time (a complete body includes a head, a torso, two legs, two arms, two hands, and two feet). The object is to guess the word before the drawing is finished.

2 players

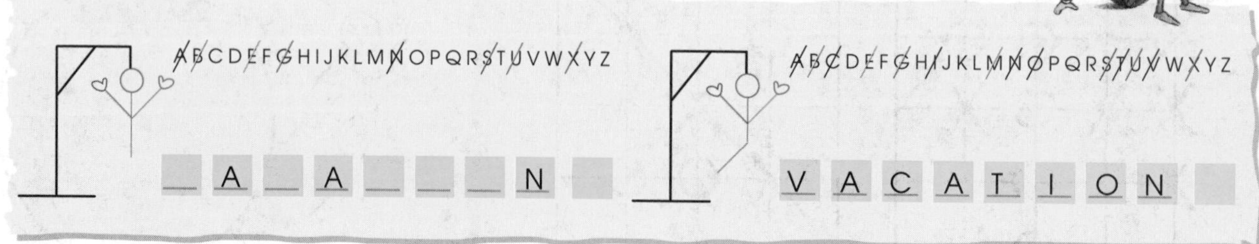

To use these blank Hangman games, draw lines under the spaces you need for your word.

Challenge!

To make this game harder, you can choose long words, phrases, or film titles.

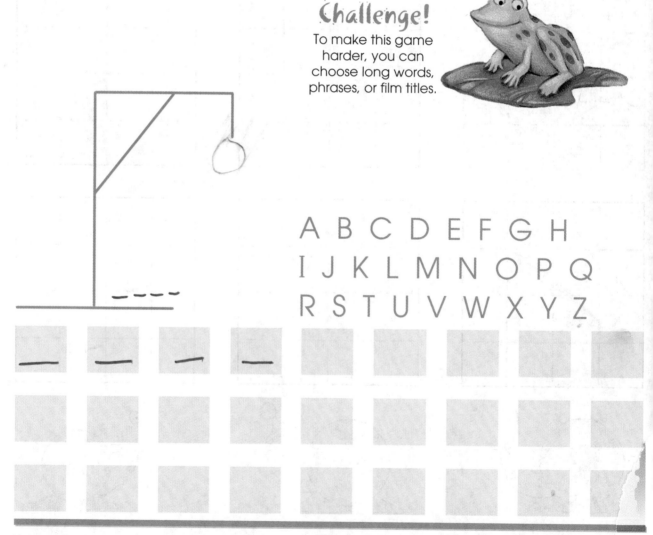

A B C D E F G H
I J K L M N O P Q
R S T U V W X Y Z

FARM ANIMALS

Farming is one of the most important occupations in the world. Nearly all the food we eat comes from crops and livestock raised on farms. In the 1700s and 1800s, the typical American family barely raised enough food for themselves. Horses plowed the fields. Since then, scientific advances have made farming increasingly specialized and productive. Today, each U.S. farmer produces enough food to feed over 150 people. Farming has become an important business run by large corporations and is no longer a way of life as it was in the past. Today, smaller, privately-owned farms provide food diversity.

Across

3. This strong animal, once used to pull a plow, is now raised mainly for riding.
4. This female bovine is often raised on a dairy farm.
5. Most of these animals are raised for meat on hog farms.
7. This animal has provided people with milk, meat, and wool since prehistoric times.
9. A domestic one is raised as a pet or for its meat and fur.

Down

1. These are among the most important animals in the world because they provide both food and wool for clothing.
2. Raising this animal for meat and eggs is a major industry.
6. This waterbird is raised for its meat and for its down (soft feathers).
8. We think of this animal as part of a traditional Thanksgiving or Christmas dinner.

HOMOGRAPHS

Some words have more than one meaning. There are two clues for each word in the puzzle. Think of a word that fits both clues. Write the word in the puzzle.

Across

4. not heavy
to set on fire

5. to conveniently arrange papers
a tool with ridges used to smooth surfaces

7. a unit of weight equal to 16 ounces
to hit with a heavy blow

8. a big dance
a round object used in sports

Down

1. a warning sound made by a kind of snake
a baby's toy that makes noise when shaken

2. an herb, a tree, or a shrub
to put in the ground so that it will grow

3. friendly, generous
sort or variety

6. part of the body at the end of the arm
to pass or give something to someone

7. to have fun
a story that is acted out on a stage

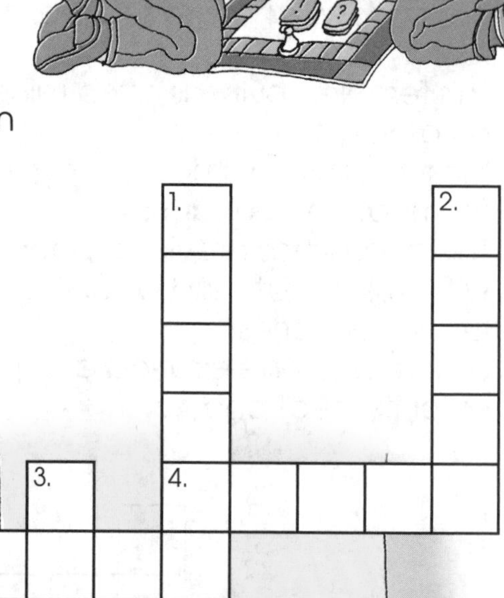

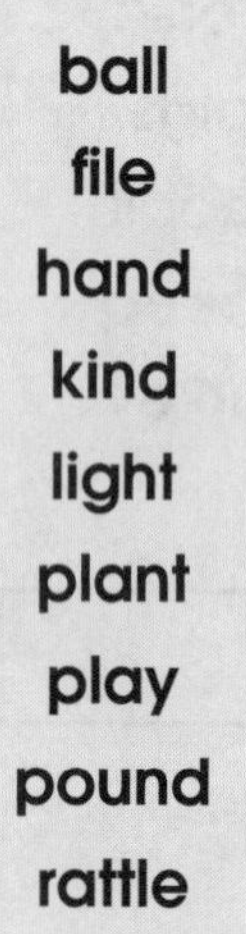

ball
file
hand
kind
light
plant
play
pound
rattle

TRUCKS

Trucking is a major industry in the United States. Trucks carry food to grocery stores, gasoline to gas stations, and manufactured goods from factories to stores. Nearly everything we eat, drink, wear, and use has been delivered by truck. Trucks vary greatly in size. Most trucks have more powerful engines than automobiles and are built for rugged work. Manufacturers produce many kinds of trucks. They are classified into three main groups: light, medium, and heavy. The groups are based on gross vehicle weight, which is the combined weight of the truck and the load it carries.

Across

1. a popular type of light-duty truck with an open cargo area
2. carries liquids, such as milk, oil, or gasoline
4. a medium-sized truck used for moving furniture or other bulky items
5. works at construction sites, unloads by the rear of the truck tilting
7. mixes and pours a strong material that has many uses, such as the foundations of buildings

concrete	**pickup**
dump	**platform**
garbage	**tank**
panel	**van**

Down

1. an all-purpose flatbed truck with rails, often used on farms
3. comes to our homes and businesses to collect trash
6. a light-duty truck popular with small businesses, such as floral shops, for delivering their goods

NURSERY RHYMES

A nursery rhyme is a rhythmical poem that amuses or soothes young children. Nursery rhymes have been passed on verbally for centuries. Every culture has its own nursery rhymes, plus additional ones that have been adopted from other countries. Many nursery rhymes pass on cultural information and values and help children appreciate the sounds and rhythms of a language. There are many origins for the rhymes. Ballads, prayers, proverbs, tavern songs, and fragments of ballads account for many of the rhymes.

Across

2. Who went up the hill?
4. What jumped over the moon?
5. Who was a pumpkin eater?
7. What bridge is falling down?
9. What ran up the clock?
10. Who fell off a wall?

Down

1. What went up a waterspout?
2. Who jumped over a candlestick?
3. Who lost her sheep?
6. How many men were in a tub?
8. Who lived in a shoe?
9. Who had a little lamb?

cow
Humpty Dumpty
Jack
Jack and Jill
Little Bo Peep
London
Mary
mouse
old woman
Peter
spider
three

INSECTS

Insects are small six-legged animals. An insect's body has three main parts. Most adult insects have wings. They smell mainly with their antennae, and some taste with their feet. Many insects hear by means of their bodies. Others have ears on their legs or antennae. Although many insects do harm, they are an important part of the food chain. They are also an important part of food production as they pollinate crops. Insects live almost everywhere on Earth, although few insects are found in the oceans.

ant
bee
butterfly
dragonfly
firefly
horsefly
ladybug
mayfly
mosquito
termite

Across
1. queen rules
4. unsaddled
6. terminator
7. spring bug
8. picnic pest
9. does not breathe fire

Down
1. won't melt
2. vampire insect
3. pyromaniac
5. female bug

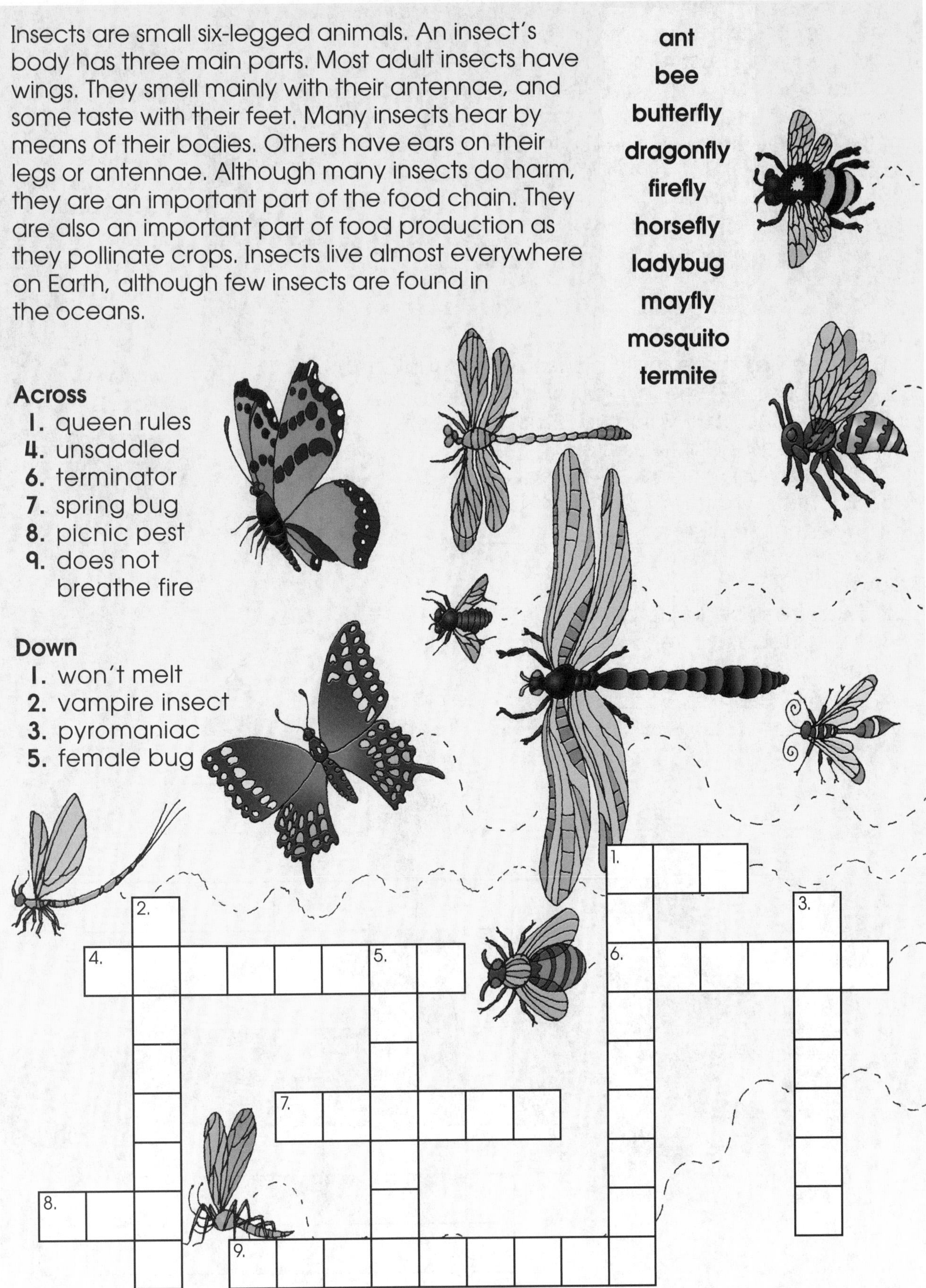

TREES

Trees are the largest of all plants. The giant sequoias of California are the oldest and largest living things. Trees continue to grow as long as they live, and some trees live for thousands of years. A tree's leaves make food that helps the tree grow and keeps it alive. Many trees lose their leaves during winter, allowing the trees to rest. Other trees keep their leaves and stay green all year long. There are thousands of kinds of trees, some of which only grow in warm regions.

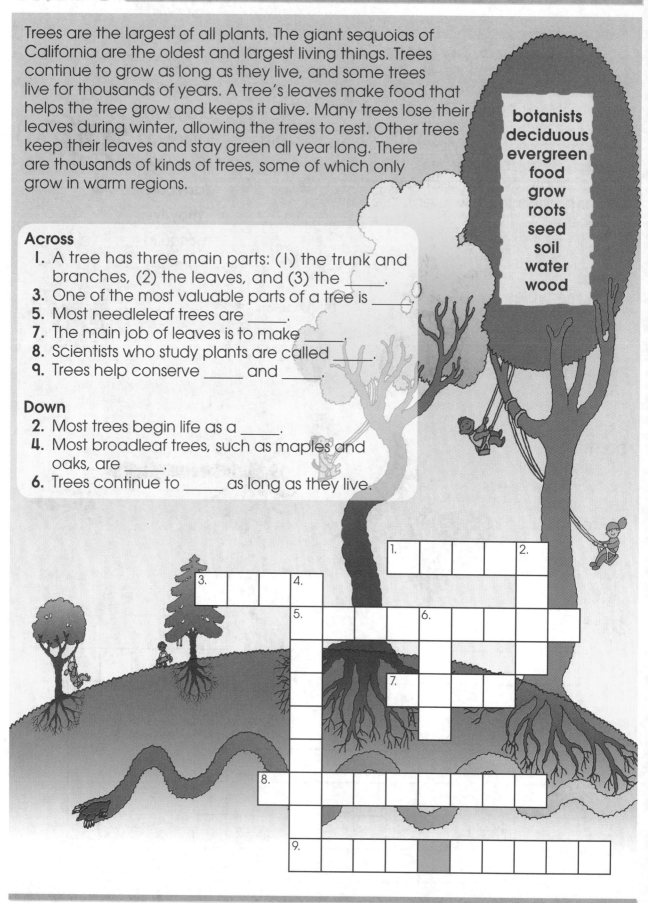

botanists
deciduous
evergreen
food
grow
roots
seed
soil
water
wood

Across

1. A tree has three main parts: (1) the trunk and branches, (2) the leaves, and (3) the _____.
3. One of the most valuable parts of a tree is _____.
5. Most needleleaf trees are _____.
7. The main job of leaves is to make _____.
8. Scientists who study plants are called _____.
9. Trees help conserve _____ and _____.

Down

2. Most trees begin life as a _____.
4. Most broadleaf trees, such as maples and oaks, are _____.
6. Trees continue to _____ as long as they live.

1. 2. 3. 4. 5. 6. 7. 8. 9.

REPTILES

Reptiles include alligators, crocodiles, lizards, snakes, turtles, and the tuatara. Reptiles are cold-blooded, which means that their body temperature is about the same temperature as their surroundings. In climates with harsh winters, they hibernate. In extremely hot climates, they are mainly active at night. Many reptiles live a long time. Some turtles have lived in captivity for more than 100 years. Reptiles live on every continent except Antarctica and in all the oceans except those in the polar regions. Some reptiles, including lizards, snakes, and crocodiles, are hunted for their skins. The United States government prohibits the importation of the skins of those reptiles classified as endangered species.

backbone
dinosaur
land
lungs
plates
reptiles
shell
temperature

Across

2. Reptiles breathe air through _____.
5. Cold-blooded animals do not have a constant body _____.
7. A spectacular reptile that is now extinct is the _____.
8. Most reptiles live on _____.

Down

1. Reptile skin is made of scales or bony _____.
3. An animal that is a vertebrate has a _____.
4. Turtles, snakes, lizards, and crocodiles are all _____.
6. Turtles are reptiles with a _____ that acts as a shield.

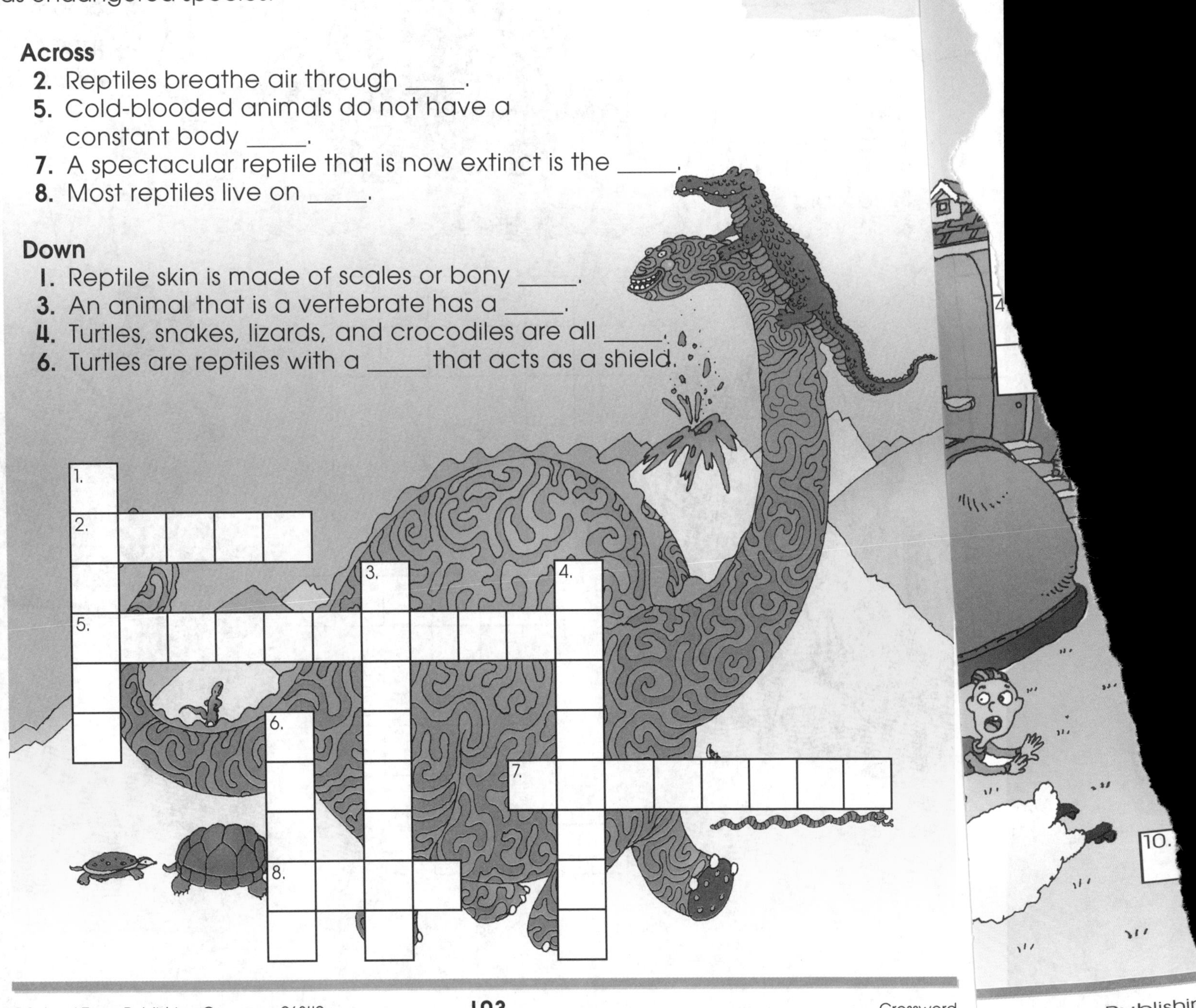

©School Zone Publishing

WORD MEANINGS

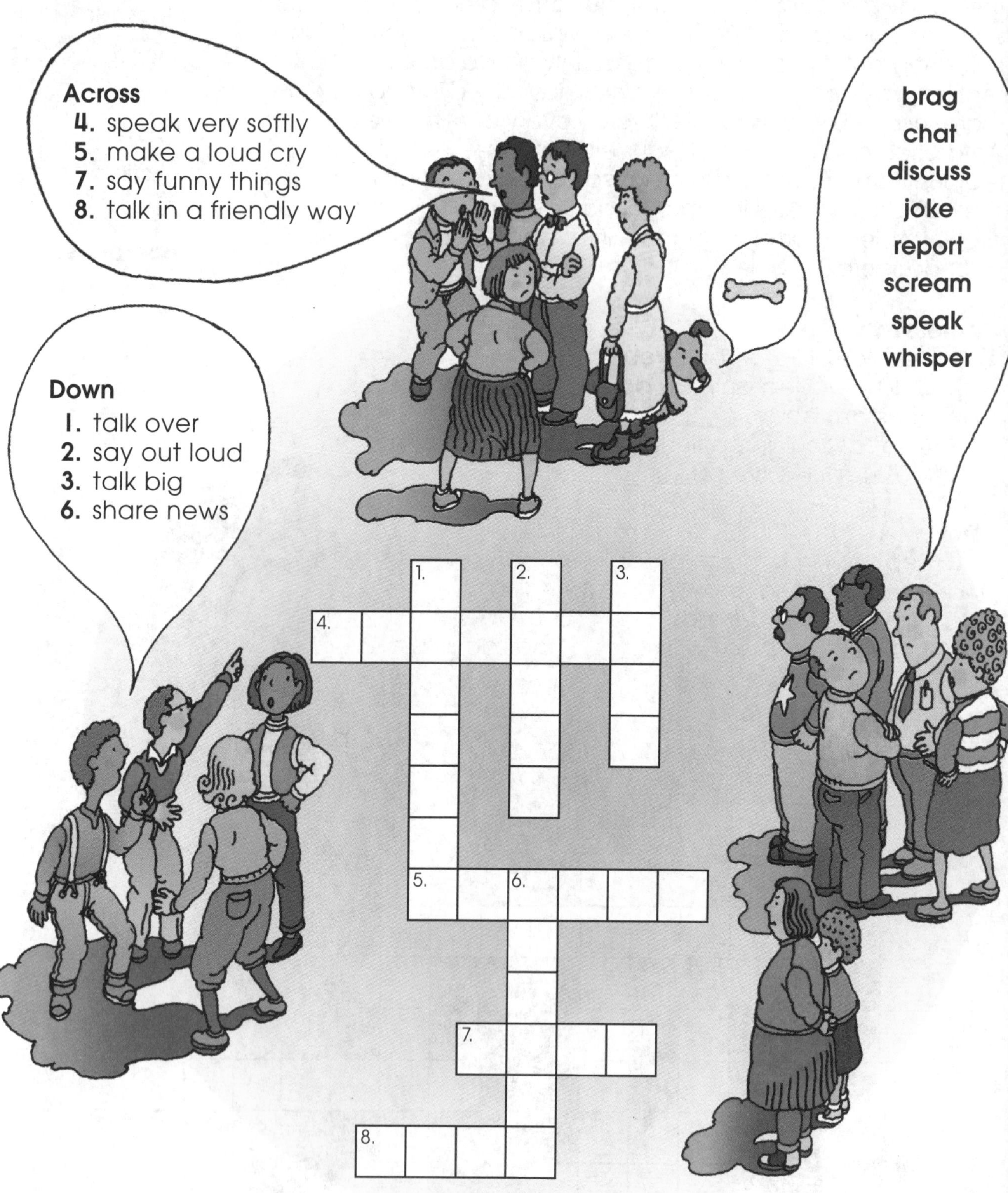

Across
4. speak very softly
5. make a loud cry
7. say funny things
8. talk in a friendly way
Down
1. talk over
2. say out loud
3. talk big
6. share news
brag
chat
discuss
joke
report
scream
speak
whisper
1.
2.
3.
4.
5.
6.
7.
8.

OCEANS

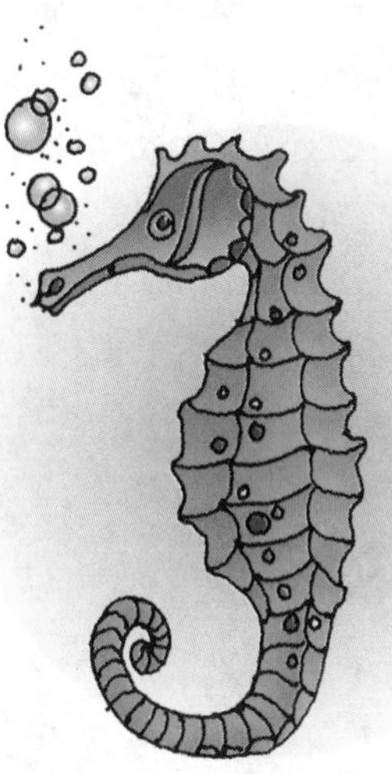

Across

3. These are places off a coast where seaweed grows as tall as trees.
6. This fish doesn't look like one.
8. Seaweed doesn't have _____ to take in water.
9. You'll find the most colorful fish here.

Down

1. These form when wind blows across the ocean.
2. This fish looks like its name and stays near the ocean floor.
4. When the tide goes out, ocean water is left here.
5. Coral reefs are formed by _____ that live together in groups.
7. The moon and sun cause the _____.

1. 2. 3. 4. 5. 6. 7. 8. 9.

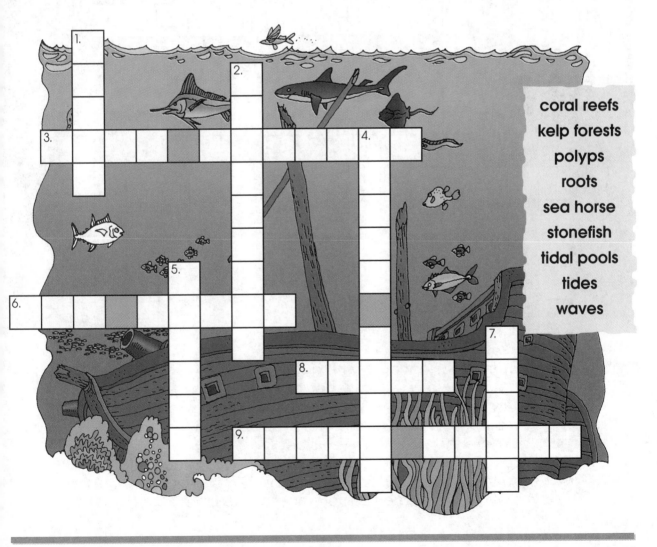

coral reefs
kelp forests
polyps
roots
sea horse
stonefish
tidal pools
tides
waves

HABITATS

The place where an animal lives is called its habitat. There are different types of habitats: mountains, grasslands, temperate forests, tropical forests, deserts, polar regions, freshwater, and oceans. Each habitat supports many kinds of animals. Most of these animals have lived in the same surroundings for centuries and have adapted to the climate. Destruction of habitats like the rainforests has caused the death of many animals, as the animals have lost their homes and sources of food.

Across

2. Tropical ____ exist in very hot and humid parts of the world.
4. Plants and animals that live in the ocean live in _____.
8. An _____ is home to fish and mammals.
10. Marshes, bogs, and swamps are all kinds of _____.

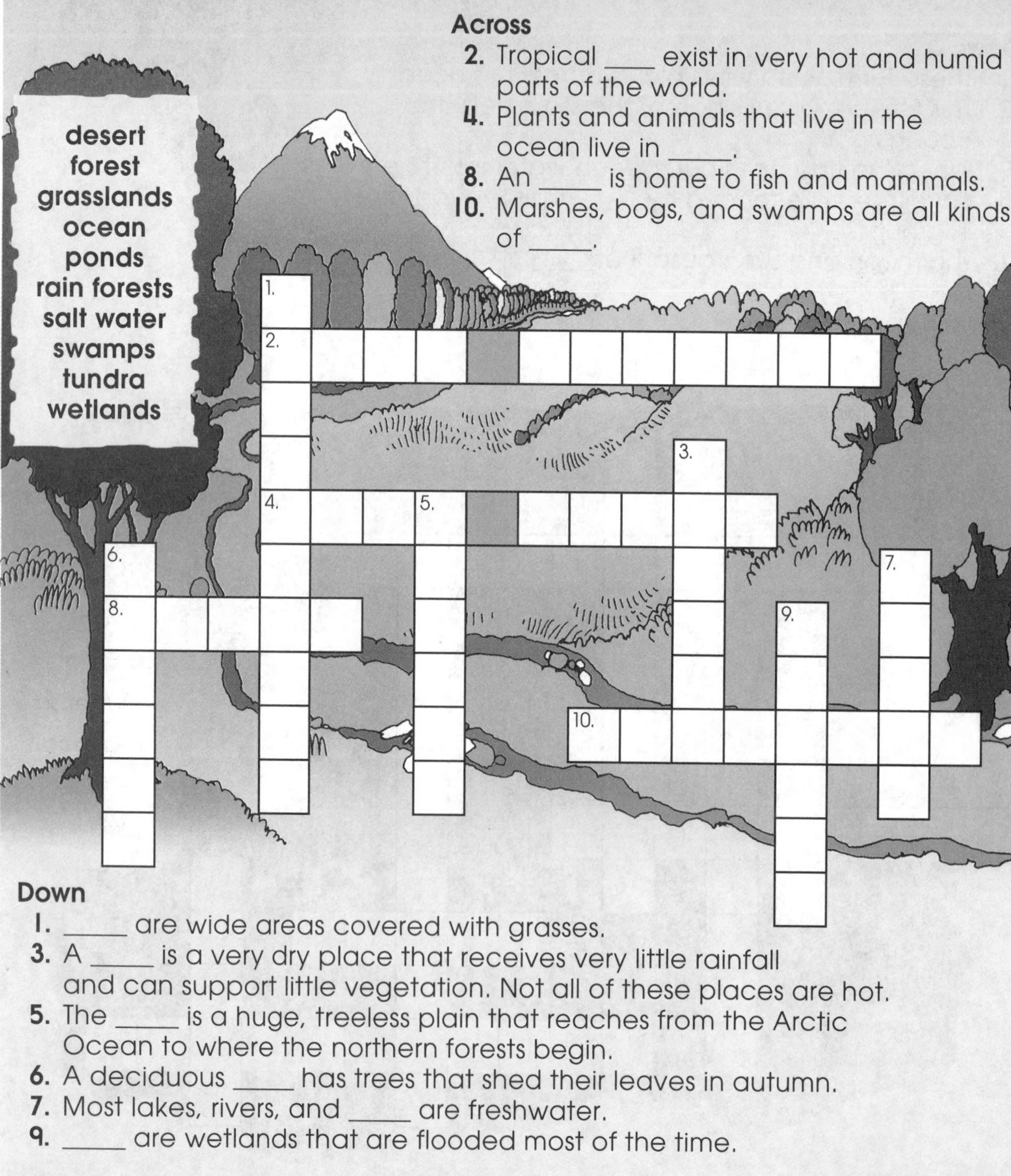

Down

1. _____ are wide areas covered with grasses.
3. A _____ is a very dry place that receives very little rainfall and can support little vegetation. Not all of these places are hot.
5. The _____ is a huge, treeless plain that reaches from the Arctic Ocean to where the northern forests begin.
6. A deciduous _____ has trees that shed their leaves in autumn.
7. Most lakes, rivers, and _____ are freshwater.
9. _____ are wetlands that are flooded most of the time.

1.
2.
3.
4.
5.
6.
7.
8.
9.
10.
11.
12.
13.

BALL GAMES

Across

3. ping-pong
5. not hardball
6. tenpins
9. pointy ball

Down

1. hands only
2. began with a bushel basket
3. What a racket!
4. not a vegetable
6. fastball
7. putter around
8. shots on goal

baseball
basketball
bowling
football
golf
soccer
softball
squash
table tennis
tennis
volleyball

BIRDS

If it has feathers, it's a bird. All birds have feathers. All birds have wings, but not all birds fly. Ostriches walk or run, and penguins use their wings for balance when they walk or as flippers when they swim. Birds hatch from eggs. There are about 10,000 kinds of birds. The fastest birds can fly at speeds over 100 miles an hour. No animal can travel faster than birds. Birds are important to humans in many ways. They scatter seeds, pollinate flowers, eat harmful insects, and are an important source of food for people. Birds live all over the world, from the polar regions to the tropics.

con
dow
frogs
humming
molt
oil
straight
toes

Across

4. ... have _____ that keeps their fe...ers dry.
5. Thes... birds can fly backwards.
8. Ostric... have two big _____.

Down

1. Herons eat fis... and _____.
2. These feathers k...ep birds warm.
3. The bottom of a bi...d's wing is _____ .
6. When birds _____, they lose feathers a few at a time.
7. Seed-eating birds have beaks shaped like this.

...DENTS

...ents are mammals with ...
...d objects. Rodents have ...
te... h. Rodents wear away ...
do ...ot wear out until late i...
teeth keep growing until th...
many kinds of rodents. The...
people. Scientists use mi...
eat harmful insects and ...
rodents have valuable ...
and the plague, are c...

Across
1. The teeth of rod...
2. Rodents are ...
4. _____ are the...
5. Some roden... the plague...
6. _____ live...
8. Most rod...

Down
1. A r... sui...
2. ...
3. R... f...
7. S...

INVENTORS

Inventing is putting ideas and materials together to make something that did not exist before. Inventions have been occurring since the Stone Age, when people began using rocks as tools. New inventions can make life easier, healthier, more comfortable, and more fun.

Benz
Daimler
Edison
Franklin
Graham Bell
Gutenberg
Kellogg
Lister
Wright

Across

3. In the mid 1400s, Johannes _____ invented printing as we know it today.
5. In the 1860s, Joseph _____ began the use of antiseptics during surgery, which almost eliminated post-surgical infection.
6. The first commercially practical electric lightbulb was invented by Thomas _____ in the late 1800s.
7. A breakfast cereal still produced today was developed by Will _____ in the 1890s.

Down

1. The _____ brothers are credited with the first successful airplane flights in 1903.
2. In 1885, Karl _____ and Gottlieb _____ built the first internal-combustion engines that were basically the same as the gasoline engines used in cars today.
3. Alexander _____ patented the telephone in 1876.
4. In 1752, Benjamin _____ flew a kite in a thunderstorm to prove lightning was electrical, which led to his invention of the lightning rod.

1.
2.
3.
4.
5.
6.
7.

HOLIDAYS

Each state has the authority to specify the holidays it will observe. Congress designates the holidays to be observed in Washington, D.C., and by federal employees throughout the country. Banks and schools usually close on a legal holiday. When a holiday falls on Sunday, it is usually observed on the following Monday. Some traditional holidays are observed by schools and organizations, although the schools and organizations do not close.

January
February
May
July
September
October
November
December

Across

4. Washington's Birthday
6. Independence Day
7. Thanksgiving
8. Christmas

Down

1. Memorial Day
2. Labor Day
3. New Year's Day
5. Columbus Day

1.
2.
3.
4.
5.
6.
7.
8.

TENNIS

Across

1. Tennis is a game played with two or four _____.
7. A _____ is used to hit the ball.
9. A zero score is called _____.
10. A game of _____ is played with four people.
11. The winner of a tennis match is determined through the best of three or five _____ .
12. A _____ is stretched across the middle of the court.

Down

1. A _____ is won when the opposing side fails to return the ball or makes an error.
2. A serve that cannot be returned is an _____.
3. _____ is a game played with two opposing people.
4. A 40-40 tie is called _____.
5. The _____ puts the ball in play.
6. Rackets are used to hit the _____ back and forth over a net.
8. Tennis is played on a flat surface called a _____.

ace
ball
court
deuce
doubles
love
net
players
point
racket
service
sets
singles

1. 2. 3. 4. 5. 6. 7. 8. 9. 10. 11. 12.

43RD ANNUAL DOG SHOW
1.
2.
3.
4.
6.
7.
8.
9.
10.
11.
1

LAND TRANSPORTATION

Land transportation is the most common kind of transportation by far. Automobiles, buses, motorcycles, snowmobiles, trains, and trucks are the chief engine-powered vehicles. Cars, buses, and trucks are the main road vehicles. Routes are predetermined for buses and for trains and subways that run on tracks. Trucks can deliver freight to where it is needed. Cars allow people to choose their routes. Transportation is a major use of energy. Cars and trucks are a major source of traffic congestion and pollution problems in cities and towns. The U.S. government has established pollution-control standards and fuel-consumption standards to help reduce these problems.

automobile
bicycle
bus
motorcycle
streetcar
subway
taxicab
train
truck

Across

2. an underground train
4. a chauffeur-driven car for hire
5. a two-wheeled vehicle that sometimes has a sidecar
7. a two-wheeled vehicle propelled by pedaling
8. a vehicle designed to move heavy objects

Down

1. a vehicle by which most families travel
2. rides on rails and transports passengers on city streets
3. a large passenger vehicle
6. a connected line of cars that ride on rails, pulled by a locomotive

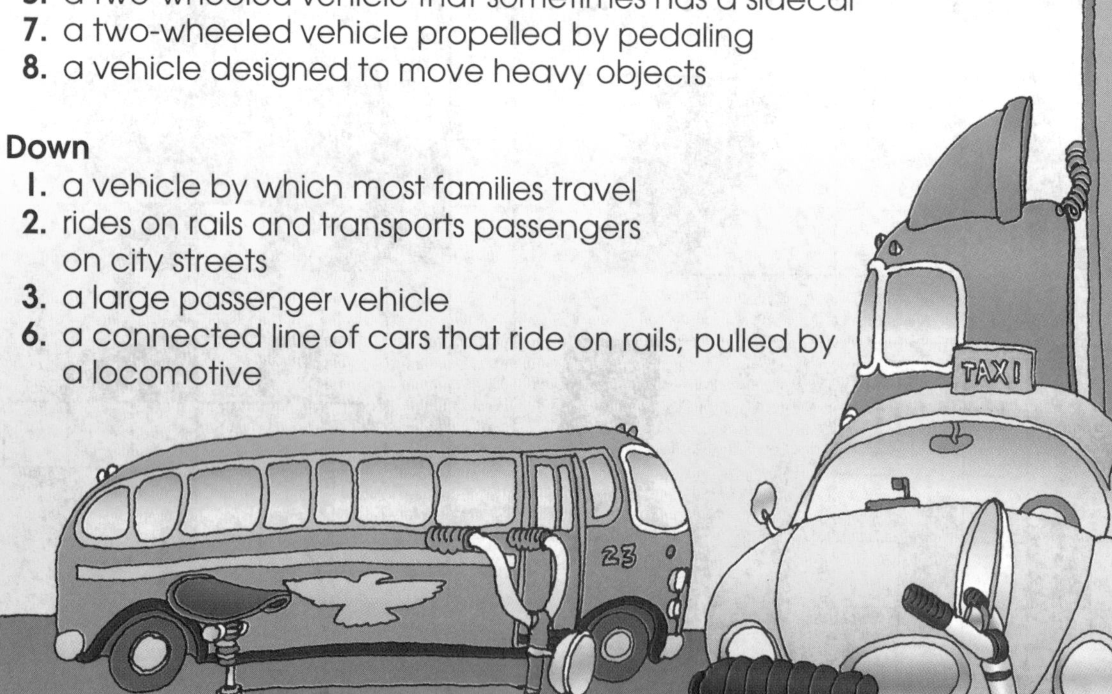

HONEST JONATHAN'S
USED VEHICLES
ONE OWNER CREAM PUFF
1.
2.
3.
4.
5.
6.
7.
8.

AIRPORTS

Across

1. people who buy tickets to travel by plane
3. where air traffic controllers direct movement in the air and on the ground.
6. where passengers board and leave aircraft from terminal locations
7. papers that show you have paid and where you are going
8. buildings in which aircraft are stored and repaired
10. what must be inspected by security employees

Down

1. a person qualified to operate an airplane
2. people who enforce security regulations
4. roads for planes to take off and land
5. the main airport building for passengers and services
9. provides energy and power to engines

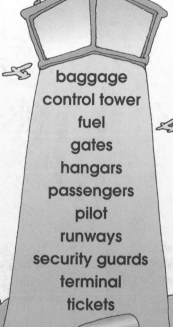

baggage
control tower
fuel
gates
hangars
passengers
pilot
runways
security guards
terminal
tickets

1. 2. 3. 4. 5. 6. 7. 8. 9. 10.

Write the names of the figures in the puzzle.

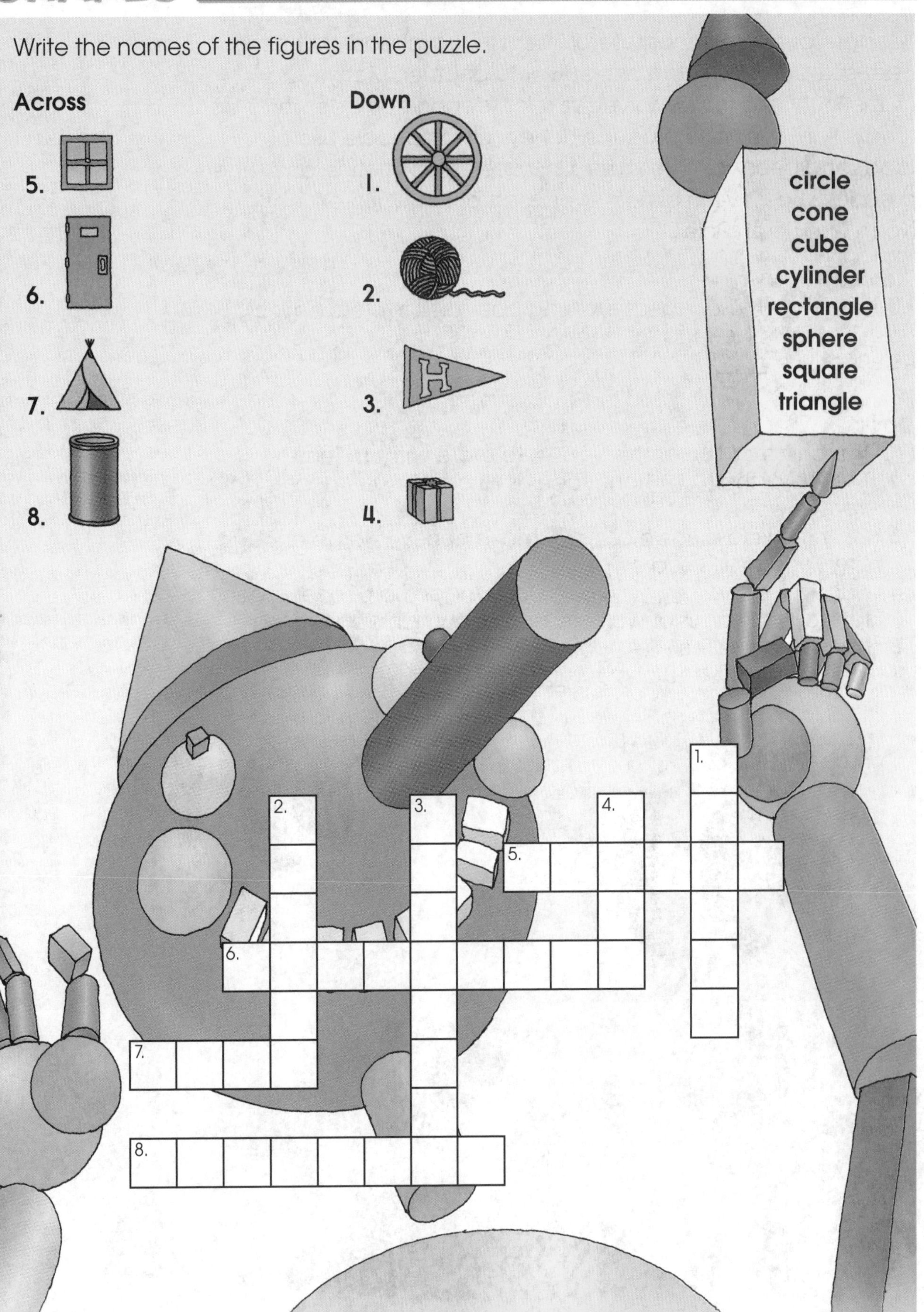

BEES

Bees are one of the most useful insects. During food-gathering, bees spread pollen from one flower to another. Many food crops, including fruits and vegetables, depend on bees for fertilization. Bees also produce honey, which people use as food, and beeswax that is used in candles, cosmetics, and other products. Bees live in almost every part of the world except the North and South Poles.

Across

3. The _____ is used to raise young bees and to store nectar.
6. _____ provide food for bees.
8. Bees are _____.

Down

1. The only function of the _____ is to mate with queens.
2. The job of the _____ honeybees is to collect nectar and pollen from flowers.
3. Only the kinds known as _____ make honey in large enough amounts to be used by people.
4. Honeybees live in _____ in a colony made up of one queen, tens of thousands of workers, and a few hundred drones.
5. Laying eggs is the _____ only job.
7. Most bees depend on their _____ for defense.

ECOSYSTEMS

Different parts of the world support a wide variety of plant and animal life. This is mainly caused by the climate in each place, which allows different kinds of living things to thrive. The climate is influenced by the physical characteristics of a region—whether it is mountainous or near the sea, for example—and its position on Earth. Each area contains communities of living things that rely on one another for survival. These communities are called ecosystems.

Across

2. An animal that eats flesh of another animal is a _____.
4. Evaporation, condensation, and precipitation are the three steps to the _____.
6. The environment in which a species lives is its _____.
7. _____ is the study of how plants and animals interact.
8. An animal that eats plants is a _____.
9. Animals that eat both plants and animals are _____.
10. The study of plants is called _____.

Down

1. A _____ is a plant or animal that lives in or on another plant or animal for its only source of food.
3. _____ is the study of weather.
5. People and animals need food, water, and _____ to live.

botany
carnivore
ecology
habitat
herbivore
meteorology
omnivores
oxygen
parasite
water cycle

1. 2. 3. 4. 5. 6. 7. 8. 9. 10.

BODY SYSTEMS

The human body has nearly a dozen interrelated systems, each designed for a special function. The skeleton is the framework. Bones and muscles work together to provide form and movement to the body. Oxygen needed to provide fuel for muscles depends on the circulatory system, which depends on the respiratory system, and so on with other related systems. Each part of our body does a special job, but all of the parts work together. The human brain separates people from all other living things. Everything you think, feel, and do is controlled by your brain.

blood
brain
ears
eyes
heart
lungs
muscles
skeleton
skin

Across

1. _____ connect with the brain through the optic nerve and provide our sense of sight.
2. _____ hold and move the skeleton and give the body its shape.
4. The _____ is a major element of the body's internal transportation system.
5. _____ draw air into the body through the mouth and nose so that oxygen can be absorbed into the bloodstream.
7. The _____ is an outgrowth at the top of the spinal cord and is the organ of thought and neural coordination.

Down

1. _____ are located at the sides of the head and are concerned with the senses of hearing, learning, and balance.
3. The _____ is the framework around which the body is built.
6. _____ is what the whole body is enclosed in and forms the body's largest organ.
7. _____ contains food, fuel, and materials for building and repairing cells vital to every tissue of the body.

1. 2. 3. 4. 5. 6. 7.

OUR SUN

Across

2. When the magnetic field in the Sun's core prevents heat from rising to the surface, these dark spots appear: _____.
5. _____ is another word for "star system."
6. The Sun shines because it gives out _____ and _____.
8. There can be no _____ without the Sun.
9. Our galaxy is named the _____.

Down

1. The center of the Sun is its _____.
2. _____ are huge eruptions of flames that appear on the Sun's surface.
3. A _____ is a huge ball of gas that gives off vast amounts of light and heat.
4. A star is made of _____ and has no solid surface.
7. Light and heat are forms of _____ .

core
energy
galaxy
gas
life
light & heat
Milky Way
solar flares
star
sunspots

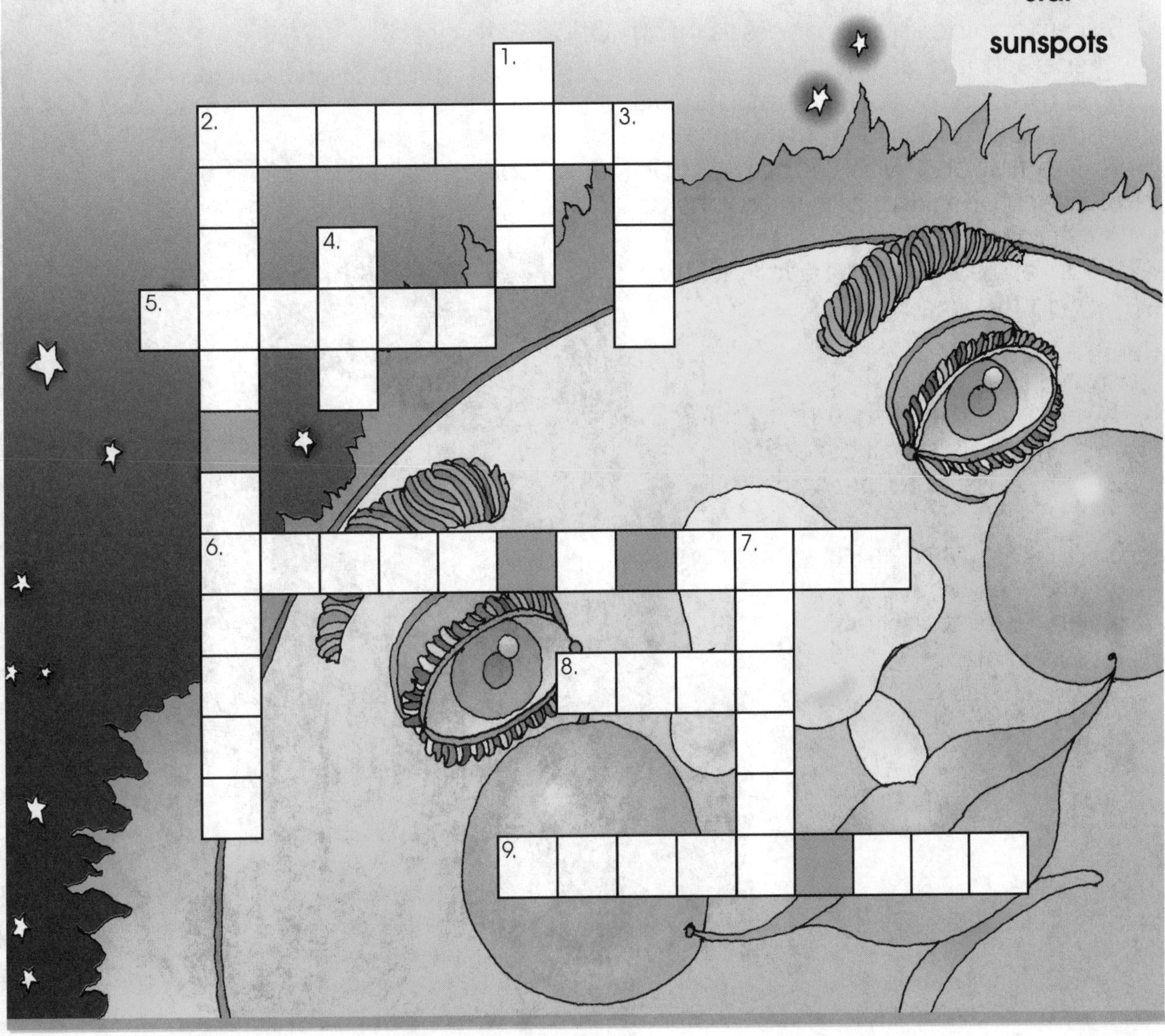

GREAT INVENTIONS

Invention is the creation of a new device, process, or product. It may involve something brand new or an improvement of something that someone else produced. Invention is closely related to discovery. Discoverers find something that already exists. For example, people discovered fire, but they invented the match to start a fire. If we compare our homes today with the homes of pioneers, we will appreciate the many inventions that have made our lives easier. Inventions can be beneficial to people, but they can also be harmful. Weapons of war are far more destructive than they once were. People invent to satisfy their needs or to make money. Many inventions fail because they do not fill a need.

airplane
camera
clock
computer
map
microscope
plow
printing press
satellite
telephone
television
wheel

Across

2. made mass communication possible before radio
3. brings pictures and sounds from around the world
4. any body that revolves around a planet—artificial ones used for communication and research
5. a machine that processes information with great speed and precision
6. a reference, sometimes printed, to help people find a destination
7. The first one was probably a potter's table.
8. used for taking photographs or making movies
9. an engine-driven machine that can fly

Down

1. an instrument that magnifies extremely small objects
2. a tool used to prepare soil for planting
3. an instrument that sends and receives sound
5. an instrument that shows time

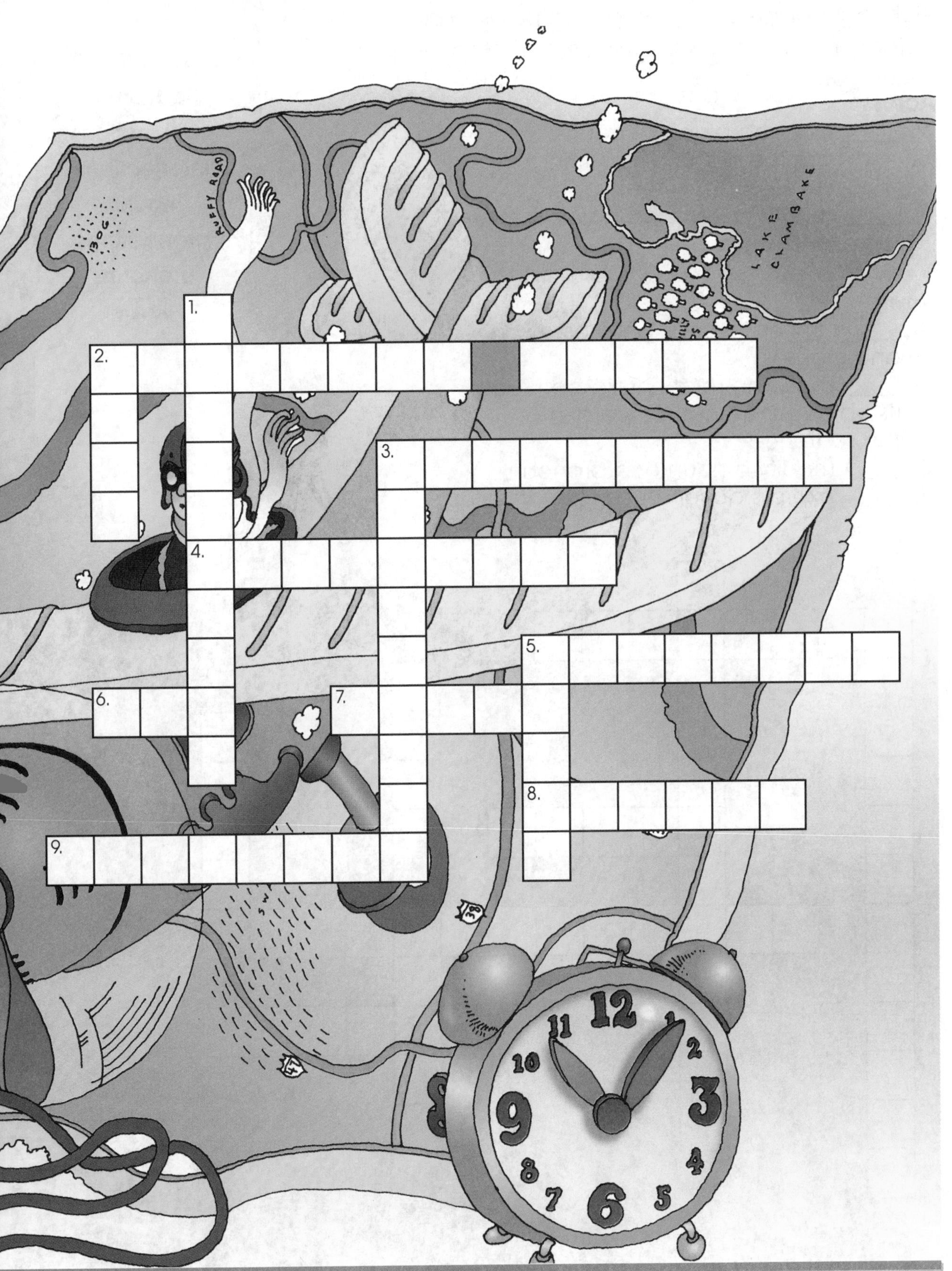
1.
2.
3.
4.
5.
6.
7.
8.
9.
BOG
RUFFY ROAD
LAKE CLAMBAKE

PARTS OF SPEECH

The eight ways in which words are used are called the eight parts of speech. A word must be used in a sentence before one can determine which part of speech it is.

adjectives
adverbs
conjunctions
interjections
nouns
prepositions
pronouns
verbs

Across

2. _____ take the place of nouns.
5. _____ are the name of anything.
6. _____ express strong feeling.
7. _____ modify a verb, an adjective, or another adverb.

Down

1. _____connect words, phrases, and clauses.
2. _____ show the relationship between its object and another word in the sentence.
3. _____ modify a noun or a pronoun.
4. _____ express action or a state of being.

1.
2.
3.
4.
5.
6.
7.
8.
9.
10.
11.
12.
13.
14.

YELLOWSTONE NATIONAL PARK

Yellowstone National Park was established in 1872 and is the oldest national park in the world. The park occupies over 3,400 square miles in Wyoming, Montana, and Idaho. Yellowstone contains many natural wonders. Geysers, hot springs, sparkling lakes and rivers, deep canyons, and acres of forests attract millions of visitors each year. Yellowstone is also known for its wildlife. A large number of animals, including elk, deer, mountain goats, buffalo, sheep, wolves, and grizzly bears, roam the park freely.

Across

1. Volcanoes and _____ shaped the landscape of Yellowstone.
4. Yellowstone Lake is one of the largest _____ lakes in North America.
5. Yellowstone Park is located mainly in _____.
7. _____ lies below the surface of the park and furnishes the heat for the park's geysers and hot springs.
9. In 1872, _____ passed a bill to establish the park and preserve its natural resources.

Down

2. The Yellowstone region was acquired in 1803 as part of the _____.
3. The park's _____ forests were caused by volcanic eruptions, which covered the trees in ash and transformed the trees from wood to minerals.
6. Old Faithful is a famous _____ in the park.
8. The park was named for yellow _____ that lie along part of the Yellowstone River.

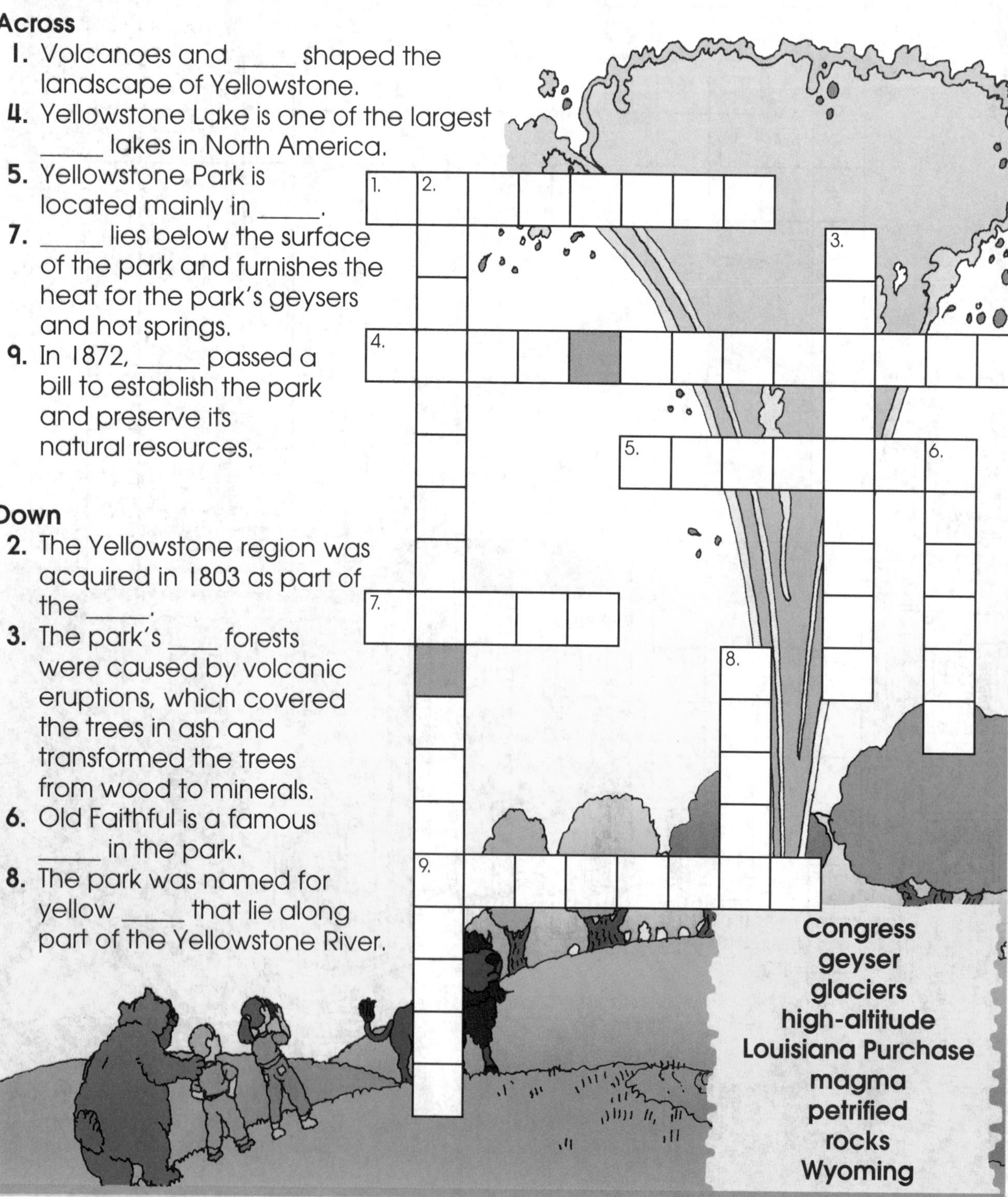

Congress
geyser
glaciers
high-altitude
Louisiana Purchase
magma
petrified
rocks
Wyoming

POLITICAL ELECTIONS

Across

1. _____ provide secrecy and simplify vote counting.
3. A _____ is a person who is selected by others as a contestant for office.
4. _____ for voting must be approximately equal in population to ensure that each vote has equal power in the election process.
6. _____ is the process by which a person's name is added to the list of qualified voters.
8. _____ is the right to vote.

Down

1. The_____ outlawed discriminatory voting practices and protects the rights of all United States citizens to vote.
2. _____ is the process by which people vote for the candidate of their choice.
3. A _____ consists of paid staff members and consultants and unpaid volunteers working together to help win votes for a certain candidate.
5. Social scientists have found more _____ vote than men.
7. A _____ is the device used to record the choices made by voters.

ballot
campaign
candidate
districts
election
registration
suffrage
voting machines
Voting Rights Act
women

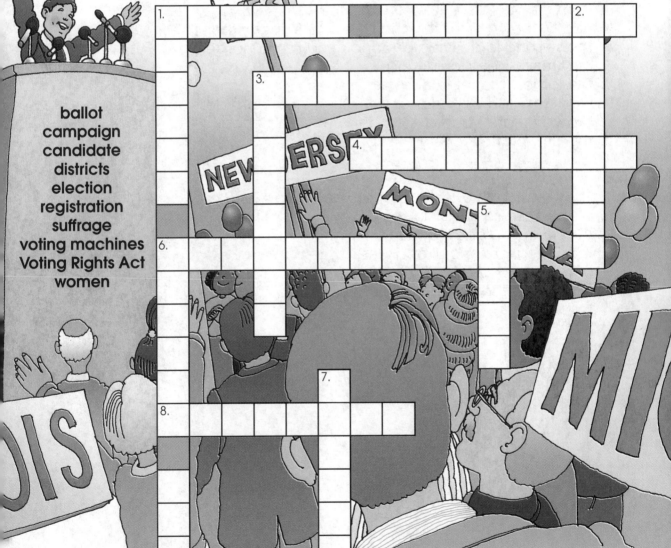

1. 2. 3. 4. 5. 6. 7. 8.

OUR SOLAR SYSTEM

A planetary system is made up of a star and the planets and other objects orbiting around it. Our solar system includes Earth and seven other planets that revolve around the Sun, which is our star. Our solar system also contains many smaller objects, such as asteroids, dwarf planets, and comets. There is also a thin cloud of dust known as the interplanetary medium. More than 100 moons, also called satellites, orbit the planets. Astronomers have discovered planets orbiting distant stars and hope to learn more about our solar system by studying the masses and orbits of those systems.

Earth
Jupiter
Mars
Mercury
Moon
Neptune
Pluto
Saturn
Sun
Uranus
Venus

Across

2. the only planet whose surface can be seen in detail from Earth
3. a satellite of Earth whose light is reflected light from the Sun, as it gives off no light of its own
4. has 27 known satellites and at least 13 rings around it
6. the second largest planet, encircled by the largest and most spectacular rings
8. the largest planet in our solar system
9. was classified as a planet until 2006, now considered a dwarf planet and a member of the Kuiper belt
10. the only planet known to support life

Down

1. known as Earth's "sister planet" because the two planets are so similar in size
2. the nearest planet to the Sun
5. a huge, glowing ball of gases at the center of the solar system
7. named for the Roman god of the sea

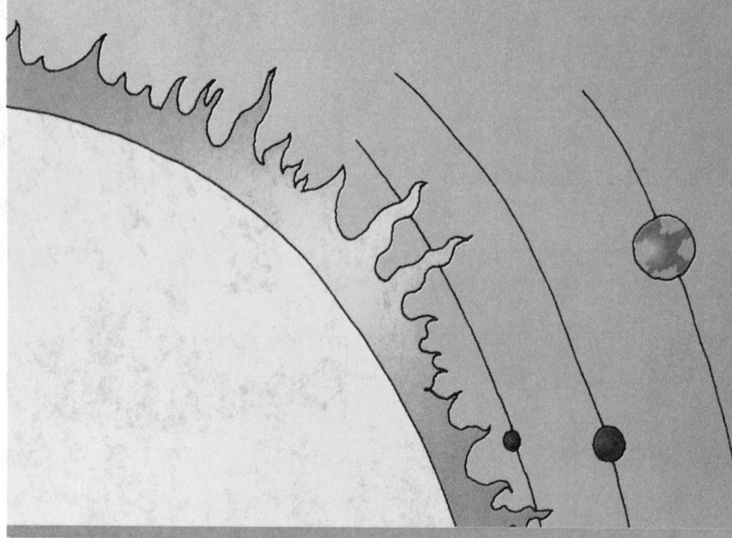

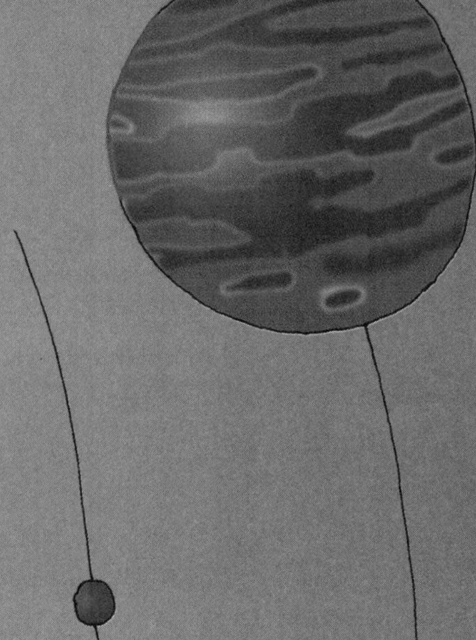

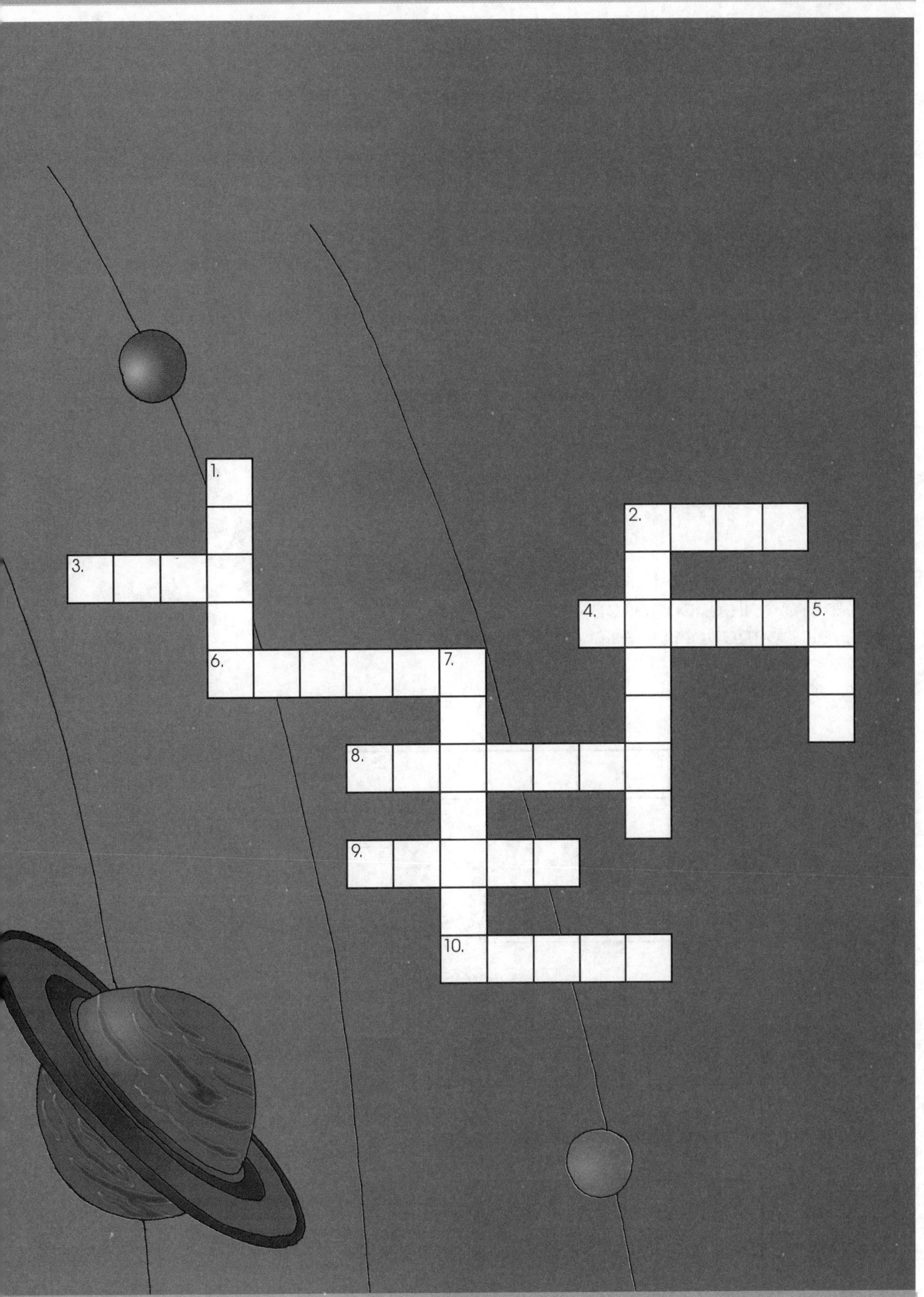
1.
2.
3.
4.
5.
6.
7.
8.
9.
10.

ARCHITECTURE

Architects design more than one kind of structure. Houses, schools, stadiums, and skyscrapers are a few of the many kinds of structures that skilled builders have created throughout history. The Great Pyramid in Egypt was built some 4,500 years ago as a tomb. An immense amount of stone was used to build it. In today's world, advances in engineering have eliminated the need for heavy walls. Modern buildings can be much taller than those of the past and can be built of lightweight outer frameworks of steel and glass. Some of the world's tallest buildings are in cities where people live and work. Architecture is one of the oldest art forms, and many important works of architecture have survived for centuries.

Across

1. a large structure for spectators that is built around a field
3. a place where people go to be taught
4. the home fortress of a monarch
7. where medical services are provided

Down

1. an exceptionally tall building
2. where collections of objects are displayed
5. a place that provides overnight lodging for the public
6. a single building where people live

castle
hospital
hotel
house
museum
school
skyscraper
stadium

SOUTH AMERICA

Across

1. Only the Nile River is longer than the _____ River.
3. Venezuela is one of the world's leading producers and exporters of _____.
4. _____ is the largest country in South America in both area and population.
5. The _____ Mountains, which stretch along the western coast of South America, are the world's longest mountain range above sea level.
7. _____ is bordered by five countries, the Pacific Ocean, and the Caribbean Sea.
8. Most of the Amazon Basin is covered by _____.

Down

1. _____ in Venezuela has the longest drop of any waterfall in the world.
2. The _____ is a fertile plain with a mild climate, which makes it ideal for farming and grazing cattle.
6. _____ was named for the equator, which crosses the country.

Amazon
Andes
Angel Falls
Brazil
Colombia
Ecuador
Pampa
petroleum
rainforests

1.
2.
3.
4.
5.
6.
7.
8.

ROCKS

To learn more about Earth's crust, geologists examine various rock samples. By using a microscope, they can study the different minerals that make up a rock's composition. Minerals are made up of atoms and molecules of different degrees of hardness. Diamond, the hardest, can cut glass. A mineral's hardness is often used to identify it. Minerals form three kinds of rock: sedimentary, metamorphic, and igneous. Sedimentary rocks are formed in thin layers from materials that were part of older rocks or of plants and animals. Over the years, the mass is compressed by the weight of more sand and solidified into sedimentary rock. Geologists can tell the age of a bed of sedimentary rock by examining the fossils that it contains. Metamorphic rock is made when other rock is altered by extreme heat or pressure. Ninety percent of the upper part of Earth's crust is made from igneous rock formed from hot magma (molten rock) that wells up from Earth's interior. The materials rocks are made of are continually recycled to make new rocks in a process called the rock cycle.

Across

3. atoms and molecules of varying degrees of hardness
4. The hardest mineral is _____.
6. Geologists use a _____ to examine rocks.
8. Rocks that are formed in thin layers are _____ rock.

Down

1. Ninety percent of Earth's crust is made from _____ rock.
2. Minerals can be identified by their _____.
3. Heat and pressure change other rock into _____ rock.
5. The age of sedimentary rock can be determined by _____ found in it.
7. Igneous rock is formed from hot _____ rock.

diamond
fossils
hardness
igneous
magma
metamorphic
microscope
minerals
sedimentary

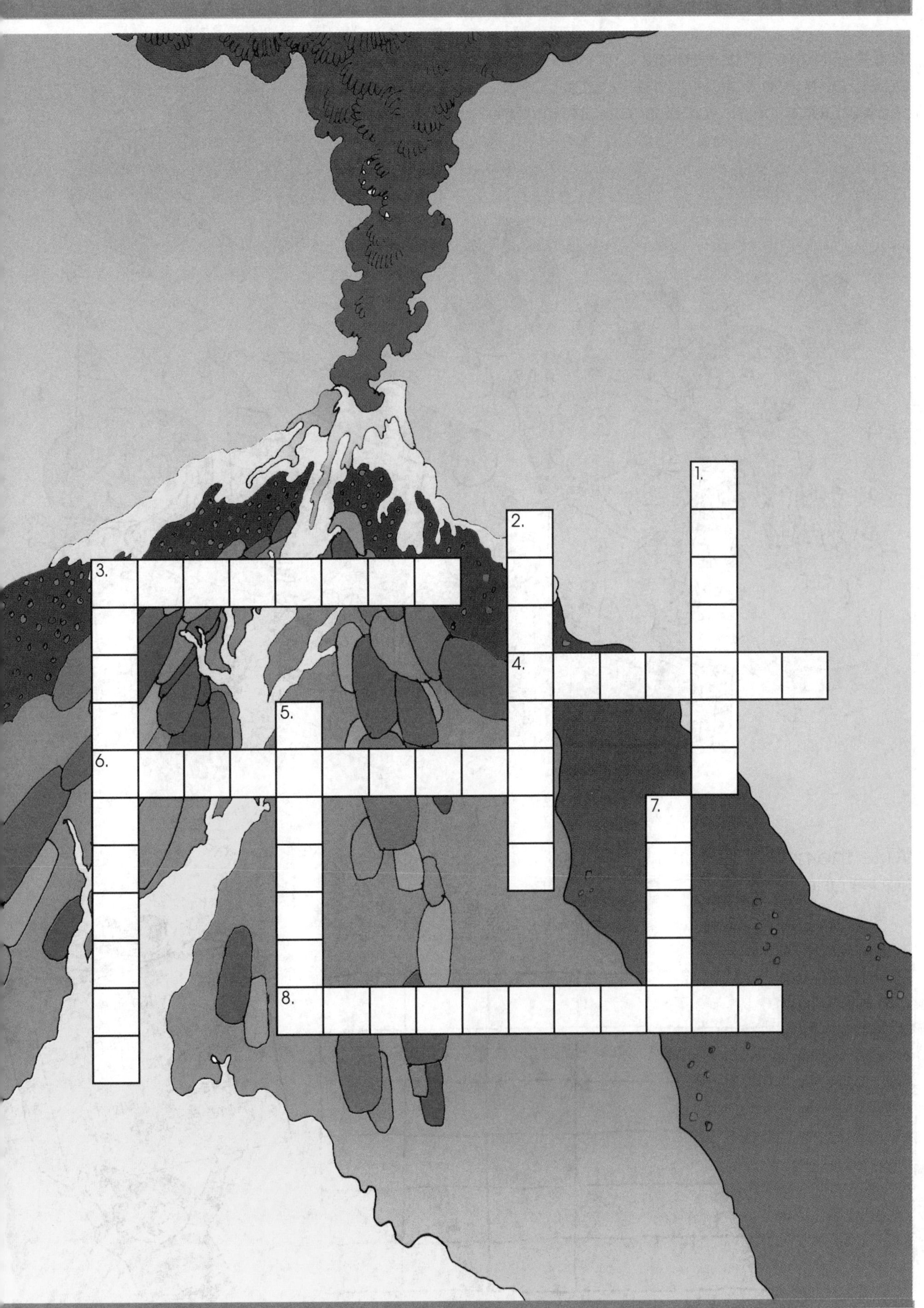

1.
2.
3.
4.
5.
6.
7.
8.

GUESS WHAT?

You're invited to Kevin's party if you can circle one of each of these solid figures: cube, cylinder, cone, sphere, rectangular prism, and a square pyramid.

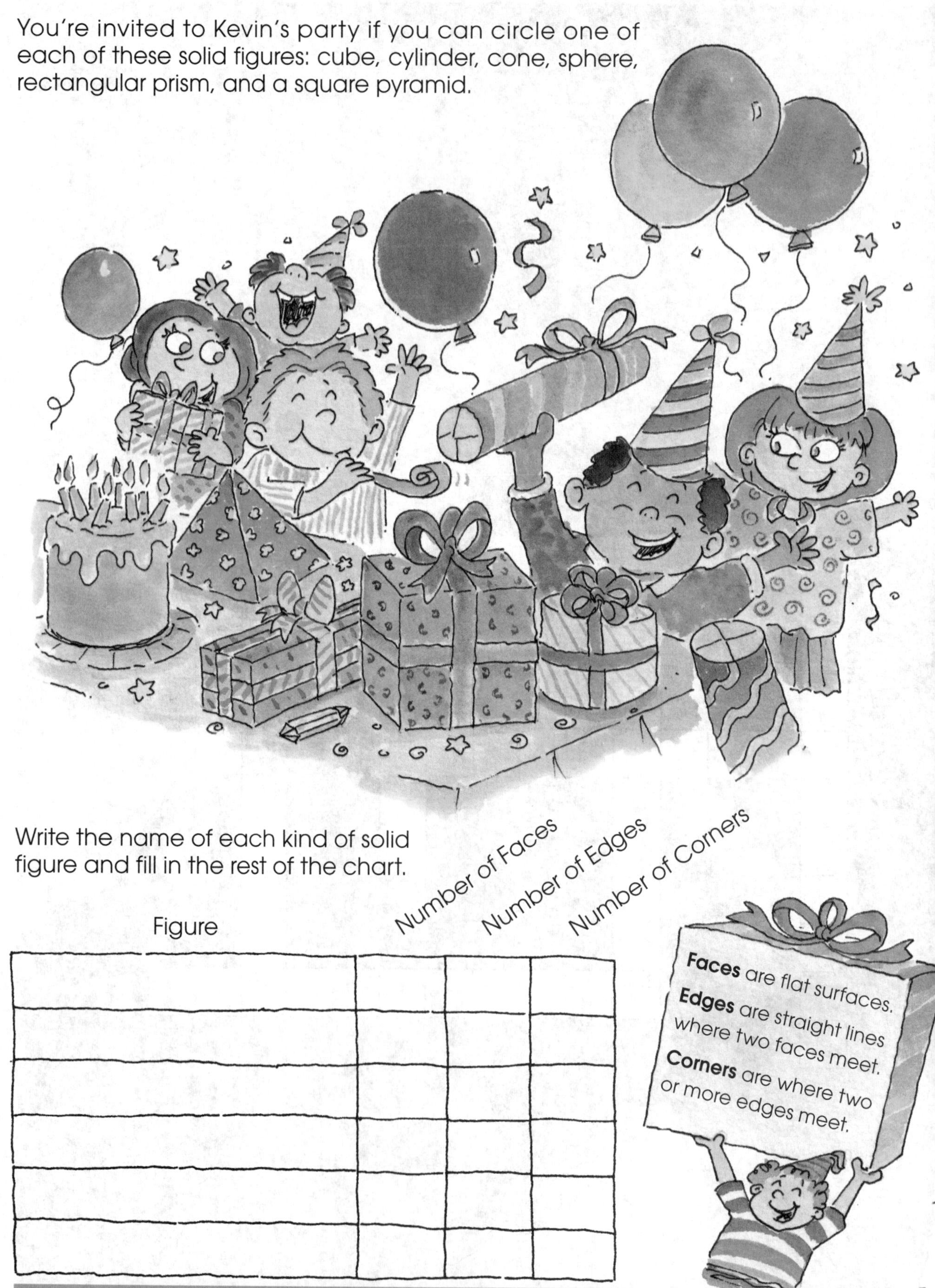

Faces are flat surfaces.
Edges are straight lines where two faces meet.
Corners are where two or more edges meet.

Write the name of each kind of solid figure and fill in the rest of the chart.

Figure	Number of Faces	Number of Edges	Number of Corners

PET IT OR EAT IT?

Seth's mother has several gifts for him. Help Seth crack the code and find out what his gifts are.

First, finish writing the code.

1 = A	2 = B	3 = C	4 = D	5 =	6 =	7 =	8 =	9 =	10 =
11 =	12 =	13 =	14 =	15 =	16 =	17 =	18 =	19 =	20 =
21 =	22 =	23 =	24 =	25 =	26 =				

Next, write the number that completes each equation in the box below it. Then write the code letter below the number. Last, write **animal**, **vegetable**, or **mineral**.

equation	2 x 2 =	5 x 3 =	9 - 2 =				
number							
letter							
equation	4 - 1 =	8 + 7 =	4 x 4 =	20 - 4 =	$5\overline{)25}$ =	6 x 3 =	
number							
letter							
equation	12 + 7 =	2 x 7 =	1 - 0 =	5 + 6 =	10 ÷ 2 =		
number							
letter							
equation	5 + 10 =	7 x 2 =	18 ÷ 2 =	8 + 7 =	15 - 1 =		
number							
letter							
equation	9 - 6 =	3 + 2 =	4 x 3 =	25 ÷ 5 =	24 - 6 =	5 x 5 =	
number							
letter							
equation	6 x 3 =	7 x 3 =	$10\overline{)20}$ =	32 - 7 =			
number							
letter							

MONSTER APPETITES

How much pizza can these monsters eat? The survey shows the fraction of a pizza each one ate. If the monster ate less than a whole pizza, draw a line from the monster to the forest. If the monster ate more than a whole pizza, draw a line from the monster to the beach.

Which monster ate the most pizza? ______________________________

THE OPERATIONS ARE MISSING

Lots of math events happened to the citizens of the town of Digit today. Finish the equation to show what happened in each story.

1. By accident, Maxine hit a beehive with a ball. At first she only saw , but soon there were . What happened?

2. Michelle, Justin, and Drew brought to the picnic. Each took to eat. What happened?

3. Daniela borrowed from Siri and then lost them. What happened?

______ = ______ CDs

4. The class was asked to think of each for the winter play. Then the teacher said, "Make that ." What happened?

______ =

5. Daniela planned to buy for Siri but ended up buying .

What happened? ______ =

6. Kurt selected , then decided to buy half that many instead. What happened?

______ = ______ bananas

7. Marshall and Tyler fed to an elephant. Marshall fed the elephant and Tyler fed it . How many all together?

______ = ______ peanuts

ODD MAZE

You're invited to the King of Unevenville's New Year's dinner! Help him find his way to the dining room. Trace a path through the number grid on the odd numbers, starting at 1. You may only go across or down, but not diagonally.

1	3	14	6	90	4	102
66	17	11	29	58	88	30
64	32	12	67	54	20	18
100	78	53	91	40	36	24
8	34	19	16	82	98	48
22	46	71	56	14	50	6
68	80	77	87	109	97	98
72	100	2	44	62	11	106
86	38	26	60	28	35	82
42	84	94	52	50	91	111

ROUND, ROUND, GET AROUND

Look at each middle number. Then round the number and color the correct ball. The first one is done for you.

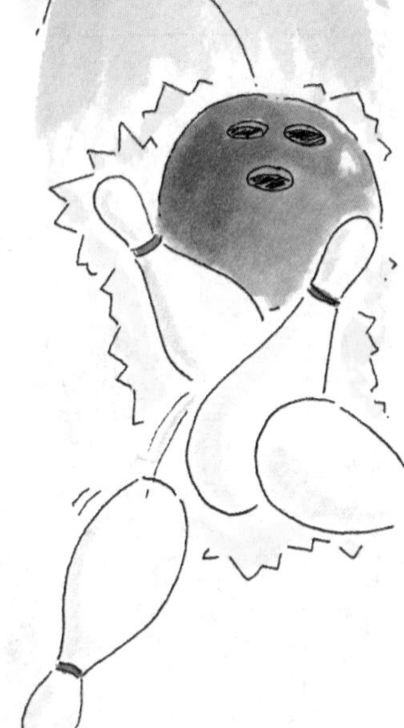

Round to the nearest tenth.

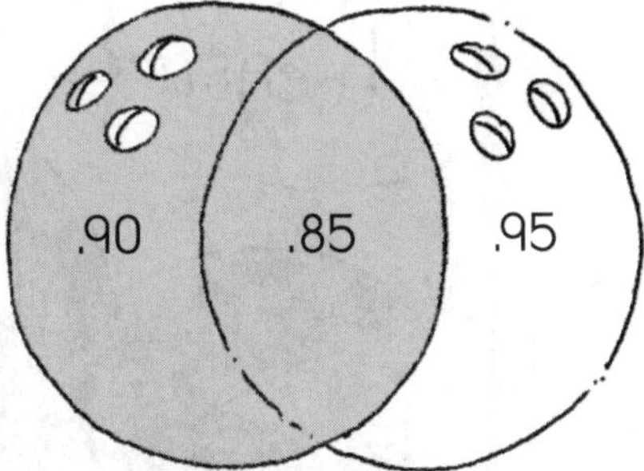

Round to the nearest hundred.

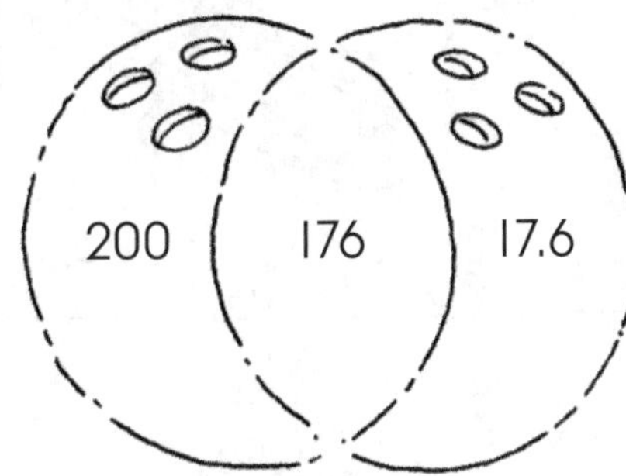

Round to the nearest one.

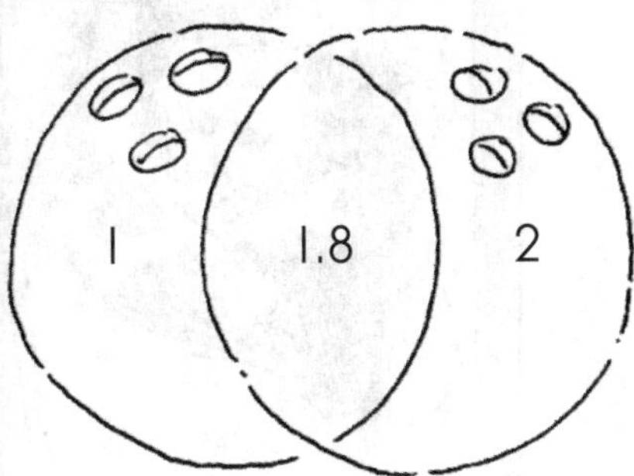

Round to the nearest ten.

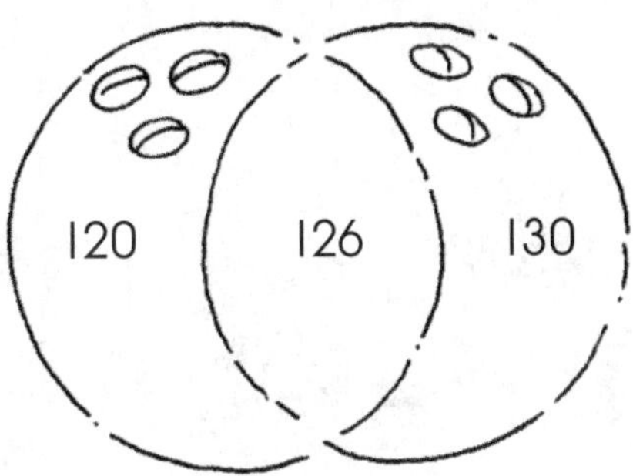

Round to the nearest hundreth.

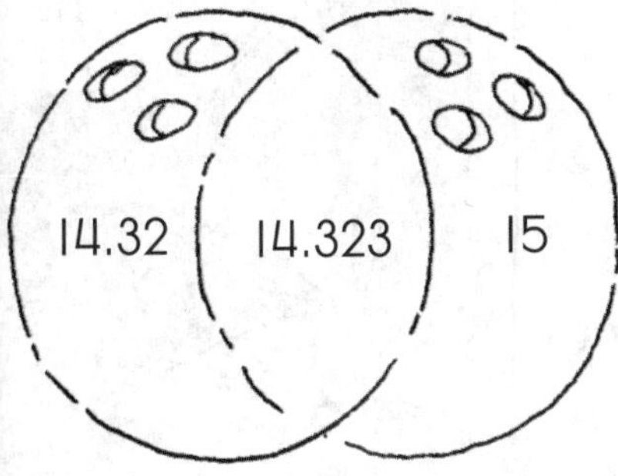

Round to the nearest thousand.

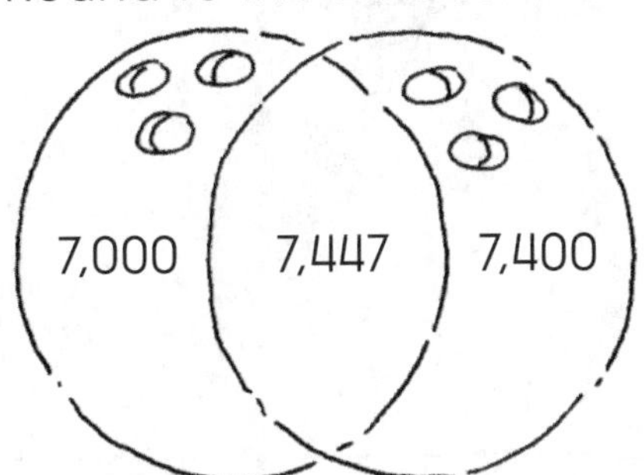

Round to the nearest tenth.

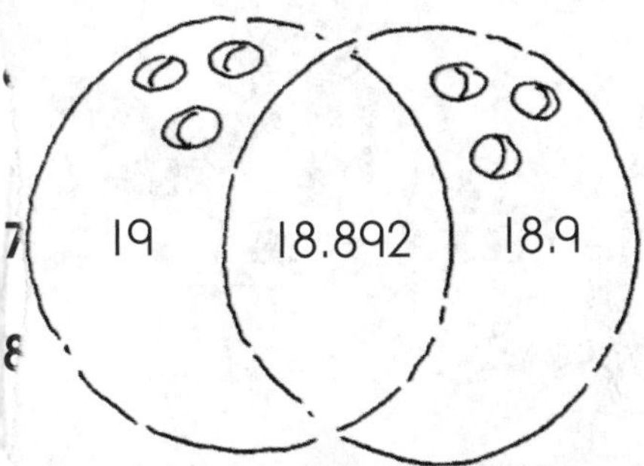

Round to the nearest ten thousand.

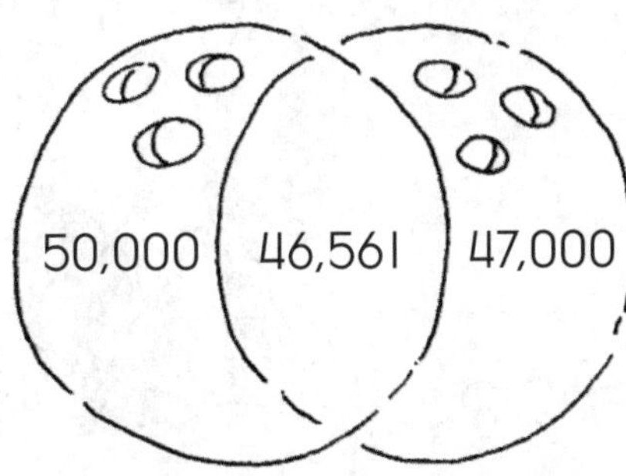

ACK! TREASURE!

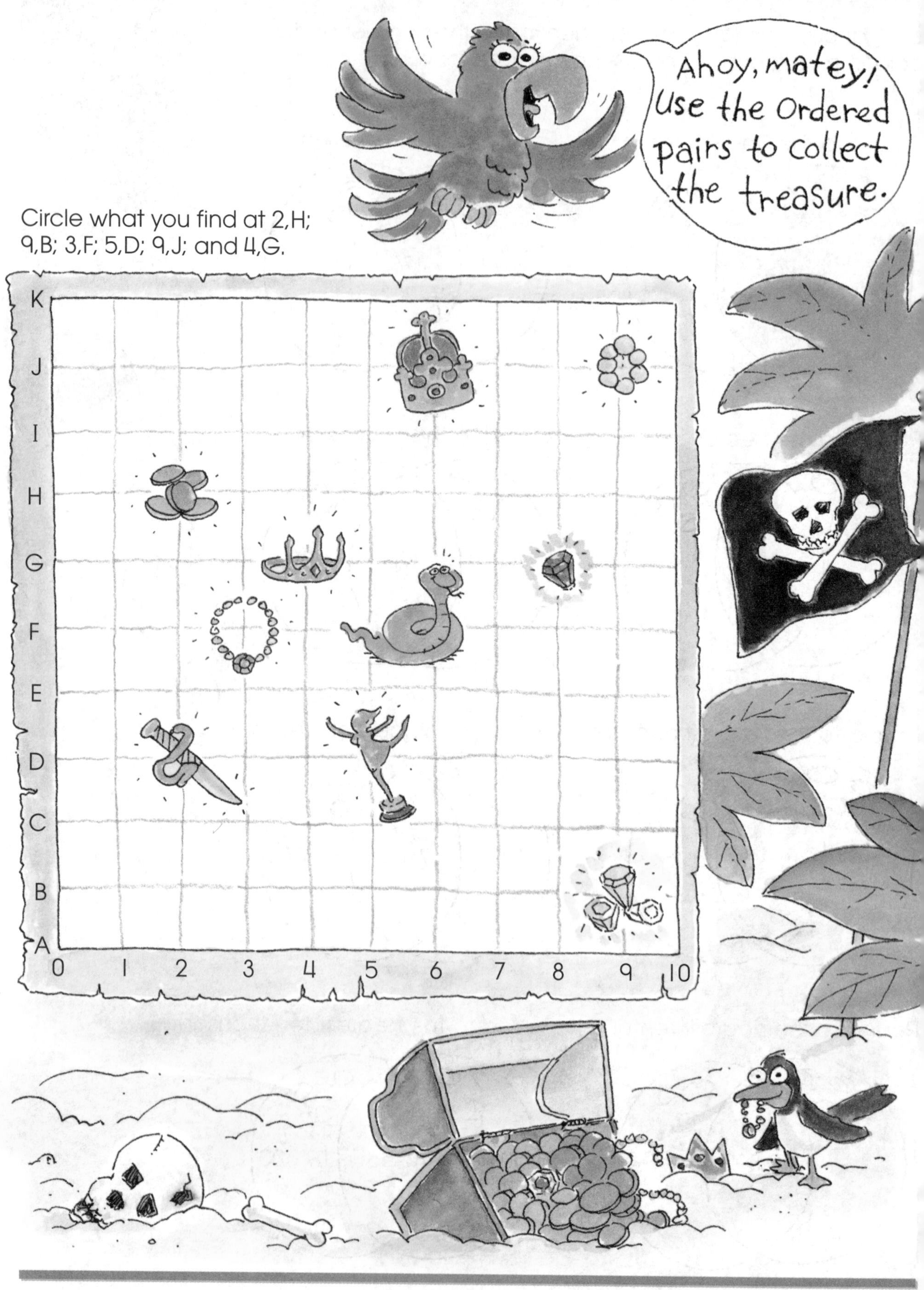

Circle what you find at 2,H; 9,B; 3,F; 5,D; 9,J; and 4,G.

POCKET MONEY

Come to a yard sale with Pauline.
She has these coins in her pocket.

Pauline wants to buy one thing. Put an **X** on every item she can afford. Put a ✔ on things she can buy with exact change.

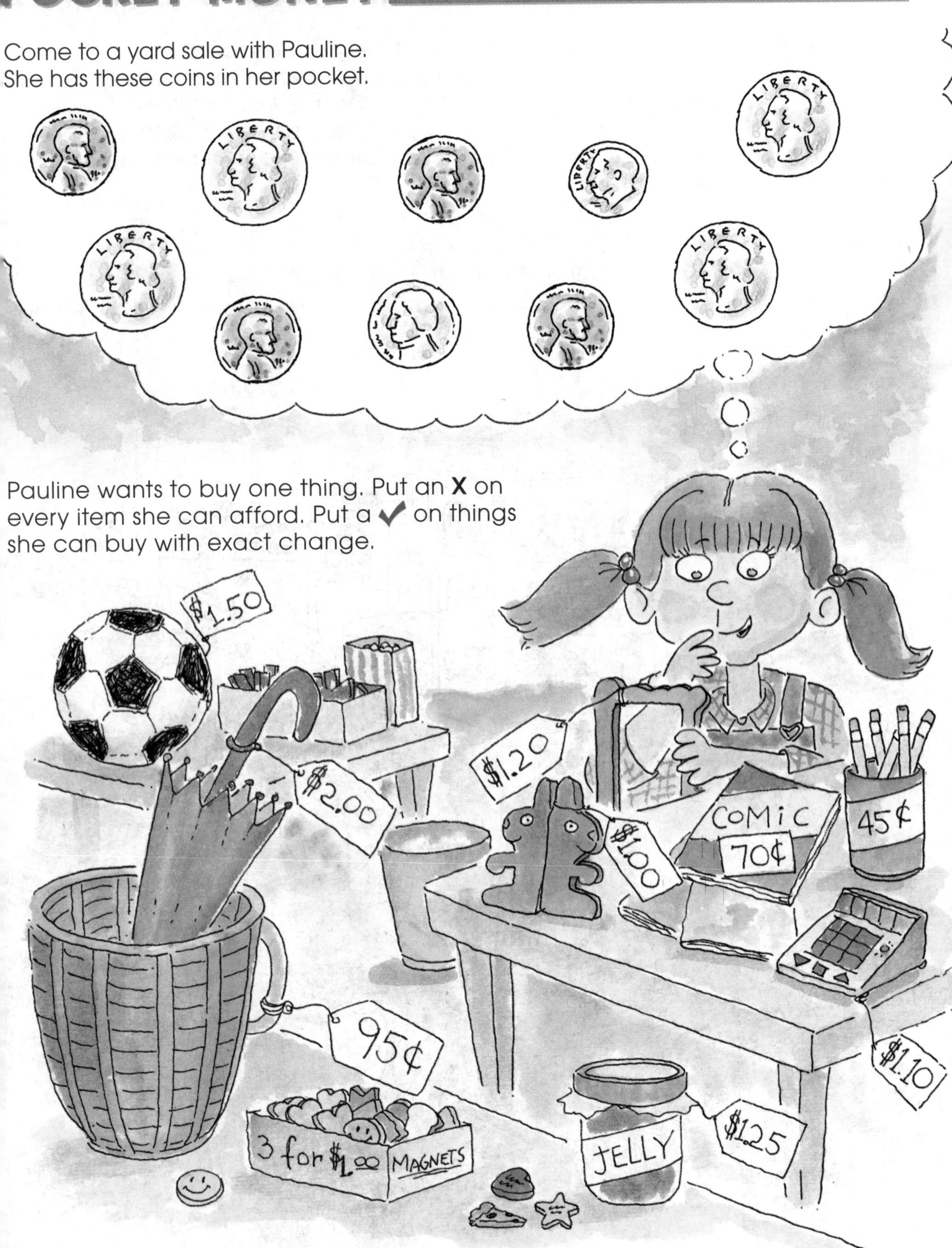

TOY FACTORY

Mrs. Chasen's class of 16 students went on a field trip to a toy factory. The whole class brought lunch, but only half the students brought sandwiches. Three-fourths of the students who didn't bring sandwiches brought fruit. Of the children who brought sandwiches, half brought two sandwiches; the rest brought one. One-fourth of the children who brought sandwiches also brought fruit.

1. How many children brought fruit? ________
2. How many children brought one or more sandwiches and fruit? ________
3. The children lost all their sandwiches during their tour! How many sandwiches were lost? ________

Circle the lost sandwiches.

RUG SHAPES

Wow! How did they make these interesting patterns? Write **slide**, **flip**, or **turn**.

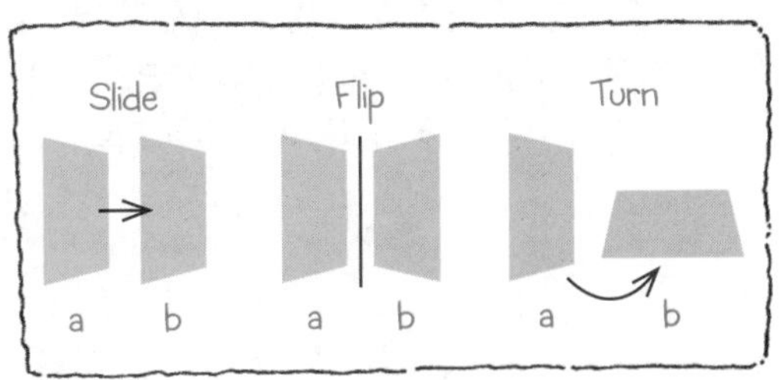

1. ____________________

2. ____________________

3. ____________________

4. ____________________

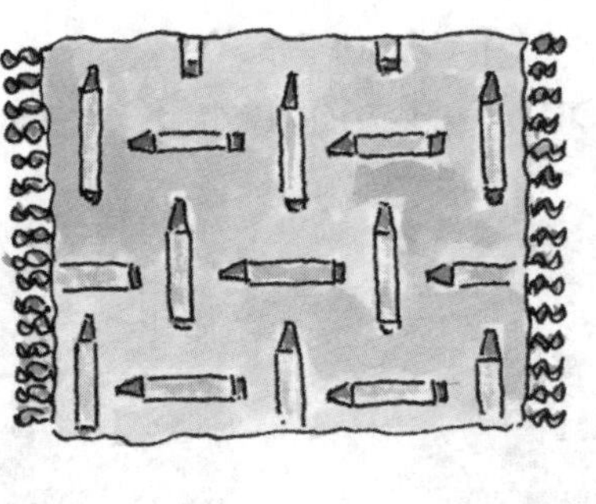

5. ____________________

6. ____________________

7. ____________________

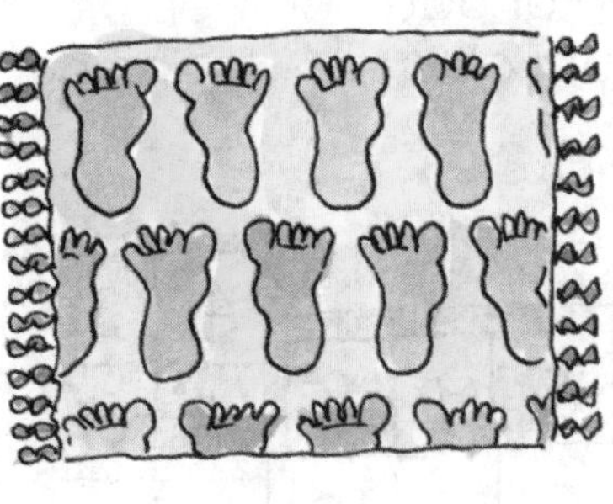

8. ____________________

9. ____________________

EQUAL OR UNEQUAL?

The kids are playing games. But wait a minute! Some of these games aren't fair. Can you figure out which games they have an equal chance of winning?

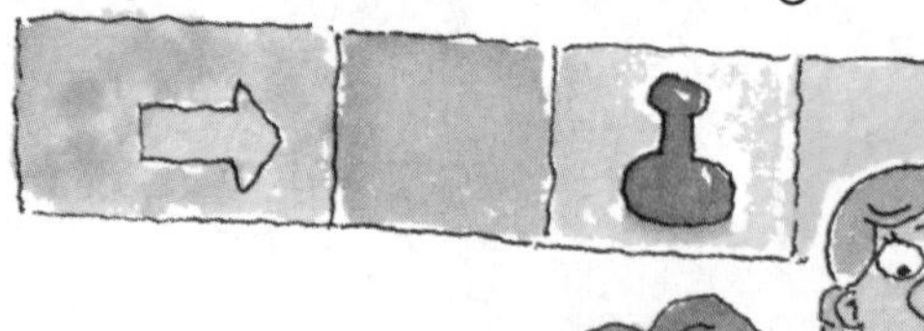

In this game, underline the spinner that has the greatest chance of landing on green.

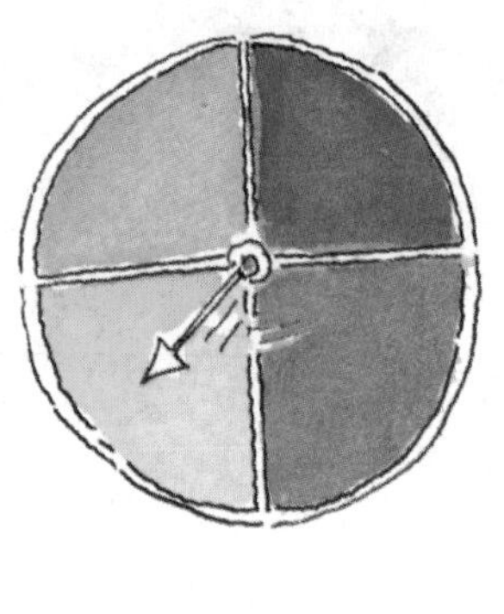
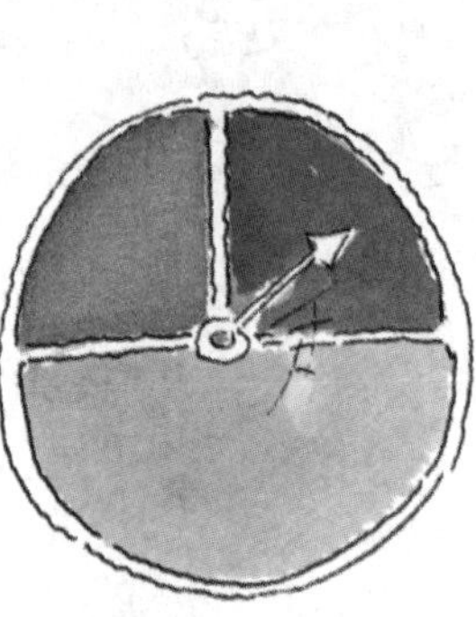
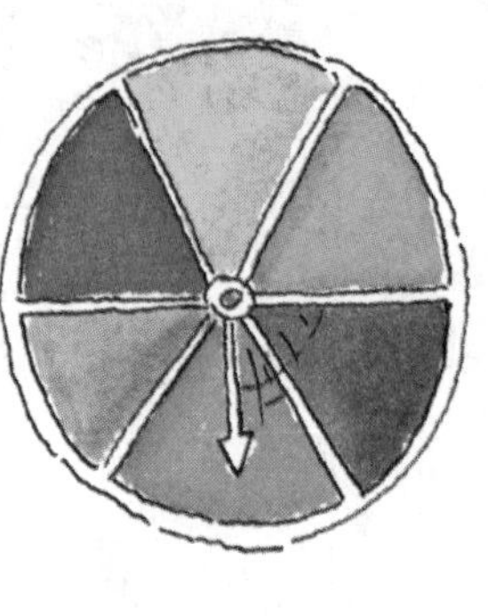
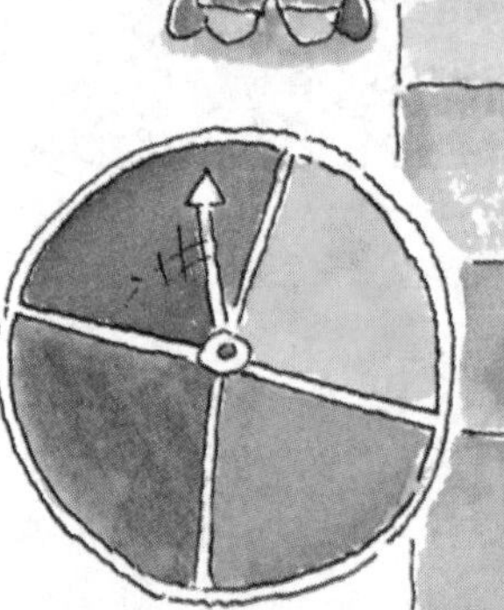

In this game, try to pick a marble of your chosen color. Circle the bags that you have an equal chance of winning. **X** the bags that are unequal.

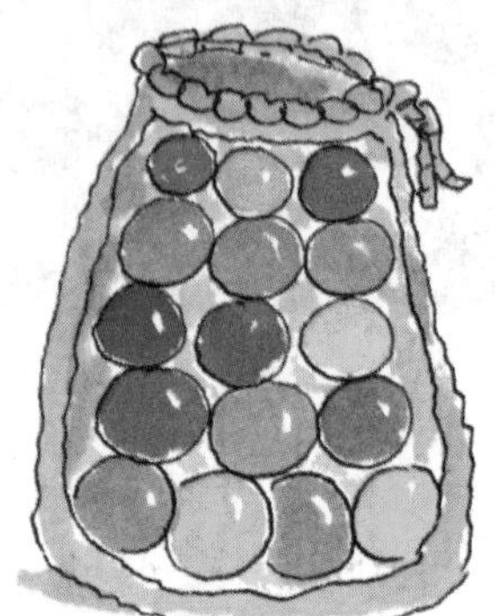
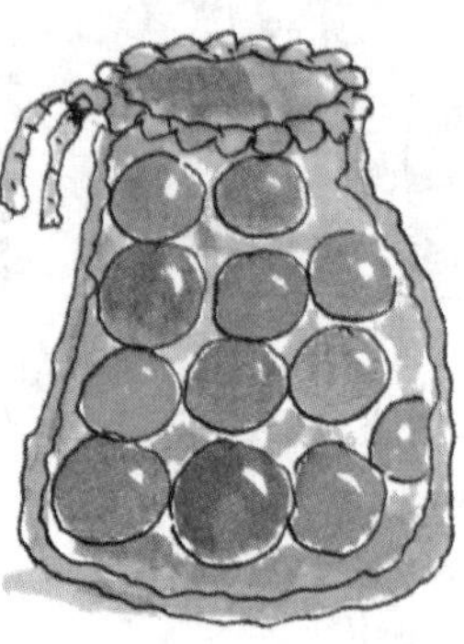
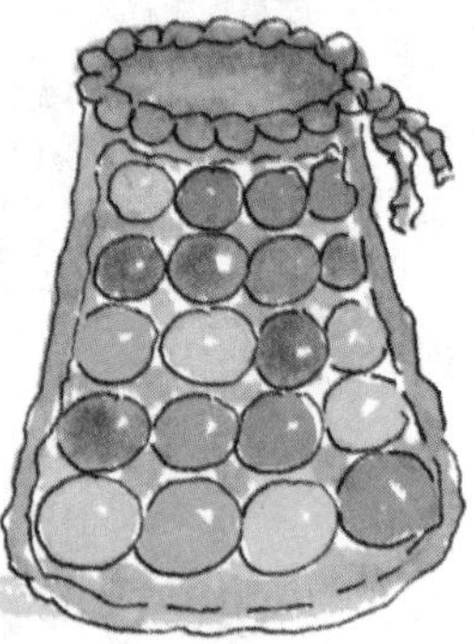

In this game, choose an even or odd number. Underline the boards that you have an equal chance of winning. **X** the boards that are unequeal.

CROSS OUT AND GRIN

Fill in the blanks. Then cross out the answers in the puzzle. The letters that are left answer this riddle: Which dog tells the best time?

WHAT TIME IS IT?

WHERE'S THE DOG, DEAR?

1. There are 1,000 millimeters in one ____________.

2. There are 60 minutes in an ____________.

3. There are 3 feet in a ____________.

4. There are 24 hours in a ____________.

5. There are 16 ounces in a ____________.

6. There are 100 centimeters in a ____________.

7. There are 40 nickles in two ____________.

8. There are 1,000 meters in about 5/8 of a ____________.

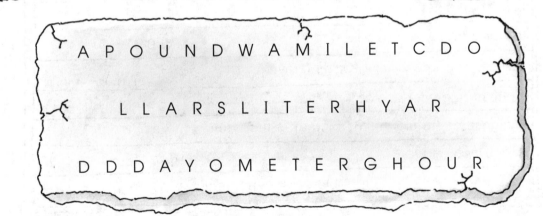

A P O U N D W A M I L E T C D O

L L A R S L I T E R H Y A R

D D D A Y O M E T E R G H O U R

MISSING DECIMAL POINTS

A summer storm hit the town of Decimal and blew away all the decimal points! Help the townsfolk restore the decimals. Add a decimal point to each number in the chart.

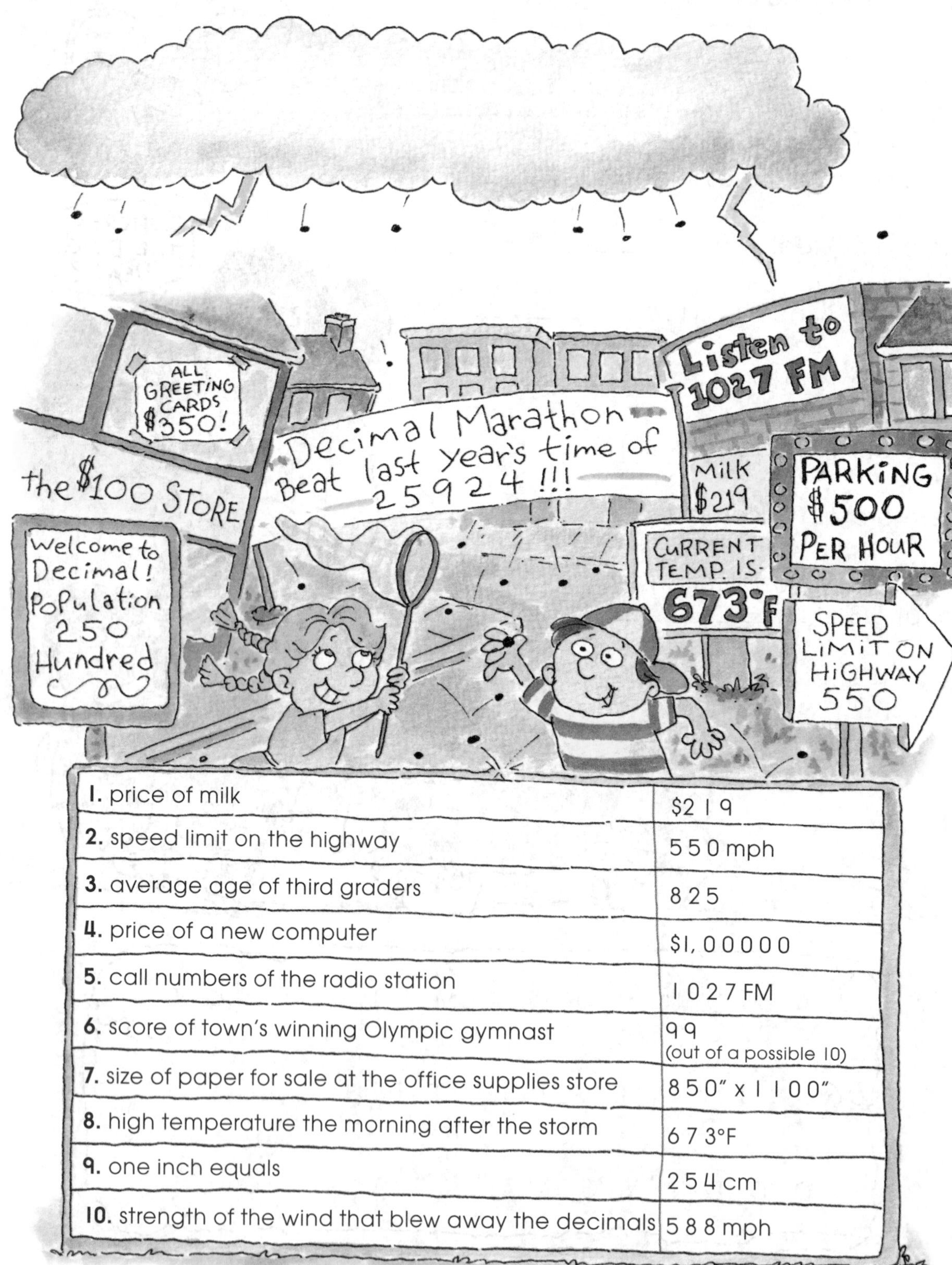

1. price of milk	$2 1 9
2. speed limit on the highway	5 5 0 mph
3. average age of third graders	8 2 5
4. price of a new computer	$1, 0 0 0 0 0
5. call numbers of the radio station	1 0 2 7 FM
6. score of town's winning Olympic gymnast	9 9 (out of a possible 10)
7. size of paper for sale at the office supplies store	8 5 0″ x 1 1 0 0″
8. high temperature the morning after the storm	6 7 3°F
9. one inch equals	2 5 4 cm
10. strength of the wind that blew away the decimals	5 8 8 mph

MENTAL ADVENTURE

While you're exploring an exotic temple in a dense jungle, a door suddenly slams shut. You struggle to open it, but no luck. You're trapped! The only way to save yourself is to complete a legendary numbers grid. You may not work out the answers on paper—the only thing you may write is the answer to each question. If you disobey the door will never open!

DOTS A LOT OF HEARTS!

Estimate the number of dots and hearts in the towers. If you're close, you win the dots and hearts! How will you come up with fairly accurate estimates?

Estimate: ___________

Strategy: ___________________________________

____

Estimate: ___________

Strategy: ___________________________________

____

Answer each clue with a mammal from the word search. Then write the letters in the boxes.

A. I can swing in trees using my tail. ________________

B. My face is marked like a bandit. ________________

C. I make clicking sounds underwater. ________________

D. I am the largest land animal. ________________

E. I am the tallest land animal. ________________

F. You might mistake me for a flying mouse. ________________

G. I like to float on ice. ________________

H. I am the only animal with bones called antlers. ________________

INSECTS

Both people and insects are animals, but they differ in many ways. Insects have a hard outside shell instead of bones. Insects have six legs, and most adult insects have wings.

An insect's body has three parts. The head has eyes, antennae (an-**ten**-ee), and the parts that eat. The thorax is behind the head. The wings and legs are connected to the thorax. The abdomen is the tail end. Some insects, such as bees, have a stinger on the end of the abdomen.

Think About It!

Design an insect that could live underwater.

Fireflies are bioluminescent, which means they give off light. A chemical reaction in the bug's abdomen creates the flashing or glowing light.

Label the insect parts below. Use the words in the box to help you.

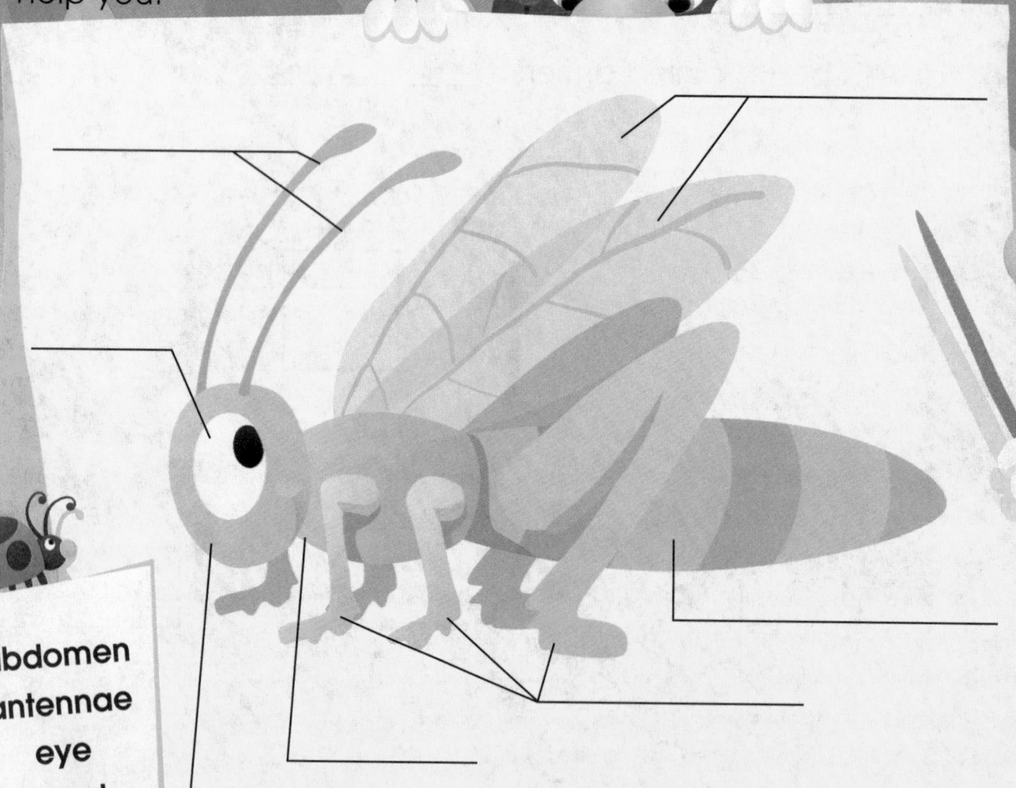

abdomen
antennae
eye
head
legs
thorax
wings

Use the code to learn the names of some unusual reptiles and amphibians.

A	D	E	F	G	I	K	L	N	O	R	S	T	U	Z

1. This amphibian grips smooth surfaces with sticky suction pads on its toes.

2. If threatened, this reptile spreads a flap of skin around its neck.

3. This reptile has spines on its back and can live for over 100 years.

4. This amphibian lives in mountain streams with fast currents.

5. This type of young newt can grow a new leg if one is injured.

6. This poisonous reptile gives a warning before it strikes.

BIRDS

Think About It!

Why do birds fly? Does flight give them an advantage over other animals?

Birds are special animals because they have feathers. Most birds use the feathers on their wings for flying. Feathers also keep birds warm in cold weather and dry in water.

Birds use their beaks to eat different kinds of food. Birds that eat hard seeds have short, cone-shaped beaks. Hawks and owls have hooked beaks for tearing apart their prey. Ducks have flat beaks to filter tiny plants and animals from the water.

Birds' feet come in many shapes and sizes. Birds that perch on tree branches usually have three toes in front and one toe behind, for good grip. Long, wide toes keep a heron from sinking in mud. Birds of prey have long, curved claws called talons. Ducks and water birds often have webbed feet.

H A
V E
B K R M P
L I M O E R
U N W J N
E G S H G
L J F T Q U J M
H A I S C I H O
W P Y S C V N I
N U T H A T C H B
V W O S E A G U L L
P H O L D R J W K P
C D G O M D T B X K M
D R O A D R U N N E R
W O O B F P F C O I B
K C P N B H P E I K L K
S J F A M I Y V C K G
J R T A N R N P I K C R E K D I
Q S G D J O S T R I C H D W T E H D U O S
W U D L S D Q C Y S P A R R O W N A T I C R F V B L N T
A H U M M I N G B I R D I S M Z N L N Y R B U H U O
C V I H S N D T P G O L D F I N C H A J A Q O W L I
W P E L I C A N C K F J M E L I J

blue jay
cardinal
duck
goldfinch
hawk
heron
hummingbird

jacana
kingfisher
nuthatch
ostrich
owl
pelican
penguin

pigeon
quail
roadrunner
robin
seagull
sparrow
woodpecker

The bar-headed goose is believed to be the highest flyer. It has been known to fly at an altitude of over 25,000 feet.
The peregrine falcon is thought to be the fastest diver at over 200 miles per hour.
The bee hummingbird is the smallest bird at about 2 inches long and weighing about 2 grams.
The male African ostrich is the largest bird. It can be 9 feet tall and weigh 300 pounds.
The emperor penguin can dive underwater at depths of over 500 feet.
Help the bird find the way back to its nest.

OCEAN PLANTS & ANIMALS

Close to shore or far from land, at the sunny surface or miles down in inky blackness, the ocean is filled with plants and animals. Most ocean animals are fish—about 15,000 different kinds have been identified so far. Fish usually live in the shallow water over the continental shelf.

Many animals besides fish live in the ocean, including tiny plankton and huge whales. Sharks are fish, but they don't have bones. Instead, a shark's skeleton is made of cartilage. Whales and dolphins are mammals. They are warm-blooded, they breathe air, and they give birth to live young. Many ocean animals are invertebrates. They don't have backbones. Some invertebrates are jellyfish, starfish, and squid.

Think About It!

How do oil spills and other forms of pollution affect ocean plants and animals?

```
                          D A T S G T A
                    U Q L R F K E L P H
                W J S H R I M P A J K I
              V F H H O N J M B W K D O
A           E S V K A N C S M P E B O
F C       F H H L C K L A T E Q E F L
D A R A B G D S E A H O R S E J O A D T P
O M H A S Q U I D R H R M Q P U K P F J H
  B T Y B I V H J K S A I L F I S H U A I
  J B A R N A C L E P L A N K T O N J S N
  C G K J K S O G M E Q S T A R F I S H V
  L O H A       S T L T Q A H O N Q U I
  S M D             S E A A N E M O N E
    T
```

barnacle	eel	sailfish	shark
cod	kelp	sea anemone	shrimp
coral	limpet	sea fan	squid
crab	octopus	seahorse	starfish
dolphin	plankton	seaweed	whale

ENVIRONMENTS

Think About It!

How do you think early humans adapted to different environments?

In what type of habitat do you live? How have you adapted?

Animals live all over the world, from frozen tundras to hot deserts. An animal's natural environment is called its habitat. Many animals migrate from one habitat to another. Other animals have adapted to their environment by developing special characteristics. For instance, heavy fur protects some animals from the cold.

Often, animals in similar habitats in different parts of the world have similar characteristics. For example, kangaroo rats in North America look like gerbils that live in the Sahara Desert.

coral reef
desert
forest
grassland
marshland
mountain
polar ice
rainforest
scrubland
swamp
tundra
woodland

PIONEERS

Pioneers are the first people to venture into new lands. Thousands of American pioneers left the eastern United States to settle on land between the Appalachian Mountains and the Pacific Ocean. Two major pioneer migrations are an important part of U.S. history. Around 1760, pioneers traveled from the Appalachians to the Mississippi Valley. During the second migration, which began in the 1840s, pioneers reached Oregon and California.

There are many famous pioneers, including Daniel Boone, Kit Carson, and Davy Crockett. It is important to remember that thousands of men and women faced dangers and hardships as they looked for new opportunities. Pioneers discovered important facts about geography, transportation, and agriculture.

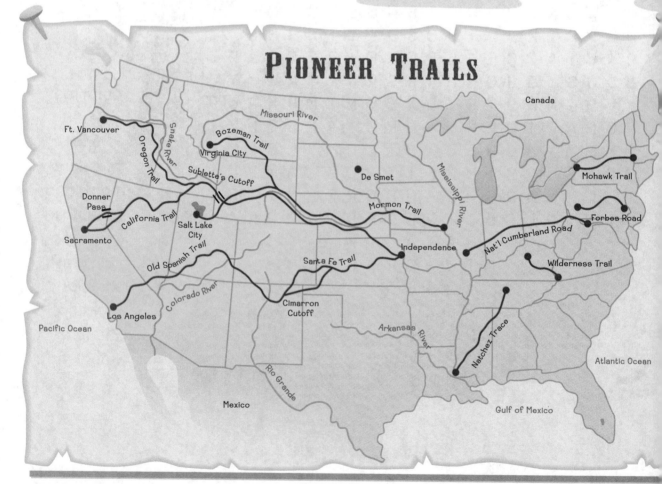

PIONEER TRAILS

Canada
Missouri River
Ft. Vancouver
Oregon Trail
Snake River
Bozeman Trail
Virginia City
Sublette's Cutoff
De Smet
Mississippi River
Mohawk Trail
Donner Pass
California Trail
Salt Lake City
Sacramento
Mormon Trail
Forbes Road
Nat'l Cumberland Road
Independence
Old Spanish Trail
Santa Fe Trail
Wilderness Trail
Colorado River
Cimarron Cutoff
Los Angeles
Pacific Ocean
Arkansas River
Natchez Trace
Atlantic Ocean
Rio Grande
Mexico
Gulf of Mexico

Northwestern totem poles serve as an emblem of a family or clan. They can tell a story or mark a grave.

Inuit live farther north than any other people. The Inuit obtain most of their food from hunting and fishing.

Hiawatha, an important leader, helped bring peace to five main Iroquois tribes. They formed an alliance called the Iroquois Confederacy.

Buffalo provided meat, clothing, and shelter for Native Americans living on the Plains.

Sacagawea, a Shoshone woman, was a guide and interpreter for the Lewis and Clark expedition to the Pacific Ocean.

Sequoyah invented a system of writing for his native language of Cherokee.

Little Big Horn Montana

Wounded Knee South Dakota

Serpent Mound Ohio

Mesa Verde Colorado

Trail of Tears To Oklahoma

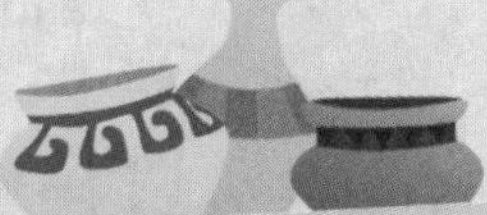

Southwestern Pueblo people lived in connected stone or adobe buildings that were up to four stories tall.

Crazy Horse, Geronimo, Osceola, and Pontiac were famous Native Americans.

CANADA

Think About It!

Canada is the second largest country in the world. It is rich in scenic beauty and natural resources. A federal government binds Canada's ten provinces and three territories in a democratic nation. Canada's closest economic and social ties are with the United States, which shares common interests and a common background.

Why do you think Canada's population is less than the United States' population even though Canada is a larger country?

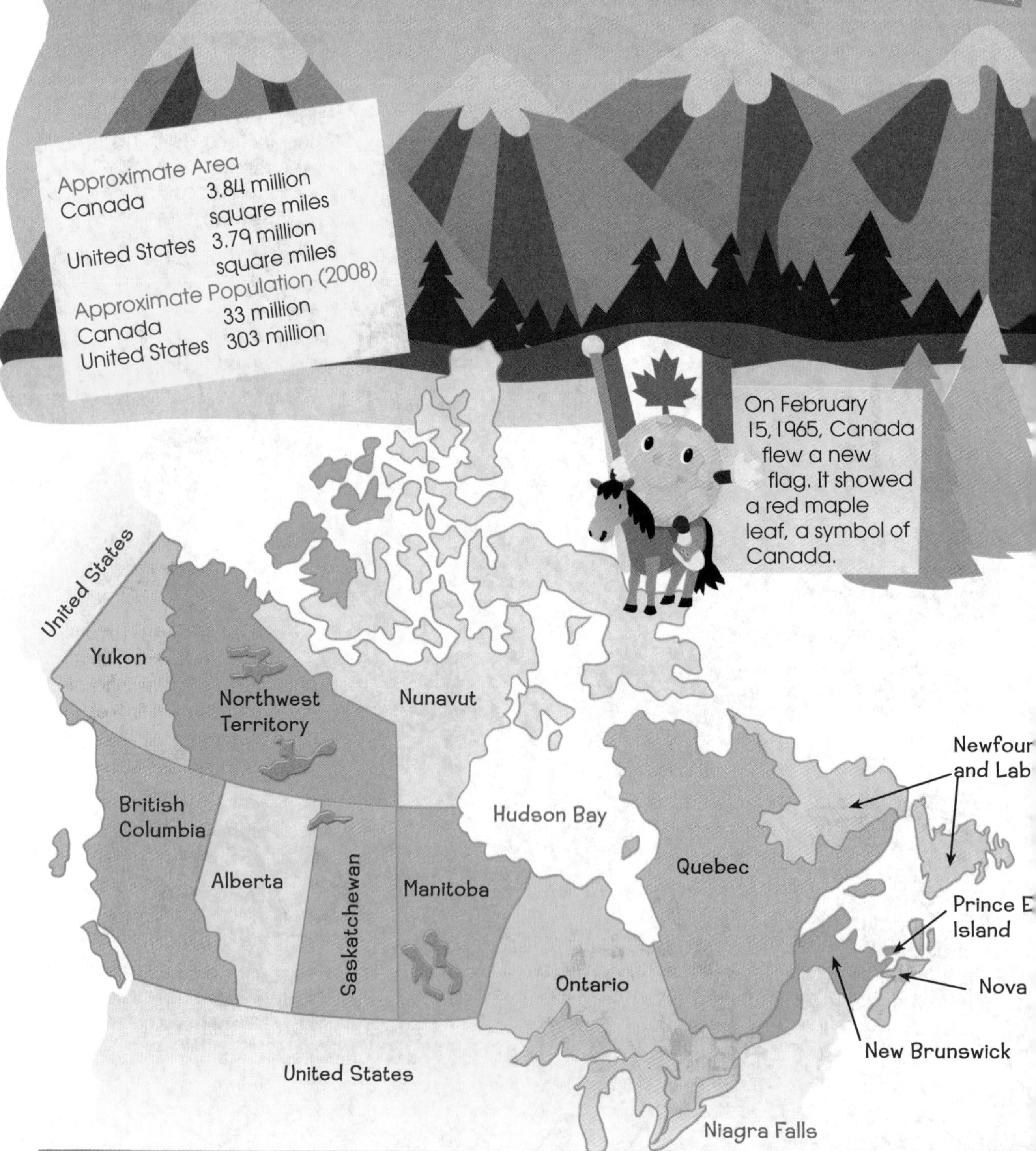

Niagara Falls is one of the greatest hydro-electric power sources in the world.

The territory of Nunavut was established in 1999. The word Nunavut means "our land" in Inuit.

Canadians celebrate Canada Day on July 1, the date in 1867 that Canada became a country. Canada still recognizes the British monarch as queen or king of Canada.

```
              S
              A B
              L R
            N B I E
O A       T U E T V       G M
  U W Q F N R I C Q K A
  S N U T A T S I H Y T
  W T N S V A H R T A H
  M L   A O W U E C S N D           E O
X U B E Z S A   V I J T A O N C H   A V N Q A T I O
N E W F O U N D L A N D A N D L A B R A D O R M R
V N O V A S C O T I A Q U O H N F N L P B S Y W
P R I N C E E D W A R D I S L A N D L R Q S A S
U W S K R T C H E O A B R I T I S H C O L U M B I A
Z P A S A S K A T C H E W A N W U Q N O E H R O
E T I A F B S I V Q N R T E P I N T M B A P
Q K Z U M A N I T O B A S A C A Q E H
N E W B R U N S W I C K N Q R U C
A T C Y K F O S J B Y S T I
N O R T H W E S T L E K I O
D F         A           A G
            Y
            U
            K
            O
            N
```

PROVINCES

Alberta
British Columbia
Manitoba
New Brunswick
Newfoundland and Labrador
Nova Scotia
Ontario
Prince Edward Island
Quebec
Saskatchewan

TERRITORIES

Northwest
Nunavut
Yukon

Canada has two official languages, English and French.

Hello! Bonjour!

EXPLORERS

Since prehistoric times, people have engaged in exploration as they searched for food and shelter. Eventually, prehistoric people populated all of the continents except Antarctica.

During ancient and medieval times, explorers from Europe, the Middle East, and Asia charted territories far from their homelands. Even so, many parts of the world remained isolated until the Europeans became active explorers during a period known as the Age of Exploration, which lasted from the early 15th century until the 17th century. By the early 20th century, most parts of the world had been mapped. New frontiers for exploration still exist deep in the oceans and outer space.

Think About It!

How do you think early explorers prepared for a journey? What kinds of transportation and tools did they have? What were some of the dangers they faced?

c. 950 - 1000

ERIK THE RED

This Norwegian explorer was named Erik Thorvaldsson He was nicknamed for his red hair. He named and colonized Greenland.

c. 1540-1595

SIR FRANCIS DRAKE

Drake was the first Englishman to sail around the world. He earned a reputation as a ruthless pirate.

1930 - 2012

NEIL ARMSTRONG

This U.S. astronaut was the first person to step on the moon. He and Edwin Aldrin, Jr. landed on the moon on July 20, 1969.

1254 - 1324

MARCO POLO

This Italian explorer became famous for his travels. His book, **The Travels of Marco Polo,** was very popular.

1491 - 1557

JACQUES CARTIER

When he explored North America, this French explorer became friends with the Iroquois people. He named Canada and based the name on the Huron-Iroquois word "Kanata," which means "village."

Amundsen, Roald
Armstrong, Neil
Cabot, John
Cartier, Jacques
Champlain, Samuel de
Clark, William
Columbus, Christopher
Cortés, Hernando

Drake, Sir Francis
Erikson, Leif
Erik the Red
Hillary, Sir Edmund Percival
Hudson, Henry
Lewis, Meriwether

Livingstone, David
Magellan, Ferdinand
Marquette, Jacques
Polo, Marco
Ponce de León, Juan
Soto, Hernando de

Jeanne Baré was probably the first woman to sail around the world. In 1766, this young Frenchwoman disguised herself as a male servant and sailed on the first French voyage around the world.

```
                         B C Y H
              L E W U N I P N L M D
D A M U N D S E N R O A C Y L W A E C
  R W Q K D C A R T I E R O D A R R L
  O T D U S Y W R N S K V L R E Q T K
  C N S F O L I E M T F T U L T U L I
  O H G G I H S G D S O G H L K E G W
  L S I Y R T I N P M T Y M E B T S F
  U R U L G I W B N A S R T N R T I I
  M E A J L I V I N G S T O N E E V
  B A K C H A M P L A I N R N H K D
  U B G L L I R Q O R T G B B G O
  S V M E A G F Y U Y H R T L N
C O R T A L C B                 F N D
T W D H F     L               D O U
  H U D S O N I M U H L E A H C P U A I P L H K
  H Y E R I K S O N C Q W T N N A C F Q O U D
    N F K A H I A R D U I U M P H B R F L H
    K T D S K M H K N I S D S X R S O T O A
      P O N C E D E L E O N T U M F K T I
```

SOUTH AMERICA

Think About It!
South America has been slow to develop its rich natural resources. Why?

South America is the fourth largest continent. South America has a wide range of climates, including dry deserts, steamy rainforests, and cold mountain peaks. Most of the continent is warm all year. The exception is high in the Andes Mountains, where it is always cold.

The Amazon River Basin supports the world's largest tropical rainforest. The Andes Mountains form the world's largest mountain range. South America is also home to many spectacular resources, landforms, and species.

The equator, which crosses Ecuador, gave the country its name.

The Amazon River flows over 4,000 miles from the Andes in Peru to the Atlantic Ocean. Only the Nile River is longer.

Much of Brazil is tropic[al] and covered by the Amazon Rainforest.

Many people living in the Andes herd llamas, alpacas, and vicuñas. The hair and fur of these animals is used to make clothing.

Gauchos are the cowboys of Argentina and Uruguay. They wear wide-brimmed felt hats and baggy pants called bombachas.

MAP BASICS

A **map** is a picture of a place. Maps can show land, water, highways, mountains, and many other things.

LEGEND

A **legend** or **key** is a box that contains symbols used on a map. The legend explains what those symbols mean. Here are some of the symbols you will find in this book:

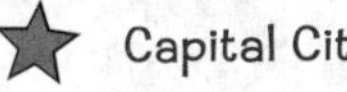

	Capital City		Indian Reservation
	City		Mountains
	Interstate Highway	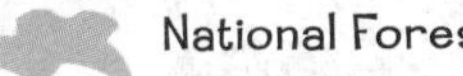	Lake
	National Park		National Forest
	City Area		Military Area
	River		National Monument

SCALE

How can you tell the distances shown on a map? You use a **map scale**. Here's one:

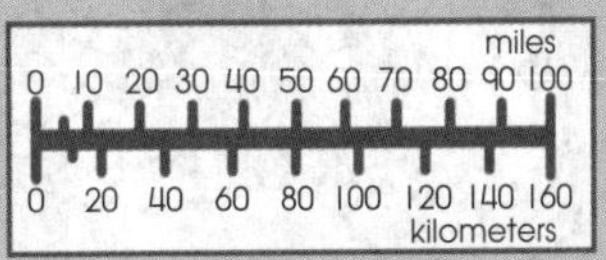

COMPASS ROSE

A **compass rose** shows the cardinal directions on a map: north, south, east, and west. It may show the in-between directions, too: northeast, southeast, southwest, and northwest.

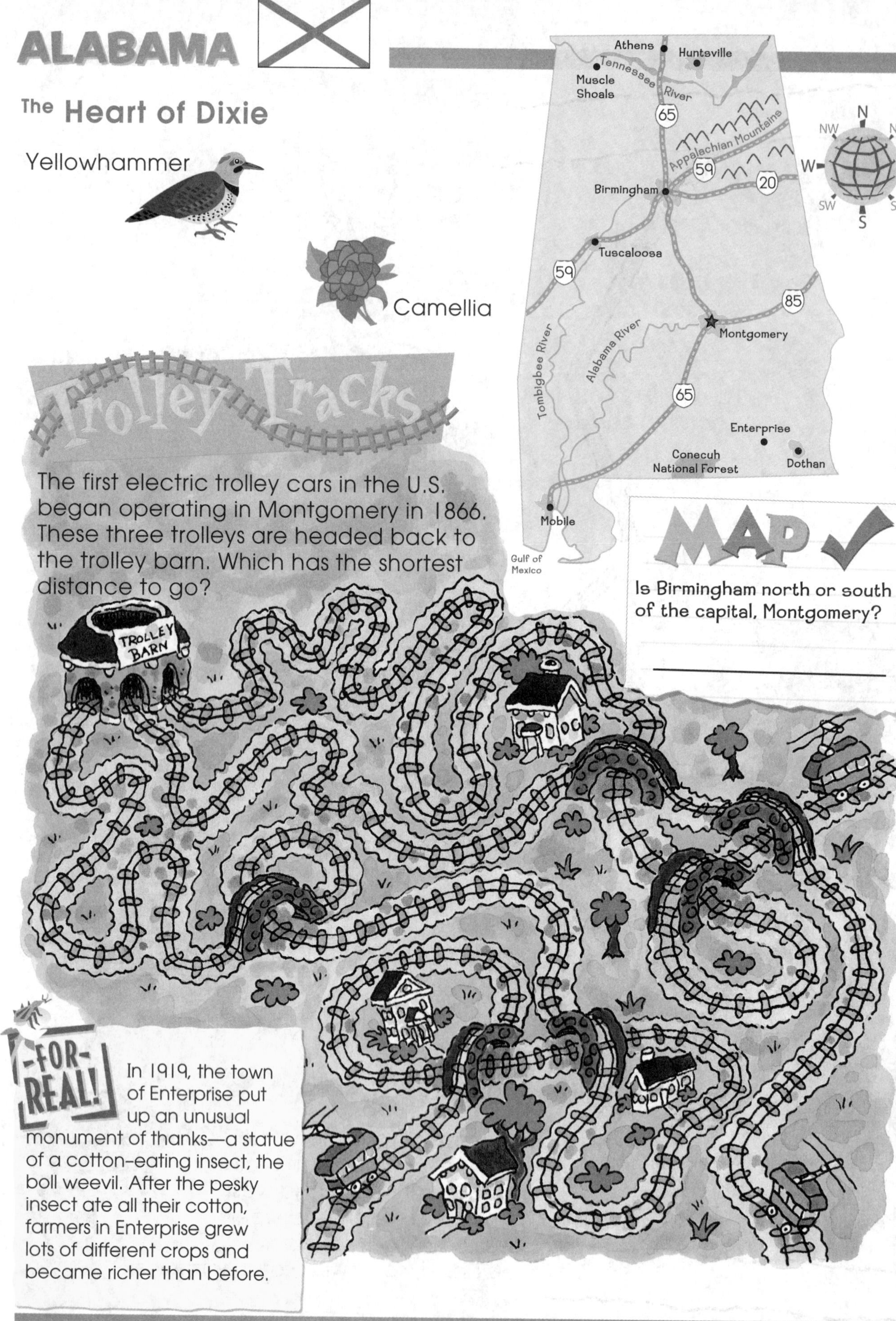
ALABAMA
The Heart of Dixie
Yellowhammer
Camellia
Athens
Huntsville
Tennessee River
Muscle Shoals
65
Appalachian Mountains
59
20
Birmingham
Tuscaloosa
59
85
Montgomery
Alabama River
Tombigbee River
65
Enterprise
Conecuh National Forest
Dothan
Mobile
Gulf of Mexico
N
NE
NW
W
SW
S
SE
Trolley Tracks
The first electric trolley cars in the U.S. began operating in Montgomery in 1866. These three trolleys are headed back to the trolley barn. Which has the shortest distance to go?
TROLLEY BARN
MAP ✓
Is Birmingham north or south of the capital, Montgomery?
-FOR-REAL!
In 1919, the town of Enterprise put up an unusual monument of thanks—a statue of a cotton-eating insect, the boll weevil. After the pesky insect ate all their cotton, farmers in Enterprise grew lots of different crops and became richer than before.

ALASKA

The Last Frontier

Willow Ptarmigan

Forget-Me-Not

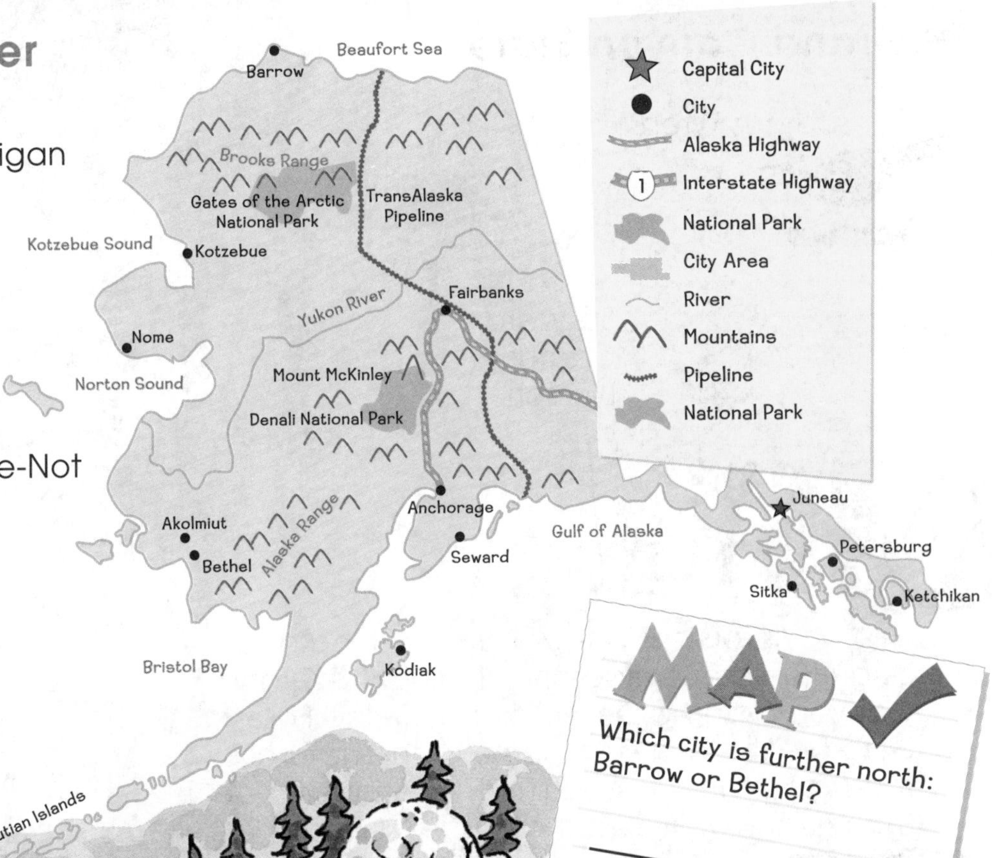

Capital City
City
Alaska Highway
Interstate Highway
National Park
City Area
River
Mountains
Pipeline
National Park

Beaufort Sea
Barrow
Brooks Range
Gates of the Arctic National Park
TransAlaska Pipeline
Kotzebue Sound
Kotzebue
Yukon River
Fairbanks
Nome
Norton Sound
Mount McKinley
Denali National Park
Anchorage
Juneau
Akolmiut
Alaska Range
Bethel
Seward
Gulf of Alaska
Petersburg
Sitka
Ketchikan
Kodiak
Bristol Bay
Aleutian Islands

MAP ✔

Which city is further north: Barrow or Bethel?

____

Hidden Resources

Alaska has more than any other state. More what? Cross off the **v**s, **x**s, **y**s, and **z**s to find out.

x x i v v y x n x x y v v l x x v

z z a v x y n x v d y w y z z z

v a x y t v z z y e v z r z z

____

FOR REAL! Temperatures in Alaska can drop as low as –80 °F and go as high as 100 °F. That's quite a range! Better pack your mittens AND your swimsuit!

ARIZONA

The Grand Canyon State

Cactus Wren

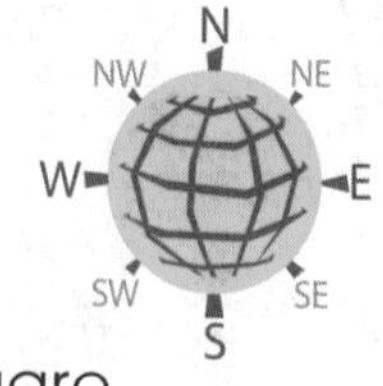

Saguaro Cactus Blossom

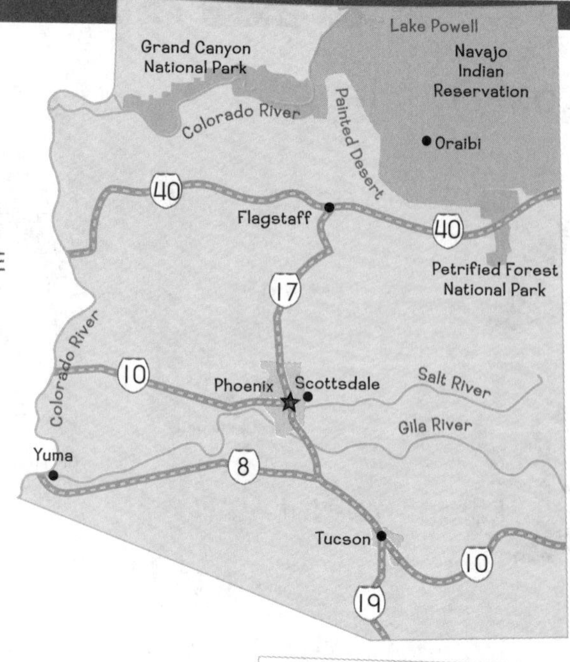

Nature Search

Visitors enjoy Arizona's amazing and beautiful scenic places, including the Grand Canyon, Painted Desert, and Petrified Forest. Here are the names of some of the natural features, plants, and animals of Arizona. How many can you find in the puzzle?

Which interstate highway goes through Flagstaff?

____

A	K	S	A	K	B	C	R	O
C	B	S	A	G	U	A	R	O
P	E	O	S	A	T	N	T	K
I	A	N	B	L	T	Y	Y	D
N	R	P	I	C	E	O	L	E
N	C	K	E	S	A	N	L	E
A	Y	H	C	V	I	T	O	R
C	R	P	O	A	M	E	S	A
L	M	Y	N	L	T	R	U	P
E	P	E	L	L	L	R	K	M
Y	C	L	S	E	Y	A	S	L
C	I	K	N	Y	U	C	C	A
H	S	P	B	K	I	E	L	H
B	A	N	T	E	L	O	P	E

-FOR- REAL! Oraibi may be the oldest town in the U.S. Hopi Indians built the settlement over 800 years ago, and people have lived there ever since.

ARKANSAS

The Natural State

Mockingbird

Apple Blossom

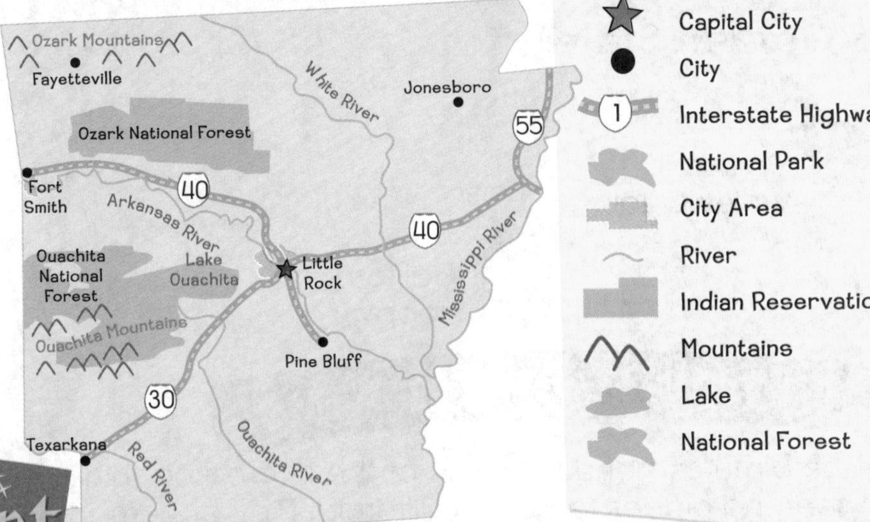

LEGEND

- Capital City
- City
- Interstate Highway
- National Park
- City Area
- River
- Indian Reservation
- Mountains
- Lake
- National Forest

Carat Hunt

Arkansas has the only working diamond mine in the United States. Visitors can keep the diamonds they find! How many diamonds can you find in this picture? ___________

Which river borders Arkansas on the east?

____

-FOR-REAL!

The city of Texarkana is divided down the middle between Arkansas and Texas. It has two governments and a post office building that stands in both states.

CALIFORNIA
CALIFORNIA REPUBLIC
The Golden State
California Valley Quail
California Poppy
California Concentration
These pictures stand for some of the interesting things to see and places to go in California. Play a memory game. Study the pictures for about 30 seconds. Then close the book. How many things can you remember?
HOLLYWOOD
Redwood National Park
Sierra Nevada Mountains
Sacramento River
Lake Tahoe
Sacramento
San Francisco
Yosemite National Park
Pacific Ocean
Sierra Nevada Mountains
Death Valley National Park
Mojave Desert
Los Angeles
San Diego
5
80
10
N
NE
E
SE
S
SW
W
NW
MAP
Which mountain range is shown on the map?
-FOR- REAL!
California's coast redwood trees are the tallest living things in the world.

COLORADO

The Centennial State

Lark Bunting

Rocky Mountain Columbine

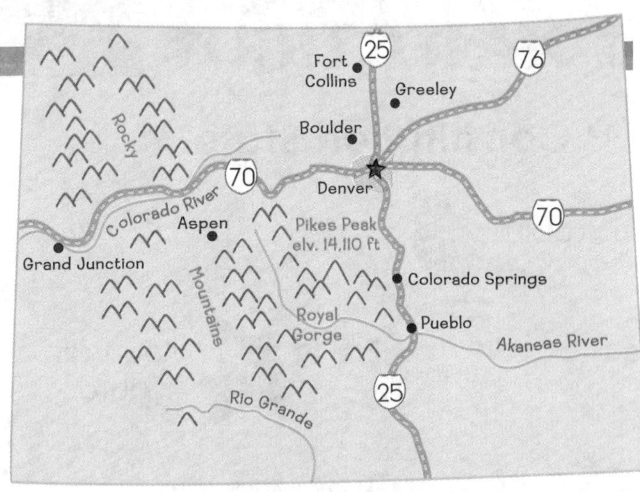

Capital Code

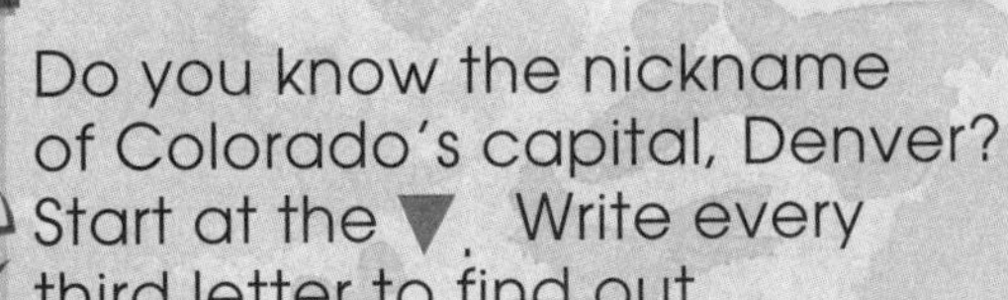

Do you know the nickname of Colorado's capital, Denver? Start at the ▼. Write every third letter to find out.

▼ C Z M B X I V W L D R E G N H S B I T Y G N K H P A C U M I J S T N W Y

First Letter

____

LEGEND

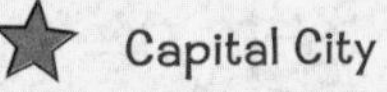

- ★ Capital City
- ● City
- Interstate Highway
- National Park
- River
- City Area
- Mountains
- Lake

MAP ✓

What is the elevation of Pikes Peak?

____

-FOR- REAL!

The Colorado River, which flows through canyons of red rock, got its name from the Spanish word **colorado**, or "colored red." The state was named for the river.

CONNECTICUT

The Constitution State

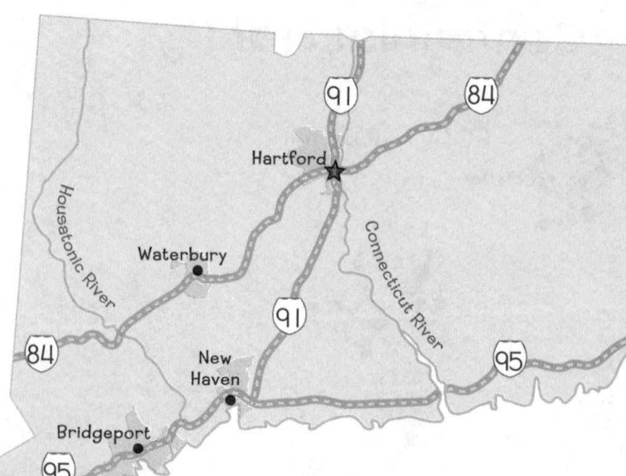

Find the Firsts!

Connecticut is the home of many historical firsts. Follow the maze to find out what some of them are. Watch out! You won't be able to find a path to the inventions that are **not** Connecticut firsts!

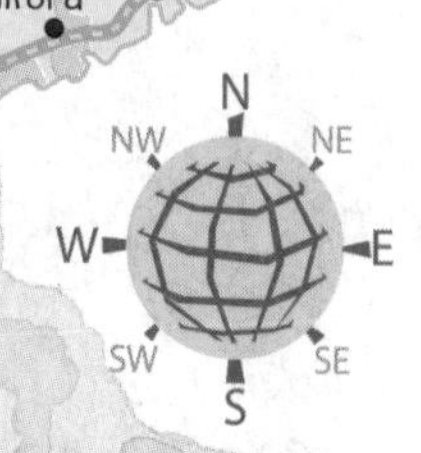

Which interstate highways go through Hartford?

____

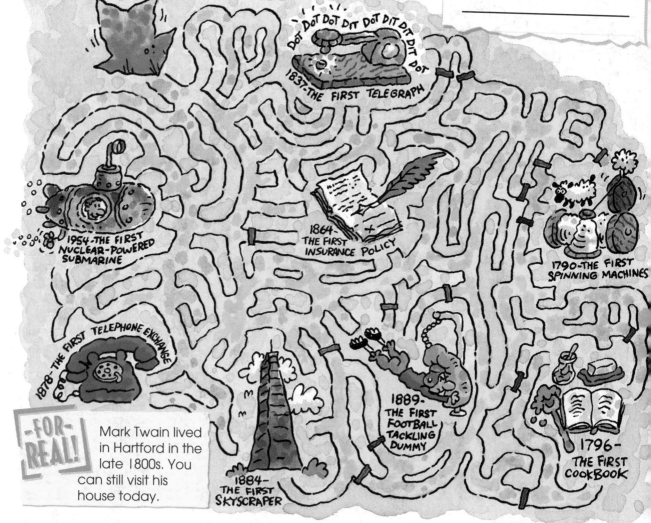

DOT DOT DOT DOT DIT DOT DIT DIT DIT DOT

1837-THE FIRST TELEGRAPH

1954-THE FIRST NUCLEAR-POWERED SUBMARINE

1864-THE FIRST INSURANCE POLICY

1790-THE FIRST SPINNING MACHINES

1878-THE FIRST TELEPHONE EXCHANGE

1889-THE FIRST FOOTBALL TACKLING DUMMY

1884-THE FIRST SKYSCRAPER

1796-THE FIRST COOKBOOK

-FOR- REAL! Mark Twain lived in Hartford in the late 1800s. You can still visit his house today.

DELAWARE

DECEMBER 7, 1787

The First State

Blue Hen Chicken

Peach Blossom

MAP ✓

Which bay is shown on the map?

____

Claymont
Elsmere
Wilmington
Newark
95
New Castle
Delaware River
Smyrna
13
Dover
Delaware Bay
Milford
Lewes
Seaford
Rehoboth Beach
Atlantic Ocean

LEGEND

Capital City
City
Interstate Highway
City Area
River
Highway

Catch the Cluckers

Broiler chickens, chickens 5 to 12 weeks old, are Delaware's most important farm product. Look at the barnyard. How many chickens can you find? ______________

T. SIRRELL

-FOR-REAL!

Chemists at the DuPont Company combined water, air, and coal by-products to produce nylon, a lightweight fabric that didn't wrinkle. The new fabric came on the market in 1938.

FLORIDA

The Sunshine State

Mockingbird

Orange Blossom

MAP ✓

What is the capital of Florida?

____

Lost in the Swamp

The Everglades is a huge, swampy area in southern Florida. You can see lots of interesting plants and animals there. How many of these plants and animals can you find in the puzzle?

cypress
myrtles
snakes
pelicans
bays
deer
fish
willows
alligators
sawgrass
panthers
mangroves

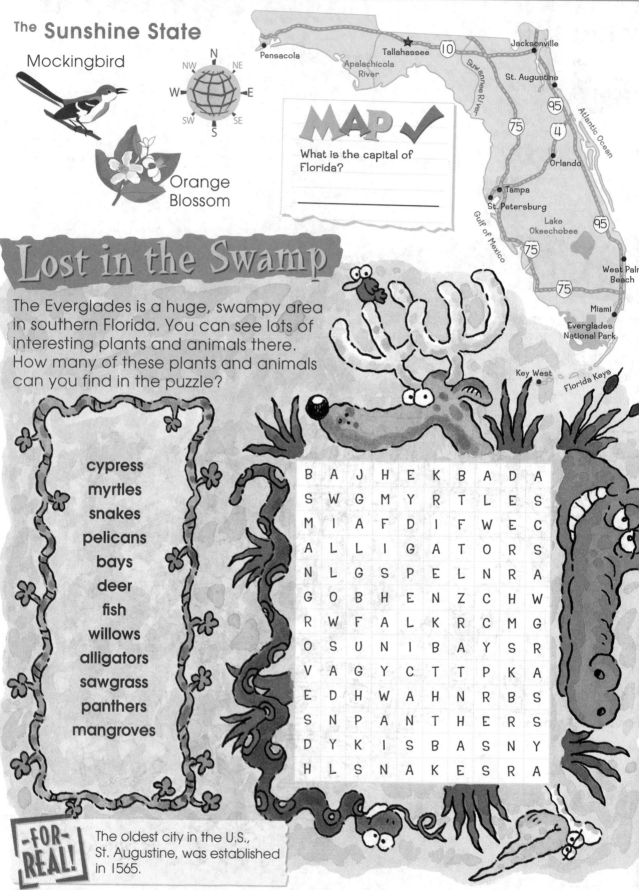

B	A	J	H	E	K	B	A	D	A
S	W	G	M	Y	R	T	L	E	S
M	I	A	F	D	I	F	W	E	C
A	L	L	I	G	A	T	O	R	S
N	L	G	S	P	E	L	N	R	A
G	O	B	H	E	N	Z	C	H	W
R	W	F	A	L	K	R	C	M	G
O	S	U	N	I	B	A	Y	S	R
V	A	G	Y	C	T	T	P	K	A
E	D	H	W	A	H	N	R	B	S
S	N	P	A	N	T	H	E	R	S
D	Y	K	I	S	B	A	S	N	Y
H	L	S	N	A	K	E	S	R	A

-FOR- REAL! The oldest city in the U.S., St. Augustine, was established in 1565.

GEORGIA

The Peach State

Brown Thrasher

Cherokee Rose

LEGEND

Capital City

City

Interstate Highway

National Park

City Area

River

Mountains

Lake

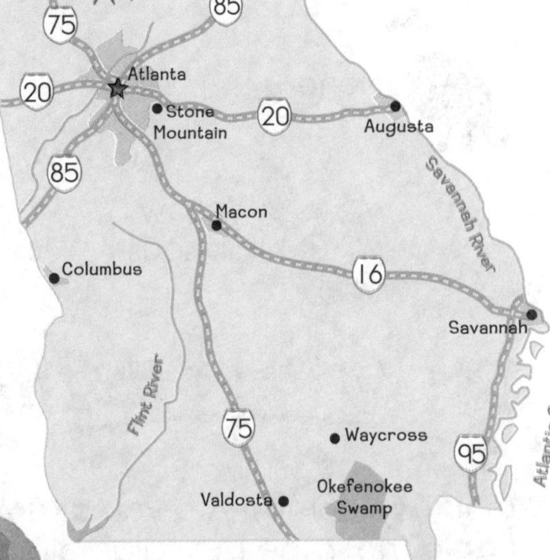

The Masters Golf Tournament is held in Augusta. In this Masters Tournament, the golf balls have really been flying! Circle the 12 hidden golf balls.

Which swamp is shown on the map?

____

-FOR-REAL!

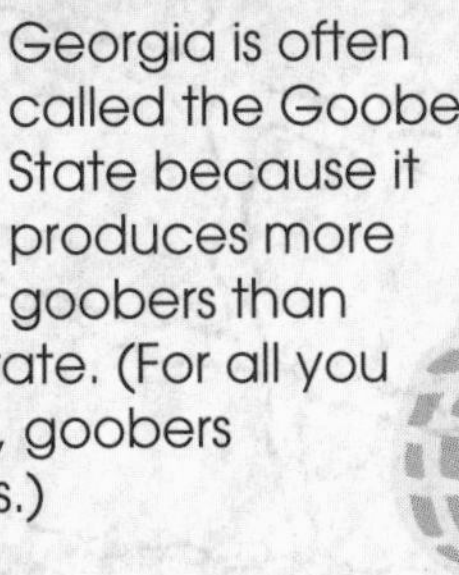

Georgia is often called the Goober State because it produces more goobers than any other state. (For all you Northerners, goobers are peanuts.)

HAWAII

The Aloha State

Nene

Yellow Hibiscus

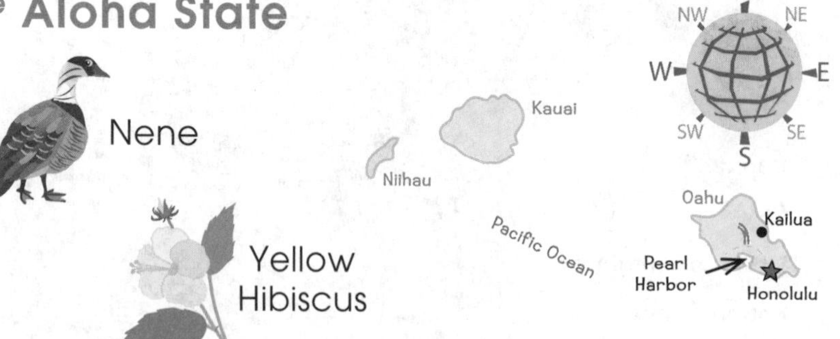

Molokai

Lanai

Kahului

Haleakala National Park

Maui

Kahoolawe

Pacific Ocean

Hilo

Hawaii

Hawaii Volcanoes National Park

How many main islands make up the state of Hawaii?

____

Nui (Great) Puzzle

Aloha (welcome)! Are you **akamai** (clever)?**Ae** (yes) or **aole** (no)? The Hawaiian alphabet has only 12 letters. You can see them on the leaves of the pineapple. How quickly can you fill the boxes on the pineapple with words made from these letters?

FOR REAL! Hawaii is a chain of over 130 islands that extends about 1,500 miles.

IDAHO

The Gem State

Mountain Bluebird

Syringa

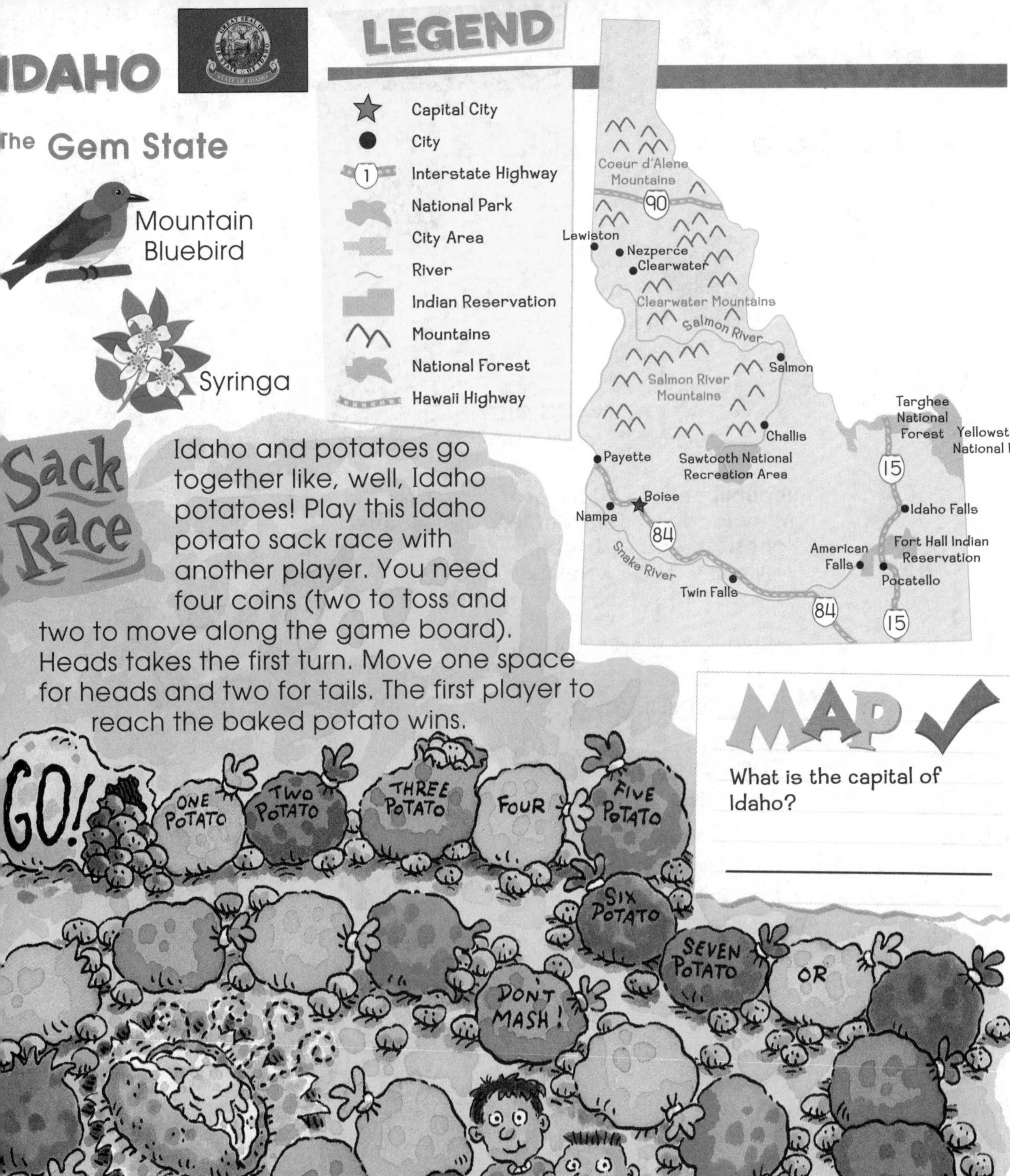

Sack Race

Idaho and potatoes go together like, well, Idaho potatoes! Play this Idaho potato sack race with another player. You need four coins (two to toss and two to move along the game board). Heads takes the first turn. Move one space for heads and two for tails. The first player to reach the baked potato wins.

MAP ✓

What is the capital of Idaho?

____

-FOR- REAL! Over 70 types of precious and semiprecious stones are mined in Idaho. Some of the stones are not found anywhere else in the world!

ILLINOIS

ILLINOIS

The Prairie State

Cardinal

Native Violet

Rockford
Lake Michiga
39
Chicago
88
Joliet
80
74
57
Peoria
Illinois River
Mississippi River
Champaign
Urbana
Decatur
Springfield
70
55
70
Wabash River
64
64
57
Carbondale
Shawnee National Forest
Ohio River

N NE E SE S SW W NW

All About Abe

Solve the crossword puzzle. Use these words if you need help:

Republican	lawyer	Civil War
Mary Todd	assassinated	seceded
Honest Abe	sixteenth	
Illinois	Kentucky	

Across

5. the state where Lincoln was living before he was elected president
7. Lincoln was our ___ president.
8. Lincoln's profession
9. Lincoln was ___ on April 14, 1865.
10. The Confederate states ___ from the Union.

Down

1. Lincoln's political party when he was elected president
2. Lincoln's nickname
3. the state where Lincoln was born
4. the war that was fought during Lincoln's presidency
6. the name of Lincoln's wife

MAP ✓

Is Joliet north or south of Chicago?

____

-FOR- REAL!

In Chicago, people say that everyone is Irish on St. Patrick's Day. One way Chicagoans celebrate is by dyeing the Chicago River green!

1. 2. 3. 4. 5. 6. 7. 8. 9. 10.

LAW

KANSAS

The Sunflower State

Western Meadowlark

Sunflower

Which military area is shown on the map?

____

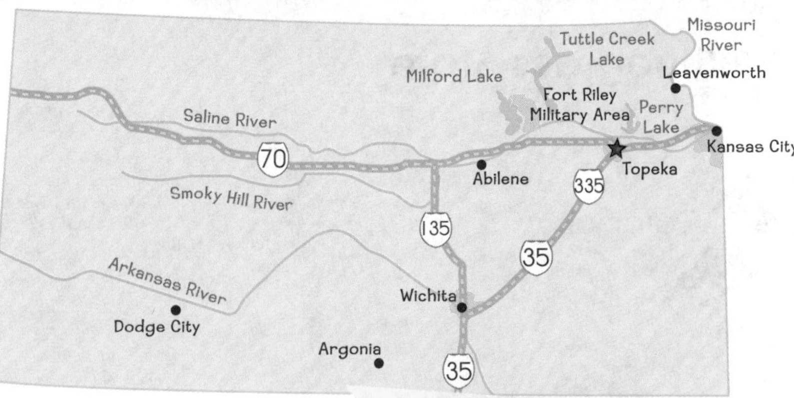

LEGEND

- Capital City
- City
- Interstate Highway
- City Area
- River
- Lake
- National Forest
- Military Area
- National Monument

Get Along Little Dogies!

In the 1860s and 1870s, cowboys herded cattle from Texas to Dodge City and other Kansas towns to be shipped all over the U.S. These longhorns just stampeded! Help the cowboys gather the herd. Can you find all 22 steers?

-FOR-REAL! The first female mayor of a U.S. city was elected in Argonia, Kansas in 1887.

KENTUCKY

The Bluegrass State

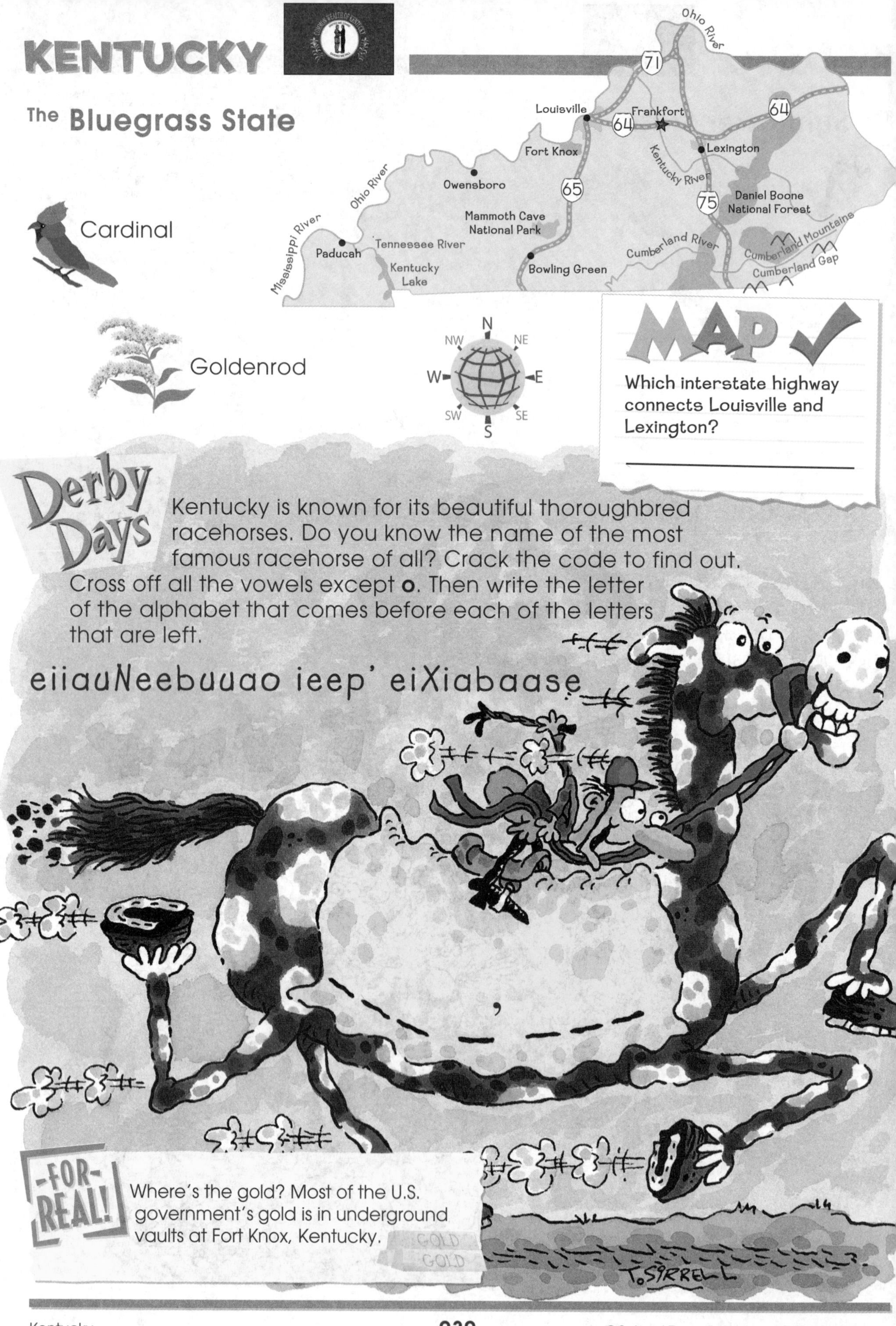

MAP ✓

Which interstate highway connects Louisville and Lexington?

____

Derby Days

Kentucky is known for its beautiful thoroughbred racehorses. Do you know the name of the most famous racehorse of all? Crack the code to find out. Cross off all the vowels except **o**. Then write the letter of the alphabet that comes before each of the letters that are left.

eiiauNeebuuao ieep' eiXiabaase

_ _ _ _ _ _ _ _ _ _ _ _ _ _ _ _ , _ _ _ _ _ _ _ _ _

-FOR- REAL! Where's the gold? Most of the U.S. government's gold is in underground vaults at Fort Knox, Kentucky.

LOUISIANA

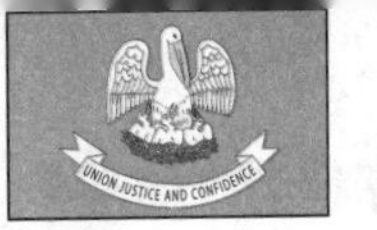
UNION JUSTICE AND CONFIDENCE

The Pelican State

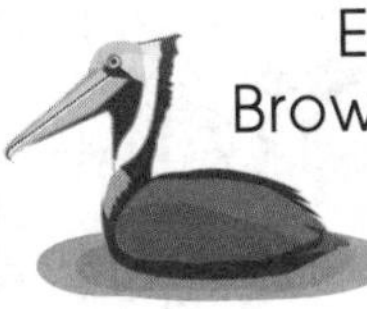

Eastern
Brown Pelican

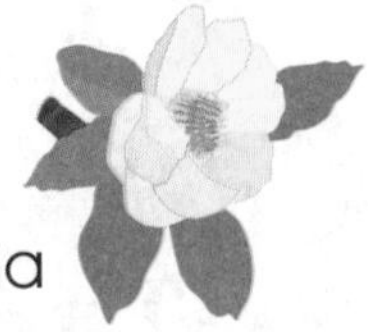

Magnolia

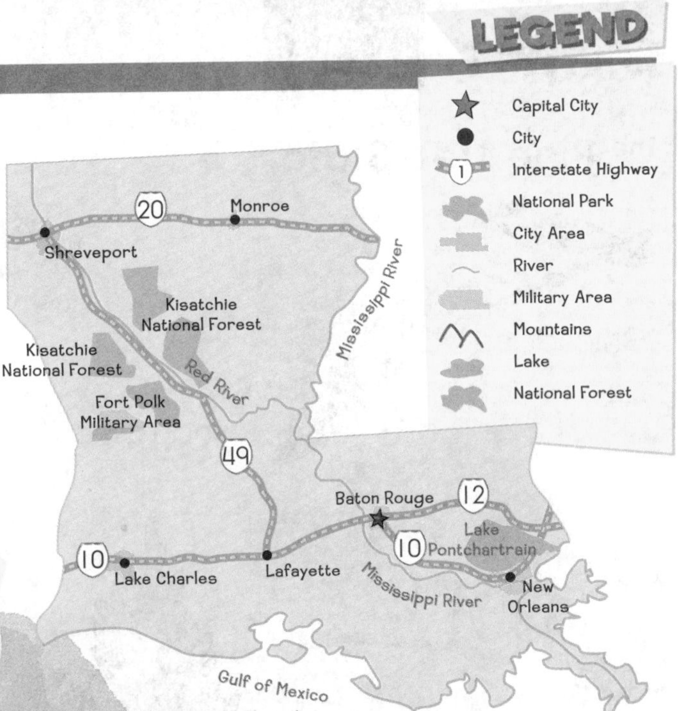
LEGEND
Capital City
City
Interstate Highway
National Park
City Area
River
Military Area
Mountains
Lake
National Forest
20
Monroe
Shreveport
Kisatchie
National Forest
Kisatchie
National Forest
Mississippi River
Red River
Fort Polk
Military Area
49
Baton Rouge
12
Lake
Pontchartrain
10
10
Lake Charles
Lafayette
Mississippi River
New
Orleans
Gulf of Mexico

Let's Party!

Every year, New Orleans hosts a wild celebration called Mardi Gras, complete with parties, parades, jazz, and costumes. Look at the Mardi Gras masks. How many pairs of matching masks can you find? ____________

MAP ✓

Which two rivers are shown on the map?

____

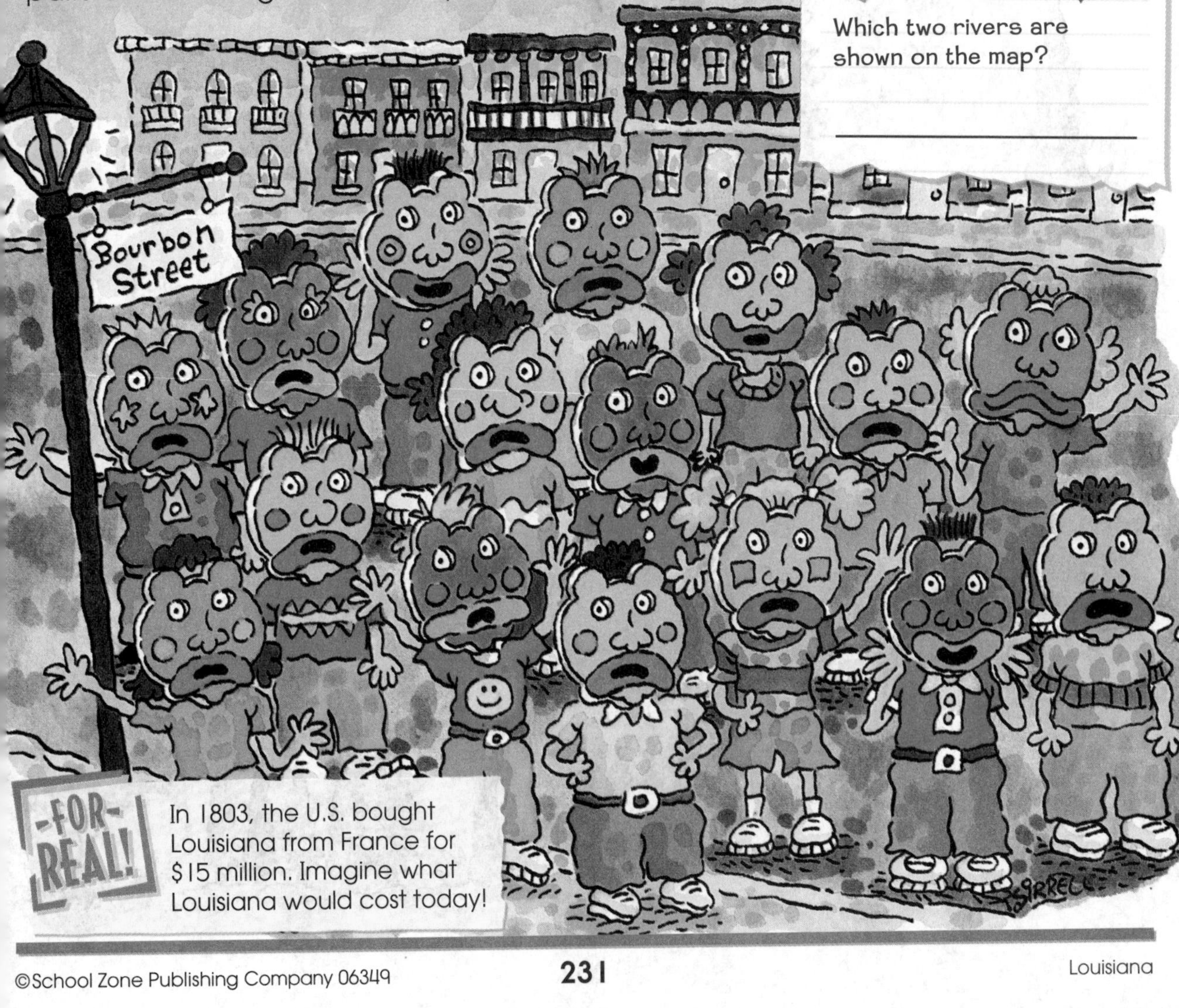
Bourbon
Street

-FOR- REAL! In 1803, the U.S. bought Louisiana from France for $15 million. Imagine what Louisiana would cost today!

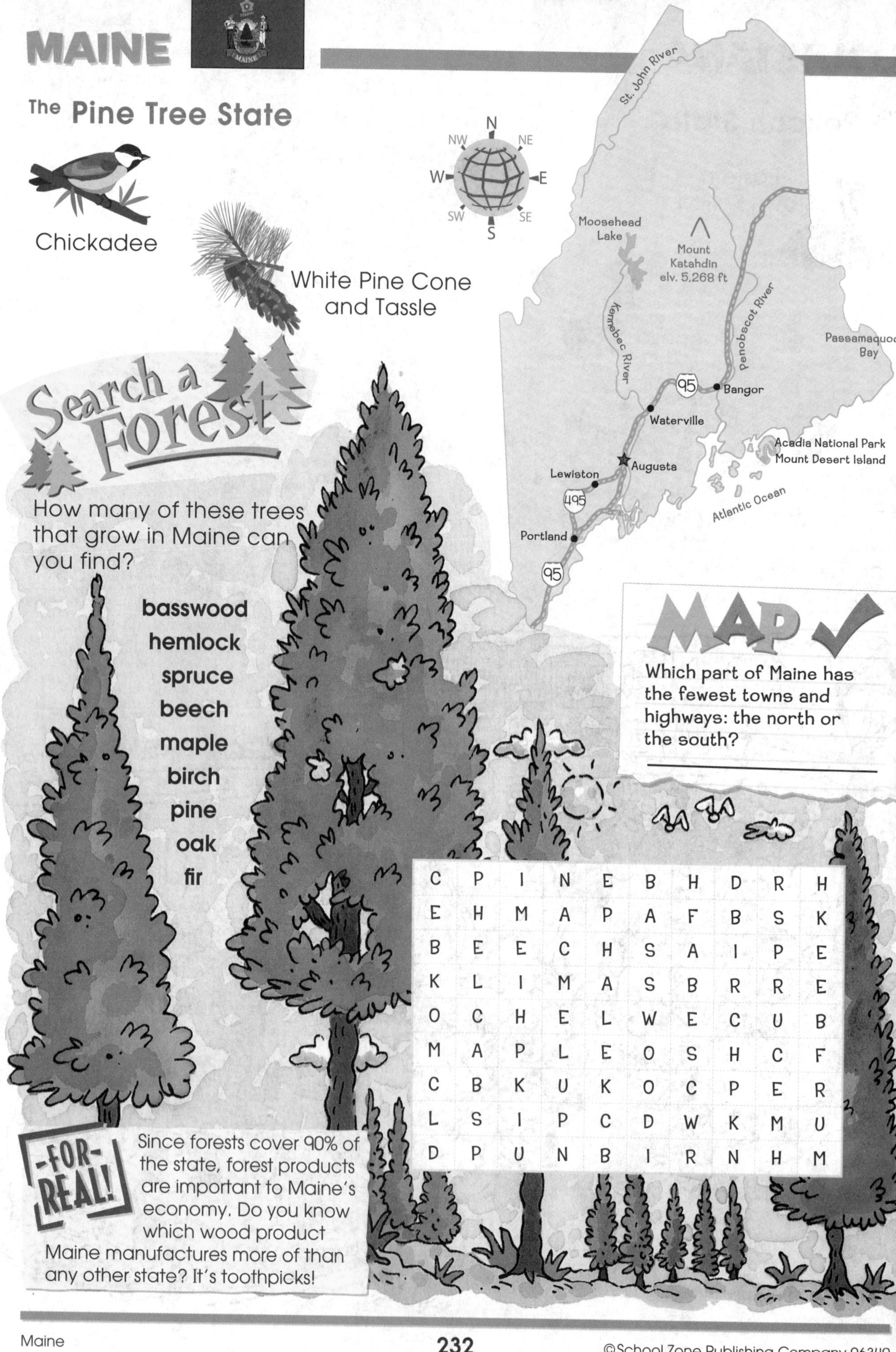

MAINE
The Pine Tree State
Chickadee
White Pine Cone and Tassle
St. John River
Moosehead Lake
Mount Katahdin elv. 5,268 ft
Kennebec River
Penobscot River
Passamaquod
Bay
95
Bangor
Waterville
Augusta
Lewiston
495
Portland
95
Acadia National Park
Mount Desert Island
Atlantic Ocean
N
NE
E
SE
S
SW
W
NW
Search a Forest
How many of these trees that grow in Maine can you find?
basswood
hemlock
spruce
beech
maple
birch
pine
oak
fir
MAP ✓
Which part of Maine has the fewest towns and highways: the north or the south?
C P I N E B H D R H
E H M A P A F B S K
B E E C H S A I P E
K L I M A S B R R E
O C H E L W E C U B
M A P L E O S H C F
C B K U K O C P E R
L S I P C D W K M U
D P U N B I R N H M
-FOR-REAL!
Since forests cover 90% of the state, forest products are important to Maine's economy. Do you know which wood product Maine manufactures more of than any other state? It's toothpicks!

MARYLAND

The Old Line State

Baltimore Oriole

Black-Eyed Susan

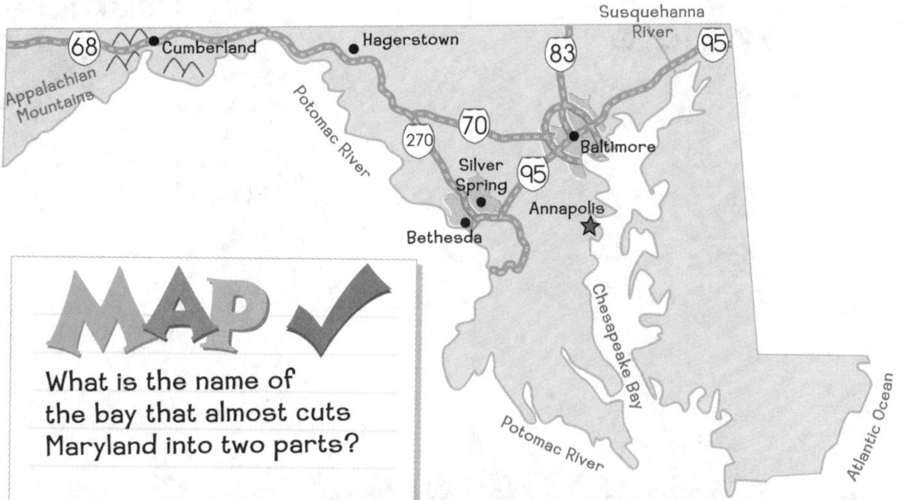

MAP ✓

What is the name of the bay that almost cuts Maryland into two parts?

____

LEGEND

- ★ Capital City
- ● City
- (1) Interstate Highway
- National Park
- City Area
- River
- Mountains
- Lake

Day & Knight

Use the code to learn the name of Maryland's official sport.

- ■ = s
- ✻ = j
- ★ = u
- ▲ = o
- ✖ = g
- ● = t
- ✺ = n
- ♠ = i

___ ___ ___ ___ ___ ___ ___ ___

✻ ▲ ★ ■ ● ♠ ✺ ✖

FOR REAL! The first American steam engine, The Tom Thumb, operated in Baltimore in 1830.

MASSACHUSETTS

The Bay State

Chickadee

Mayflower

Merrimack River
91
95
Lowell
93
Connecticut River
Concord
Salem
Cambridge
Boston
90
Worcester
90
Quincy
Housatonic River
Springfield
95
Cape Cod
Cape Cod Bay
495
Fall River
Atlantic Ocean
Nantucket Sound
Martha's Vineyard
Nantucket

LEGEND

- Capital City
- City
- School Zone Publishing
- Interstate Highway
- National Park
- City Area
- River
- National Forest

Search the Stars

Find out two famous Massachusetts firsts. Start at the ▼ and write every other letter to learn one. Start at the ▼ to learn the other.

P W O O S R T L O D F S F E I R C I E E S S

____

____

-FOR- REAL! The Salem witch trials of 1692 and 1693 resulted in the deaths of many innocent people.

MAP ✓

How many interstate highways go into Boston?

____

MICHIGAN

The Great Lakes State or The Wolverine State

Robin

Apple Blossom

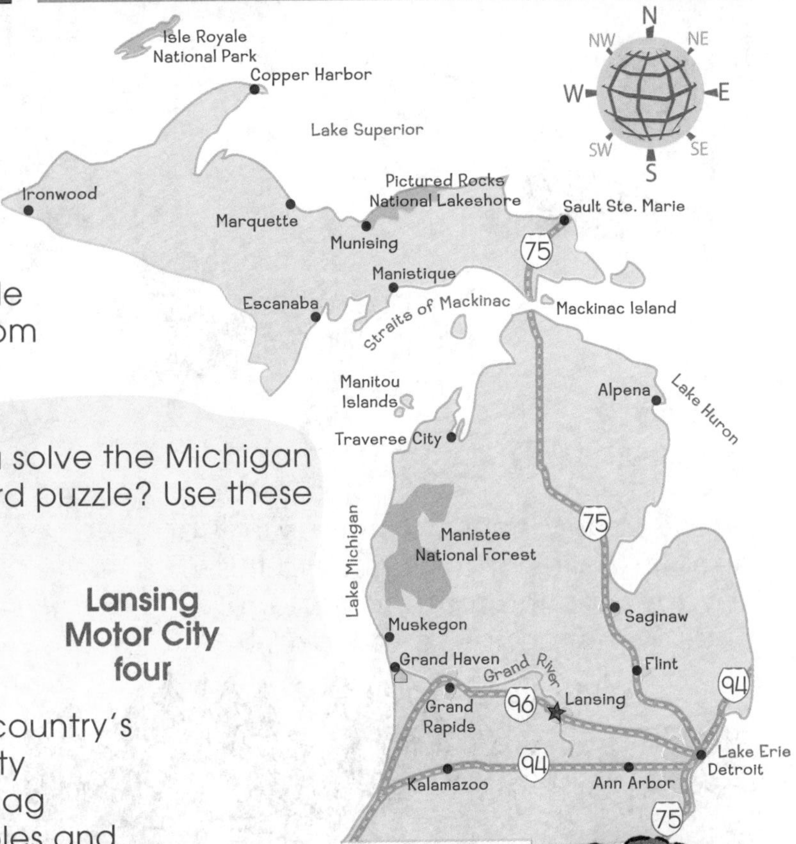

Isle Royale National Park
Copper Harbor
Lake Superior
Ironwood
Marquette
Pictured Rocks National Lakeshore
Munising
Sault Ste. Marie
Manistique
Escanaba
Straits of Mackinac
Mackinac Island
Manitou Islands
Alpena
Lake Huron
Traverse City
Lake Michigan
Manistee National Forest
Muskegon
Saginaw
Grand Haven
Grand River
Flint
Grand Rapids
Lansing
Lake Erie
Detroit
Kalamazoo
Ann Arbor

Michigan Squared

Can you solve the Michigan crossword puzzle? Use these words:

cereal **fruit** **Lansing**
wolverine **eagle** **Motor City**
tourists **two** **four**

Across

3. the nickname of Detroit, the country's leading car manufacturing city
5. the bird on Michigan's state flag
6. Michigan is famous for its apples and other kinds of ___.
8. the capital of Michigan
9. The state of Michigan has ___ parts.

Down

1. the animal in Michigan's unofficial motto
2. the number of Great Lakes that border Michigan
4. Battle Creek is the home of Kellogg and other ___ makers.
7. Michigan's scenic beauty attracts many ___ every year.

-FOR-REAL! Besides the Great Lakes, Michigan has more than 11,000 smaller lakes.

MINNESOTA

The North Star State

Common Loon

Pink and White Lady's Slipper

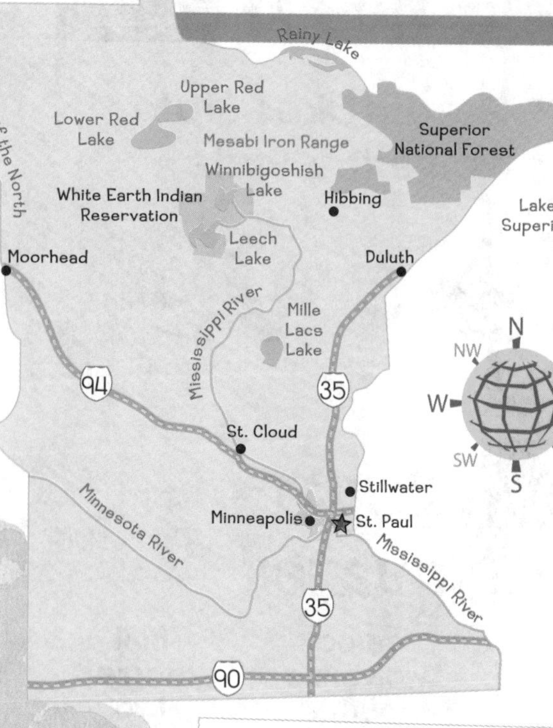

Can You Canoe?

Visitors love Minnesota's thousands of beautiful lakes and rivers. Help this voyager find the route to **portage**, or carry, her canoe to the lake.

Which national forest is shown on the map?

____

Here's a sticky fact for you. Cellophane tape was invented by Richard Gurley Drew of St. Paul. The Minnesota Manufacturing and Mining Company began making the tape in 1930.

MISSISSIPPI

The Magnolia State

Mockingbird

Magnolia

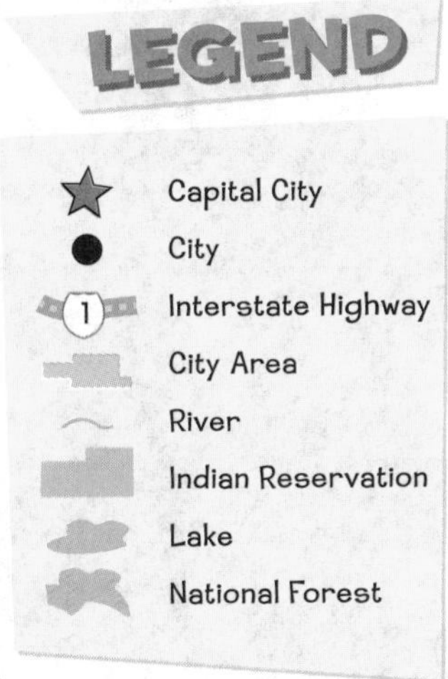

LEGEND

 Capital City

 City

 Interstate Highway

 City Area

River

 Indian Reservation

 Lake

 National Forest

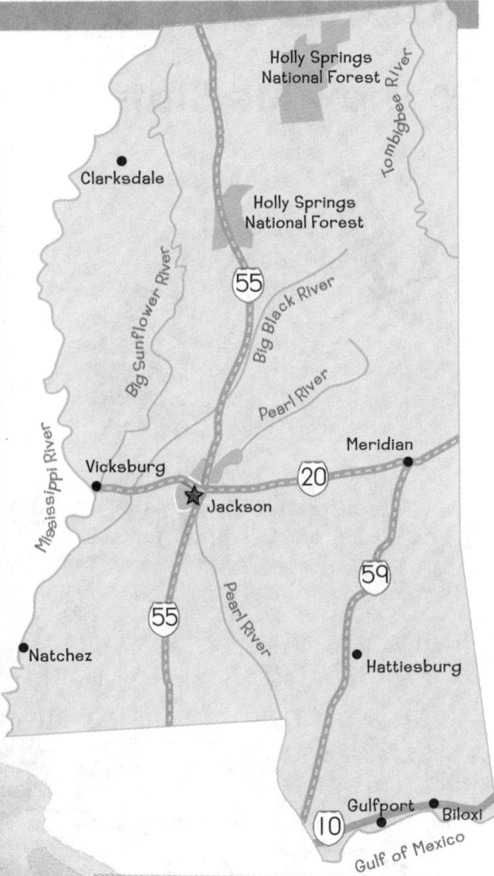

M-i-s-s-i-s-s-i-p-p-i Means What!?

Write the letters coming from the smoke stack in reverse order. Then cross off every third letter to find out what Mississippi, an early Indian name, means.

____

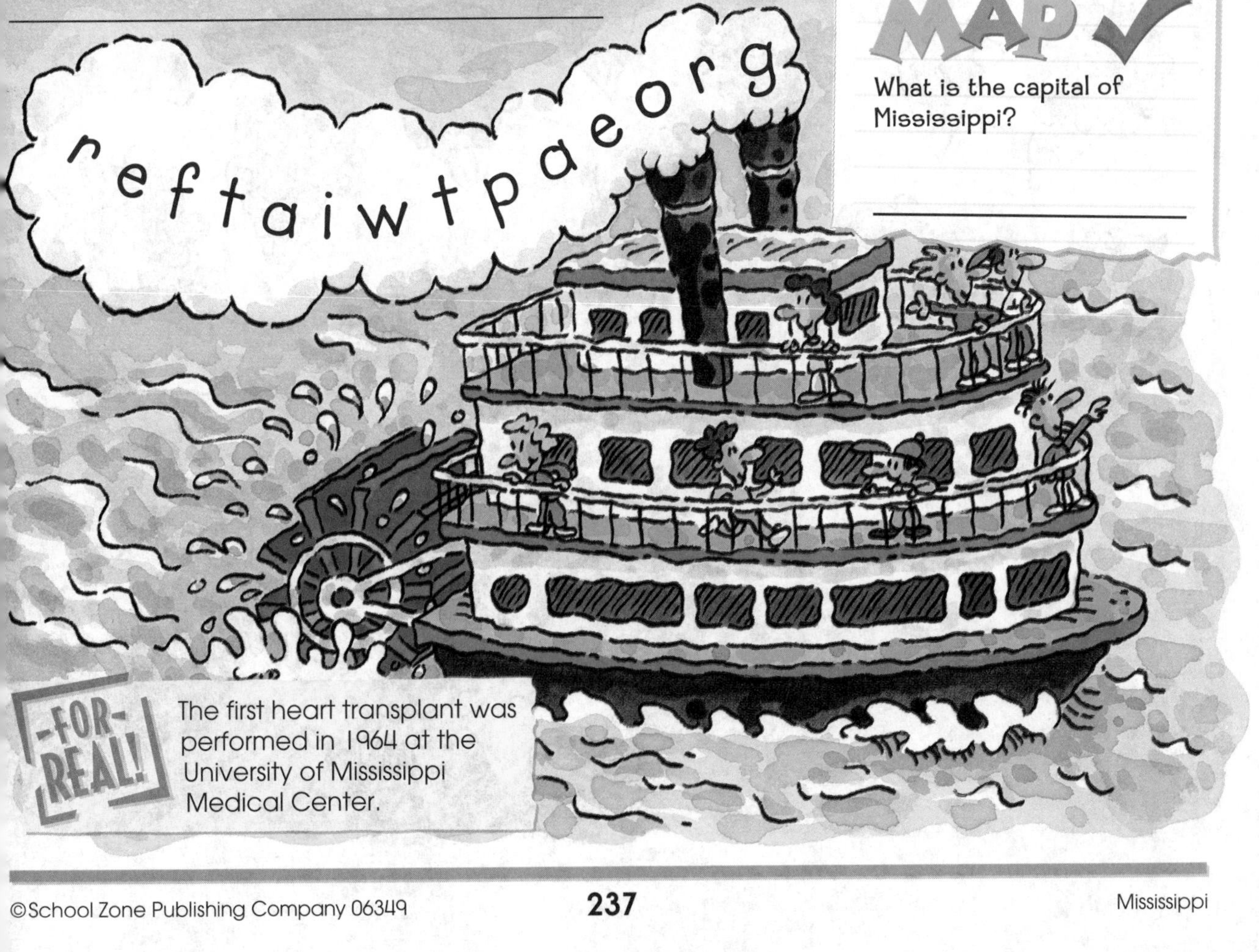

r e f t a i w t p a e o r g

MAP ✓

What is the capital of Mississippi?

____

-FOR-REAL! The first heart transplant was performed in 1964 at the University of Mississippi Medical Center.

MISSOURI

The Show Me State

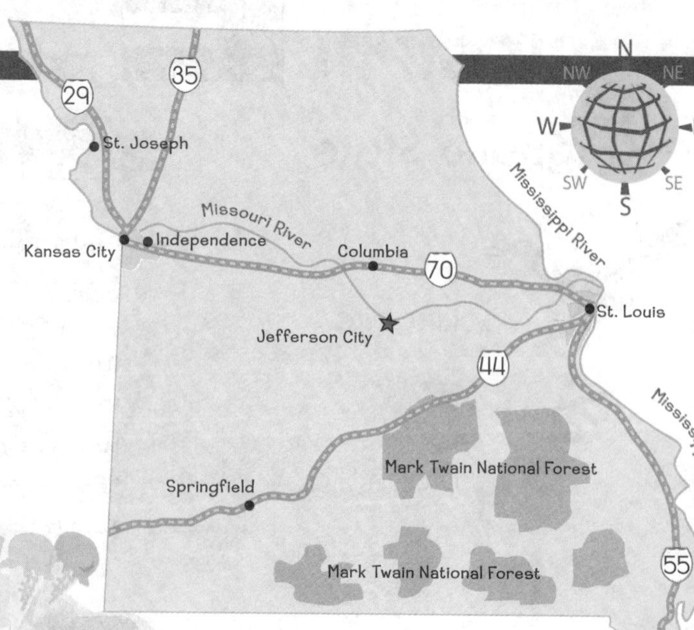

Sweet Dreams!

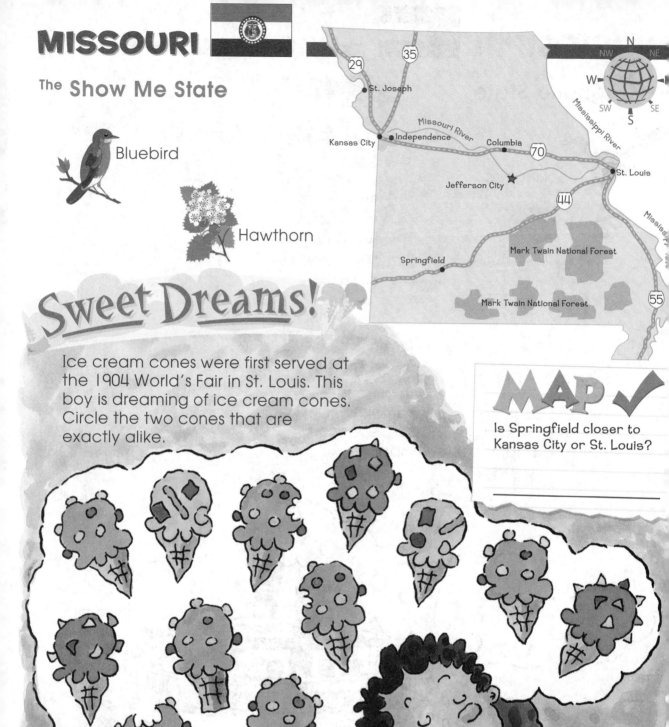

Ice cream cones were first served at the 1904 World's Fair in St. Louis. This boy is dreaming of ice cream cones. Circle the two cones that are exactly alike.

Is Springfield closer to Kansas City or St. Louis?

____

The Gateway Arch in St. Louis is the tallest monument in the U.S.

MONTANA

MONTANA

The Treasure State

Western Meadowlark

Bitterroot

Blackfeet Indian Reservation
Glacier National Park
Flathead National Forest
Flathead Lake
Rocky Mountains
15
Lewis & Clark National Forest
Great Falls
Missouri River
Fort Peck Lake
Fort Peck Indian Reservation
90
Missoula
Lewis & Clark National Forest
Helena
Yellowstone River
94
Gallatin National Forest
Billings
Butte
90
Beaverhead National Forest
Crow Indian Reservation
90
Custer National Forest
15
Gallatin National Forest
Custer National Forest
Beaverhead National Forest
Yellowstone National Park

LEGEND

Capital City
City
Interstate Highway
National Park
City Area
River
Indian Reservation
Mountains
Lake
National Forest

MAP

How many national parks and forests are on the map?

____

Treasure State Crossword

gold silver fourth
coal Sky Helena
cattle Glacier mountains
Billings Canada

Across

3. Montana has many tall, rugged ___.
5. It lies north of Montana.
6. Montana is the ___ largest state.
8. Montana's largest city
9. one of the minerals mined in Montana
10. On Montana's vast plains, ___ graze on grass.

Down

1. This popular national park is located in northwest Montana.
2. one of the minerals that give Montana its nickname
4. Montana is often called "Big ___ Country."
5. Montana's most important mining product
7. the capital of Montana

-FOR-REAL!

In 1917, Jeanette Rankin of Missoula became the first female representative to the U.S. Congress.

NEBRASKA

The Cornhusker State

Western Meadowlark

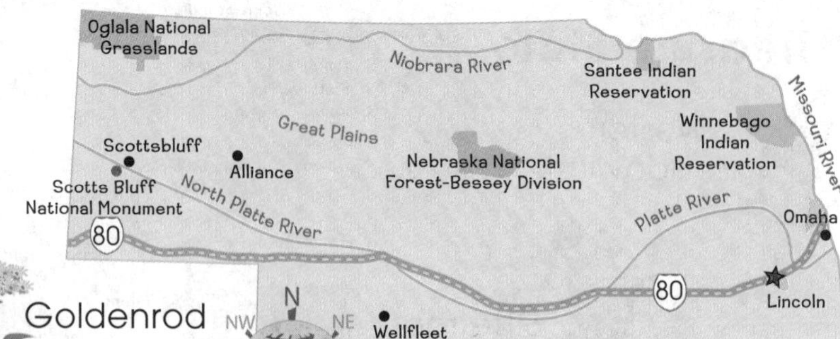

Goldenrod

Wildlife Search

Here are some plants and animals you might see in Nebraska. How many can you find?

pheasants
perch
trout
larkspurs
rabbits
skunks
badgers
cottonwoods
cedars
ducks
pike
chokecherries
poppies
raccoons
geese
coyotes
pines
hackberries

C	O	Y	O	T	E	S	H	U	P
C	S	D	U	C	K	S	R	N	I
O	L	O	P	C	B	A	C	L	K
T	R	A	E	H	U	P	E	H	E
T	A	N	R	O	I	S	D	A	S
O	B	R	C	K	E	O	A	C	G
N	B	A	H	E	S	O	R	K	P
W	I	C	G	C	M	P	S	B	H
O	T	C	U	H	B	O	U	E	E
O	S	O	D	E	I	P	T	R	A
D	R	O	O	R	E	P	L	R	S
S	N	N	W	R	S	I	Y	I	A
Y	M	S	P	I	N	E	S	E	N
B	A	D	G	E	R	S	O	S	T
N	K	Y	O	S	K	U	N	K	S

MAP ✓

On which side of the stat
is Omaha?

____

What a mammoth mammoth! The fossil of a 5 ton, 14 foot high mammoth was dug up in Lincoln county in 1922.

NEVADA

The Silver State

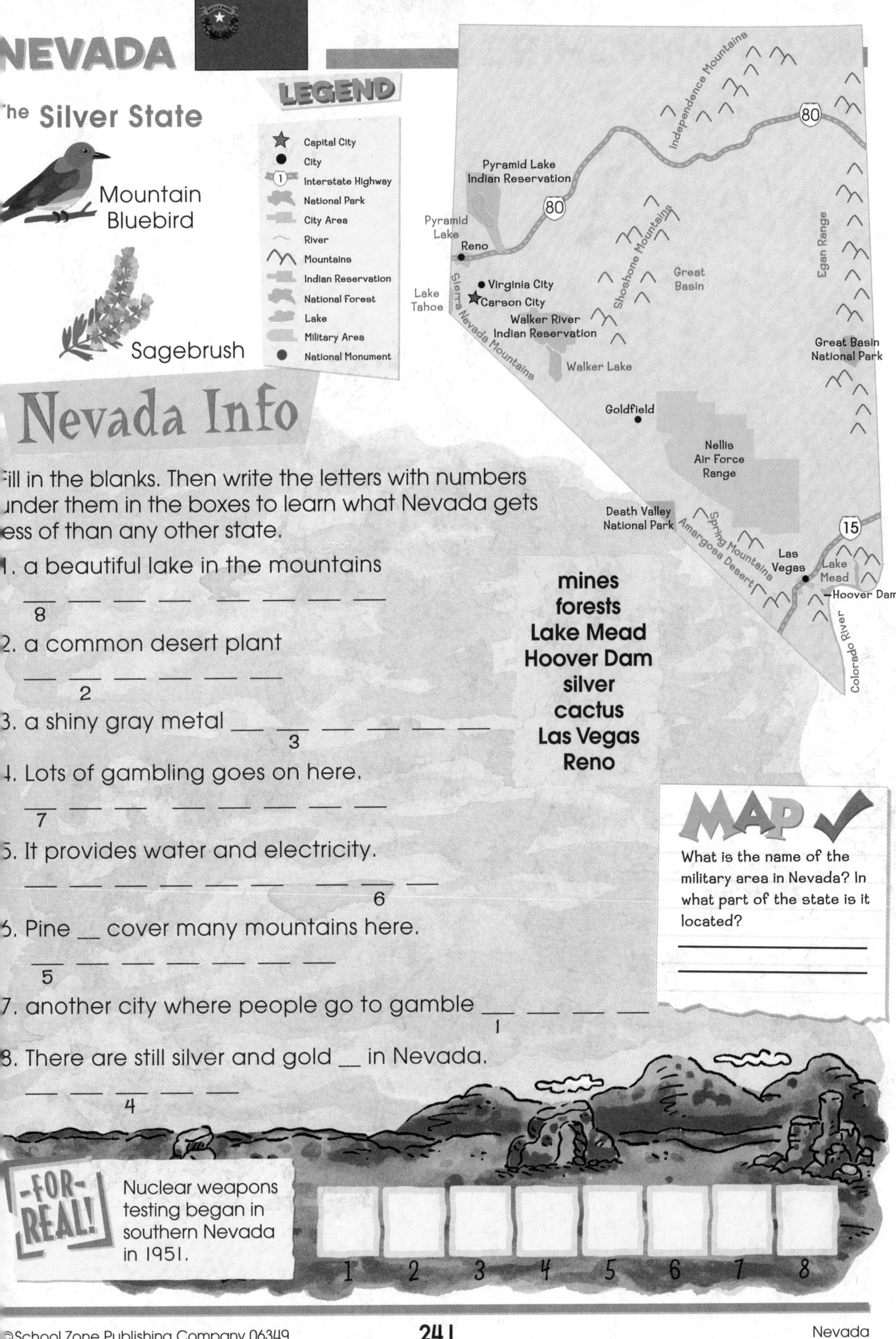

Nevada Info

Fill in the blanks. Then write the letters with numbers under them in the boxes to learn what Nevada gets less of than any other state.

1. a beautiful lake in the mountains ___ ___ ___ ___ ___ ___ ___ ___ (8)
2. a common desert plant ___ ___ ___ ___ ___ ___ (2)
3. a shiny gray metal ___ ___ ___ ___ ___ ___ (3)
4. Lots of gambling goes on here. ___ ___ ___ ___ ___ ___ ___ ___ (7)
5. It provides water and electricity. ___ ___ ___ ___ ___ ___ ___ ___ ___ ___ (6)
6. Pine __ cover many mountains here. ___ ___ ___ ___ ___ ___ ___ (5)
7. another city where people go to gamble ___ ___ ___ ___ (1)
8. There are still silver and gold __ in Nevada. ___ ___ ___ ___ ___ (4)

mines
forests
Lake Mead
Hoover Dam
silver
cactus
Las Vegas
Reno

MAP ✓

What is the name of the military area in Nevada? In what part of the state is it located?

____

____

-FOR- REAL! Nuclear weapons testing began in southern Nevada in 1951.

1	2	3	4	5	6	7	8

NEW HAMPSHIRE
The Granite State
Purple Finch
Purple Lilac
It's All Downhill!
Ski down New Hampshire's White Mountains and gather letters along the way. Once you've got them all, you'll have the name of the first American to fly in space. (He's from New Hampshire, of course!)
N
NW
NE
W
E
SW
SE
S
White Mountains
White Mountain National Forest
White Mountain National Forest
93
Lake Winnipesauke
89
Connecticut River
Merrimack River
Concord
Portsmouth
Manchester
93
Nashua
MAP ✓
On which river is Concord?
B
A
N
D
R
A
TO SIRRELL
-FOR- REAL!
The Navy's first shipbuilding yard opened in 1800 in Portsmouth. It built warships in WWI and submarines in WWII.
____ __ ________, __

NEW JERSEY

The Garden State

Eastern Goldfinch

Violet

LEGEND

- Capital City
- City
- Interstate Highway
- City Area
- River
- Military Area
- Mountains
- Lake
- National Forest

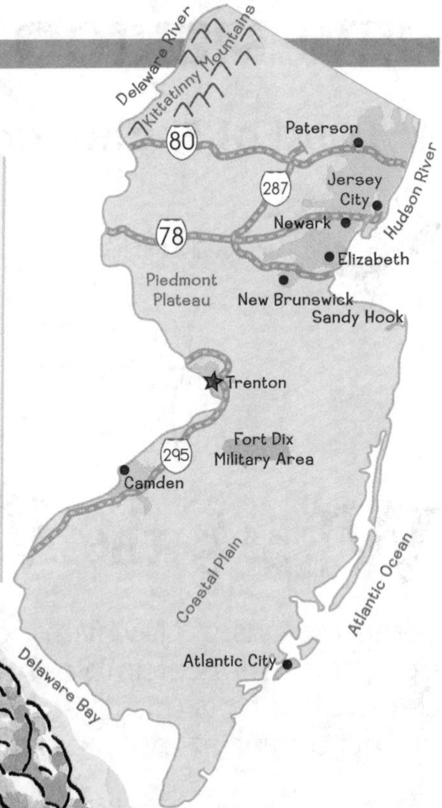

Delaware River
Kittatinny Mountains
80
Paterson
287
Jersey City
Hudson River
78
Newark
Elizabeth
Piedmont Plateau
New Brunswick
Sandy Hook
Trenton
295
Fort Dix Military Area
Camden
Coastal Plain
Atlantic Ocean
Delaware Bay
Atlantic City

Food Fight!

How many names of fruits and vegetables can you find in the Garden State word search? Are you in the mood for some competition? Challenge a friend to see who can find more names in thirty seconds.

tomatoes	snap beans	sweet potatoes
cabbages	peaches	squash
lettuce	blueberries	pumpkins
potatoes	grapes	
sweet corn	cranberries	

C	P	U	M	P	K	I	N	S	H	W	P	A
A	O	C	R	A	N	B	E	R	R	I	E	S
B	T	S	S	G	S	Q	U	A	S	H	A	N
B	A	E	K	R	P	B	I	L	N	P	C	A
A	T	O	M	A	T	O	E	S	B	K	H	P
G	O	T	E	P	L	E	T	T	U	C	E	B
E	E	S	W	E	E	T	C	O	R	N	S	E
S	S	Q	F	S	N	U	L	W	E	A	N	A
B	L	U	E	B	E	R	R	I	E	S	P	N
S	W	E	E	T	P	O	T	A	T	O	E	S

MAP ✓

If you were in Newark and wanted to travel to Trenton, which direction would you go?

____

-FOR- REAL!

Take a good look at the state flag. Liberty is on the left and Ceres, the goddess of agriculture, is on the right.

NEW MEXICO

The Land of Enchantment

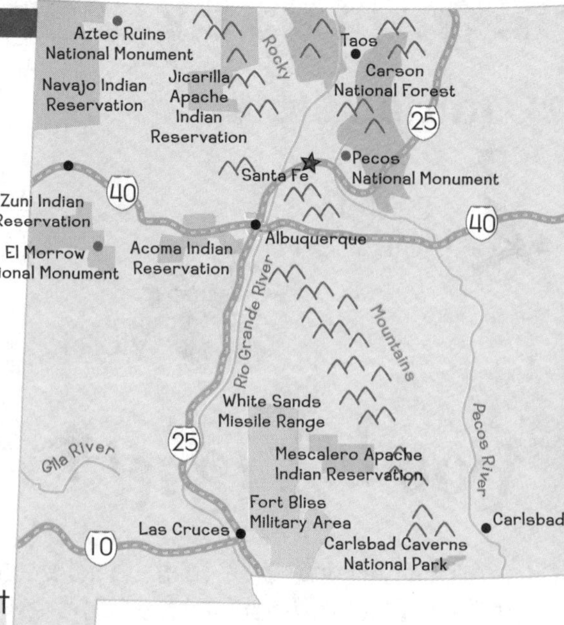

What's the Word?

Some Indians of New Mexico lived in the first apartments. Unscramble the letters on the decorated pots (just the decorated ones) to find out what these buildings are called.

Which highway connects Albuquerque and Sante Fe?

____

T U O Z D L T M S

P B E B A Q O N

POTS For SALE

Sante Fe is the highest state capital in the U.S. It is 7,000 feet above sea level!

___ ___ ___ ___ ___ ___ ___

NEW YORK

The Empire State

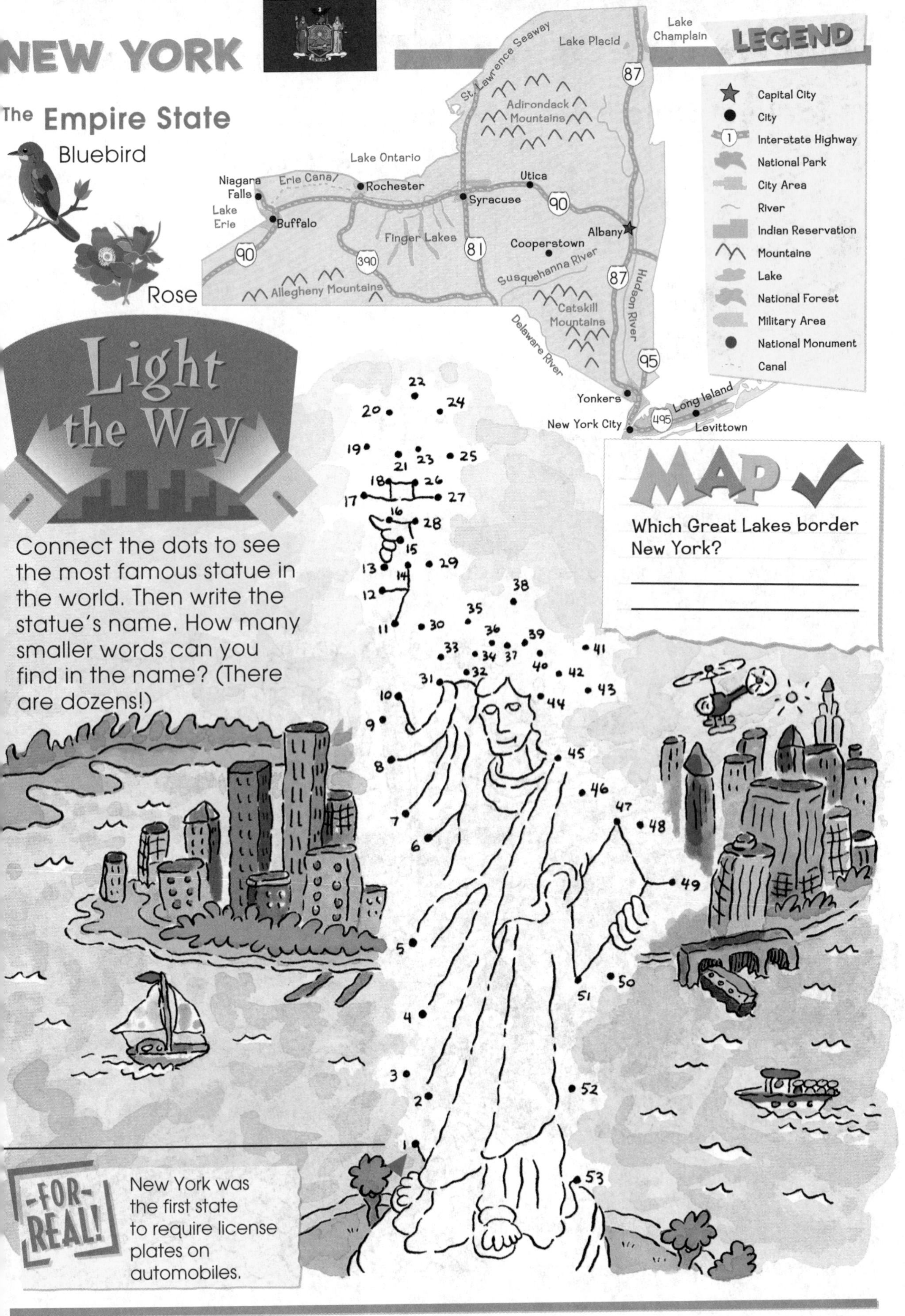

Light the Way

Connect the dots to see the most famous statue in the world. Then write the statue's name. How many smaller words can you find in the name? (There are dozens!)

____

MAP ✓

Which Great Lakes border New York?

____

____

-FOR-REAL! New York was the first state to require license plates on automobiles.

NORTH CAROLINA

The Tar Heel State

Piedmont Region
Dismal Swamp
Blue Ridge Mountains
Winston-Salem
Greensboro
Durham
Great Smoky Mountains National Park
Asheville
Raleigh
Charlotte
Hatteras
Coastal Plains
Wilmington
Atlantic Ocean
85
40
77
95

Cardinal

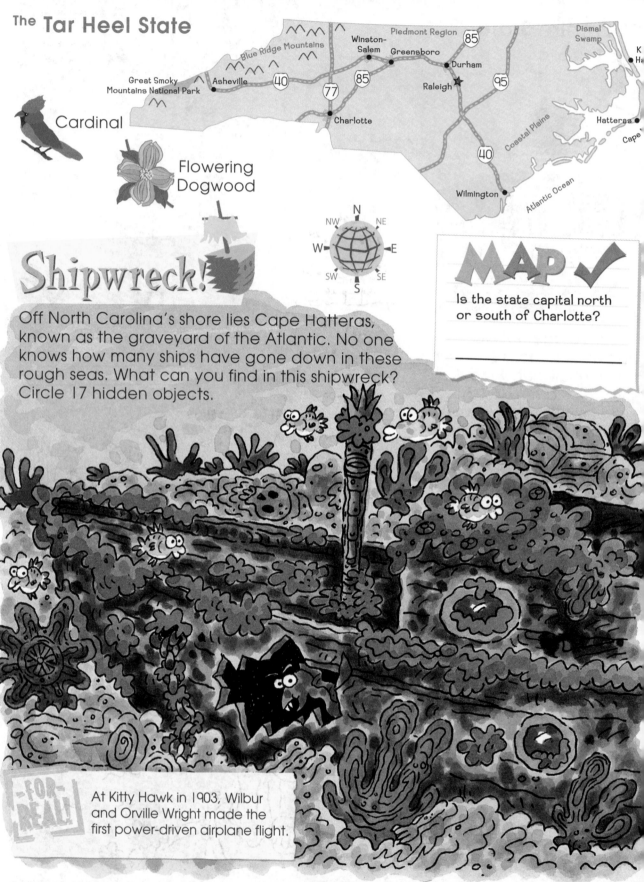

Flowering Dogwood

N NE E SE S SW W NW

Shipwreck!

Off North Carolina's shore lies Cape Hatteras, known as the graveyard of the Atlantic. No one knows how many ships have gone down in these rough seas. What can you find in this shipwreck? Circle 17 hidden objects.

MAP ✓

Is the state capital north or south of Charlotte?

____

FOR REAL!

At Kitty Hawk in 1903, Wilbur and Orville Wright made the first power-driven airplane flight.

NORTH DAKOTA

The Flickertail State

Western Meadowlark

Wild Prarie Rose

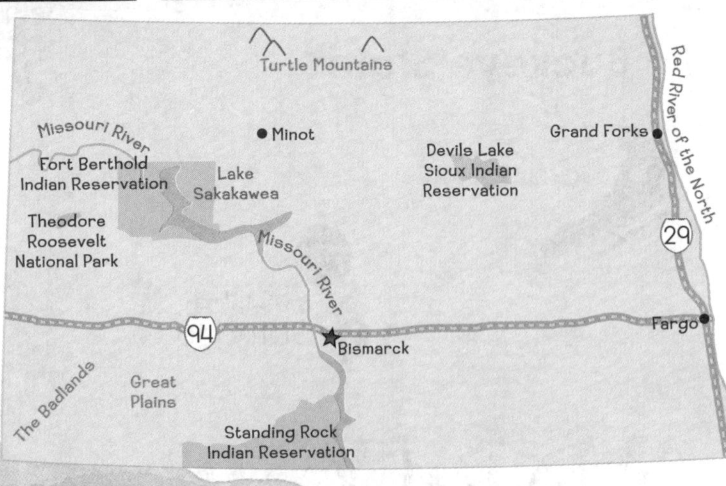

LEGEND

- Capital City
- City
- Interstate Highway
- National Park
- City Area
- River
- Indian Reservation
- Mountains
- Lake
- National Forest

MAP ✓

How many Indian reservations are shown on the map?

____

T.R.'s Place

What's the name of the area where President Theodore Roosevelt had ranches in the 1880s? (It's a national park and wildlife sanctuary now.) Give up? Cross off these letters to find out: **v, w, x, y, z**.

T	Z	W	X	Y	V
W	H	V	Y	E	W
Y	X	Z	B	W	X
A	V	D	Y	Y	L
V	A	Y	W	N	Y
W	Z	D	X	S	Z

____

Wheat brings in more farm income to North Dakota than any other crop. It's grown in every county in the state.

The **Buckeye State**

Cardinal

Scarlet Carnation

Who Did What?

Seven presidents were born in Ohio. Two of the most famous astronauts and three famous inventors were also born in Ohio. Do you know the presidents from the astronauts and the astronauts from the inventors? Write **p** for president, **a** for astronaut, or **i** for inventor in the boxes.

Which city on the map is farthest east?

____

Warren G. Harding ☐

Neil A. Armstrong ☐

William McKinley ☐

William Howard Taft ☐

Ulysses S. Grant ☐

John H. Glenn, Jr. ☐

Orville Wright ☐

Thomas A. Edison ☐

James A. Garfield ☐

The Rock and Roll Hall of fame is in Cleveland.

Rutherford B. Hayes ☐

Wilbur Wright ☐

Benjamin Harrison ☐

OKLAHOMA

The Sooner State

Scissor-Tailed Flycatcher

Oklahoma Rose

OK? OK!

Oil derricks are common sights in the Oklahoma landscape. Look at all the derricks! Can you find two that are exactly alike?

LEGEND

- Capital City
- City
- Interstate Highway
- City Area
- River
- Mountains
- Lake
- National Forest
- Military Area
- National Monument

MAP ✓

Which moutain range is further west, the Wichitaw Mountains or the Ouachita Mountains?

____

-FOR- REAL!

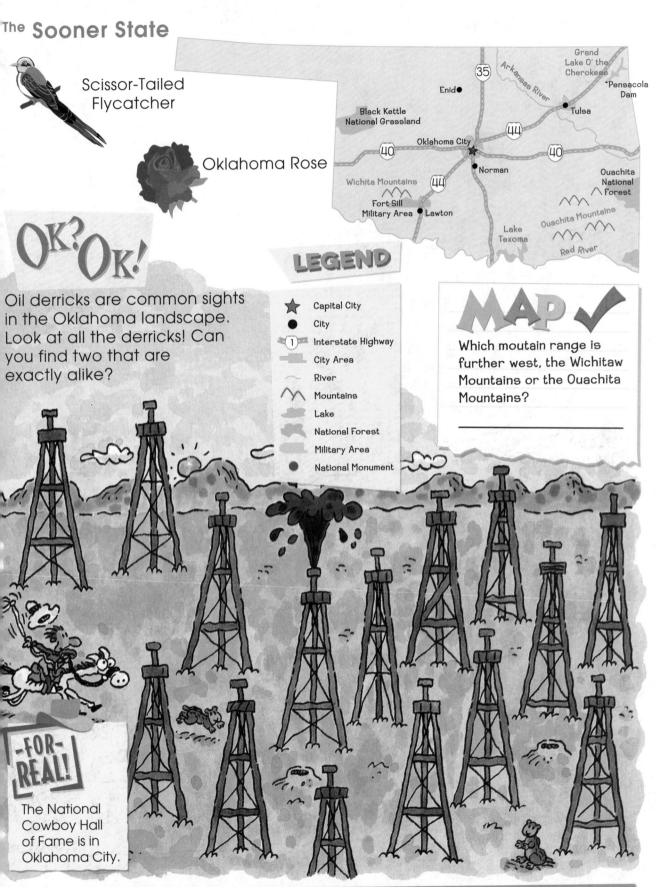

The National Cowboy Hall of Fame is in Oklahoma City.

OREGON

STATE OF OREGON
1859

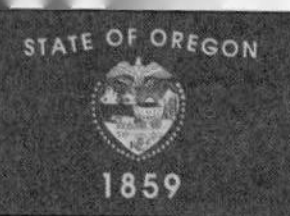

The Beaver State

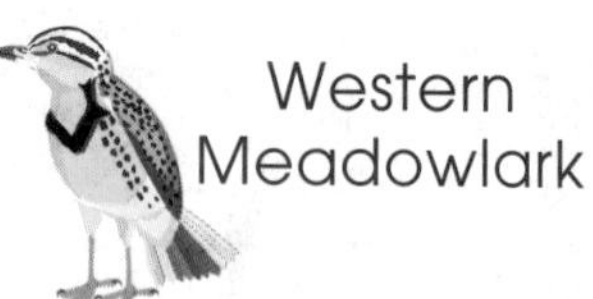

Western Meadowlark

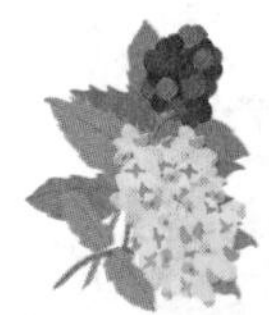

Oregon Grape

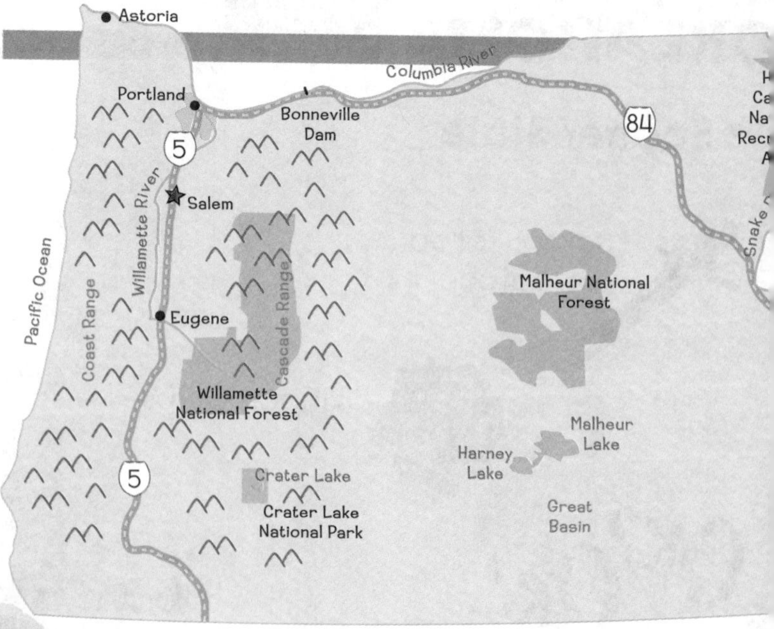

Astoria
Columbia River
Portland
Bonneville Dam
84
5
Salem
Willamette River
Pacific Ocean
Coast Range
Cascade Range
Eugene
Willamette National Forest
Malheur National Forest
Malheur Lake
Harney Lake
Crater Lake
Crater Lake National Park
Great Basin
Snake R

Trailblazers

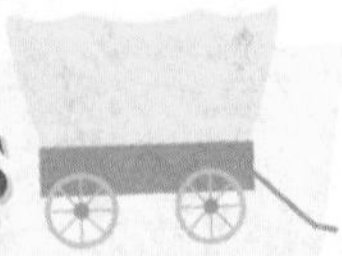

Pioneers traveled the Oregon Trail in the mid-1800s from Independence, Missouri to Oregon. Use two coins as markers to play this Oregon Trail game. Toss one coin. Heads goes first and moves two spaces. Tails moves one space. The first to reach the Willamette Valley wins.

N
NE
E
SE
S
SW
W
NW

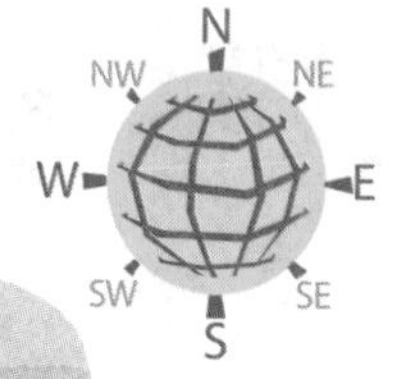

MAP ✓

Which interstate highway goes through Eugene and Portland?

____

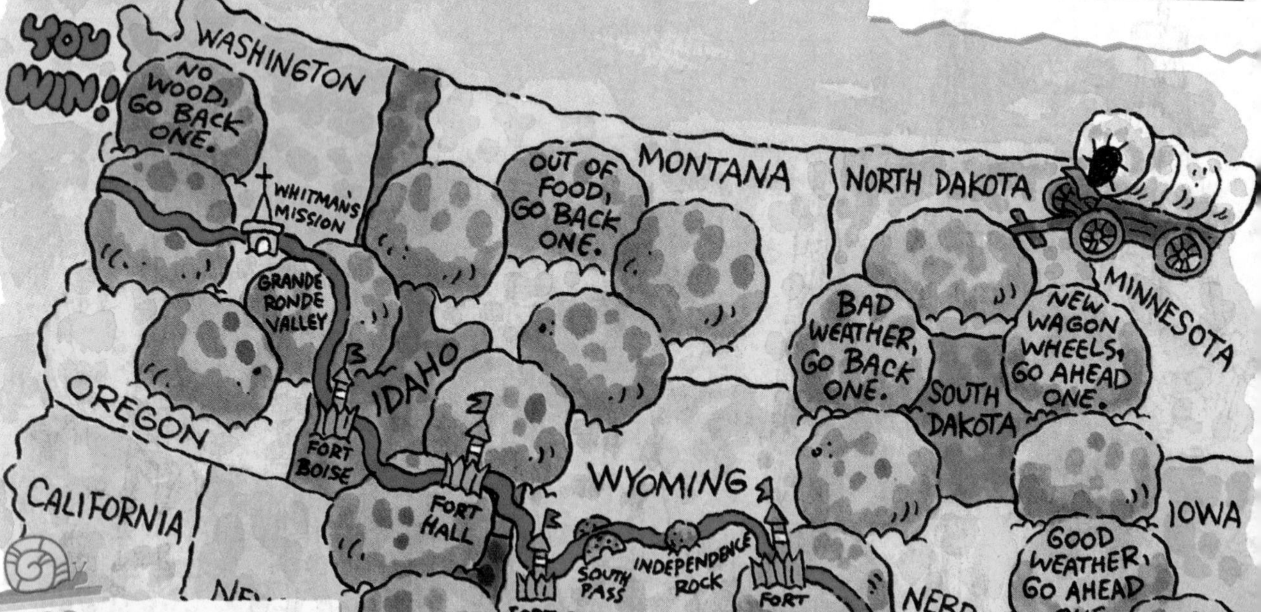

YOU WIN!
WASHINGTON
NO WOOD, GO BACK ONE.
WHITMAN'S MISSION
GRANDE RONDE VALLEY
OREGON
IDAHO
FORT BOISE
OUT OF FOOD, GO BACK ONE.
MONTANA
NORTH DAKOTA
MINNESOTA
BAD WEATHER, GO BACK ONE.
NEW WAGON WHEELS, GO AHEAD ONE.
SOUTH DAKOTA
CALIFORNIA
FORT HALL
WYOMING
SOUTH PASS
INDEPENDENCE ROCK
FORT LARAMIE
FORT BRIDGER
IOWA
GOOD WEATHER, GO AHEAD ONE.
NEBRASKA
START
UTAH
FLOODED RIVER, GO BACK ONE.
DISEASE, GO BACK ONE.
COLORADO
KANSAS
INDEPENDENCE
MISSOURI

-FOR- REAL! The world's smallest park, just two feet across, is in Portland. The tiny park was designed for leprechauns and snail races.

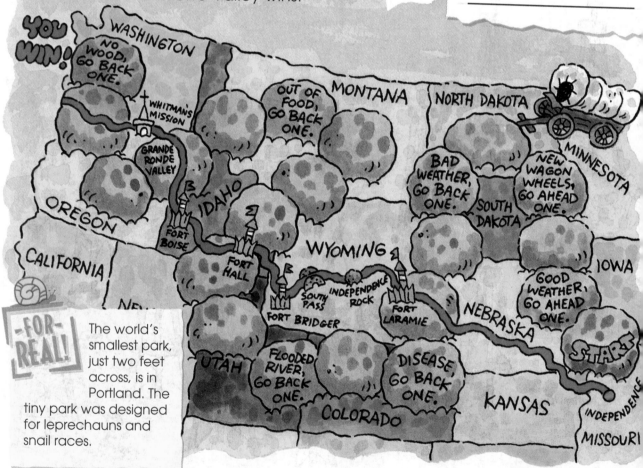

PENNSYLVANIA

The Keystone State

Ruffed Grouse

Which river runs along Pennsylvania's eastern edge?

____

Mountain Laurel

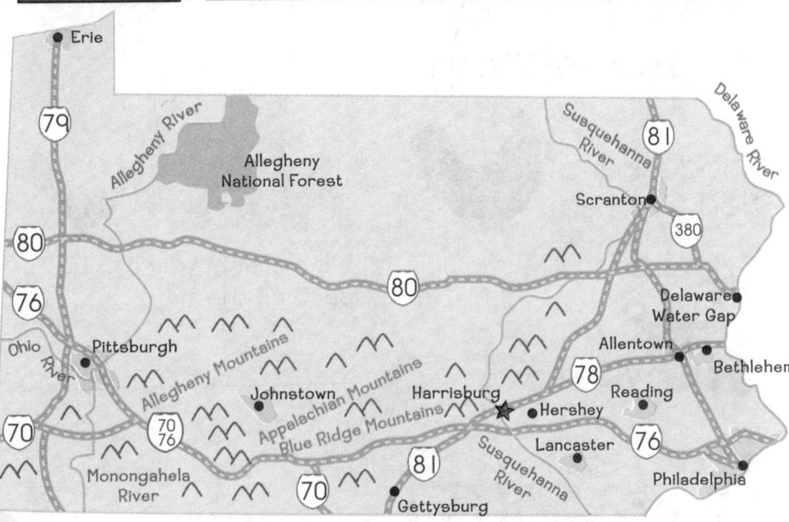

Some Pennsylvania Dutch farmers paint beautiful designs on their barns. Circle the two Pennsylvania Dutch designs that are exactly the same.

LEGEND

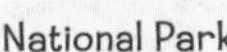

★	Capital City		Lake
●	City		National Forest
1	Interstate Highway		Mountains
	City Area		National Park
	River		

Yum! The world's largest chocolate factory is in Hersey.

RHODE ISLAND

The Ocean State

Rhode Island Red Chicken

Violet

MAP ✓

Which reservoir can be seen on the map?

____

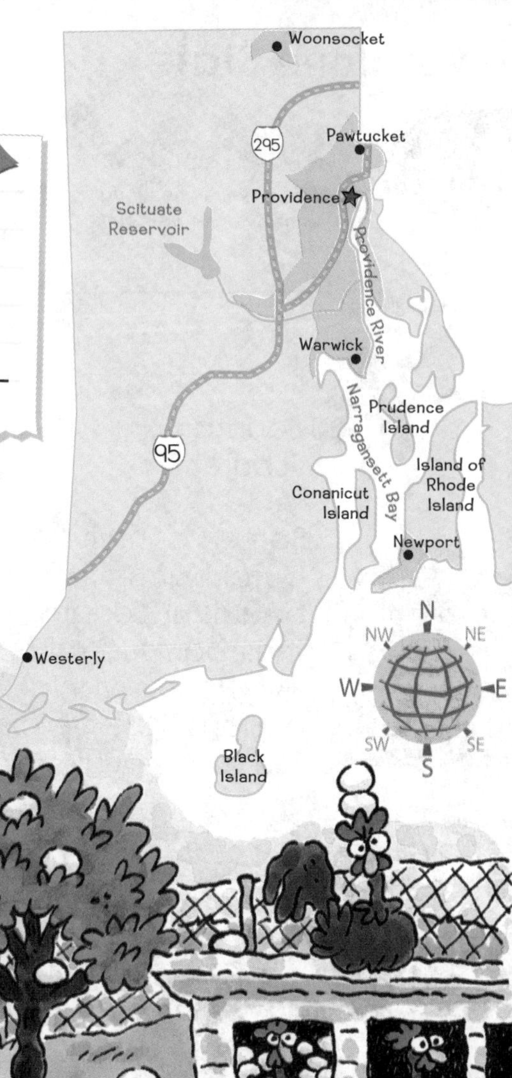

Eggsactly!

Rhode Island Red chickens began the poultry industry in the U.S. They lay lots of eggs. These Rhode Island Reds have misplaced their eggs! Can you find all 53 eggs?

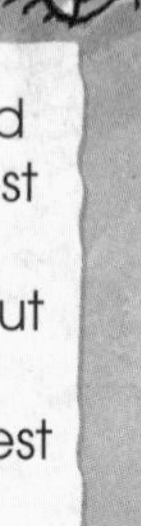

-FOR-REAL! Rhode Island is the smallest state in the U.S. It is about half the size of the next smallest state, Delaware.

SOUTH CAROLINA

The Palmetto State

Great Carolina Wren

Carolina Jessamine

MAP ✓

South Carolina is roughly what geometric shape?

____

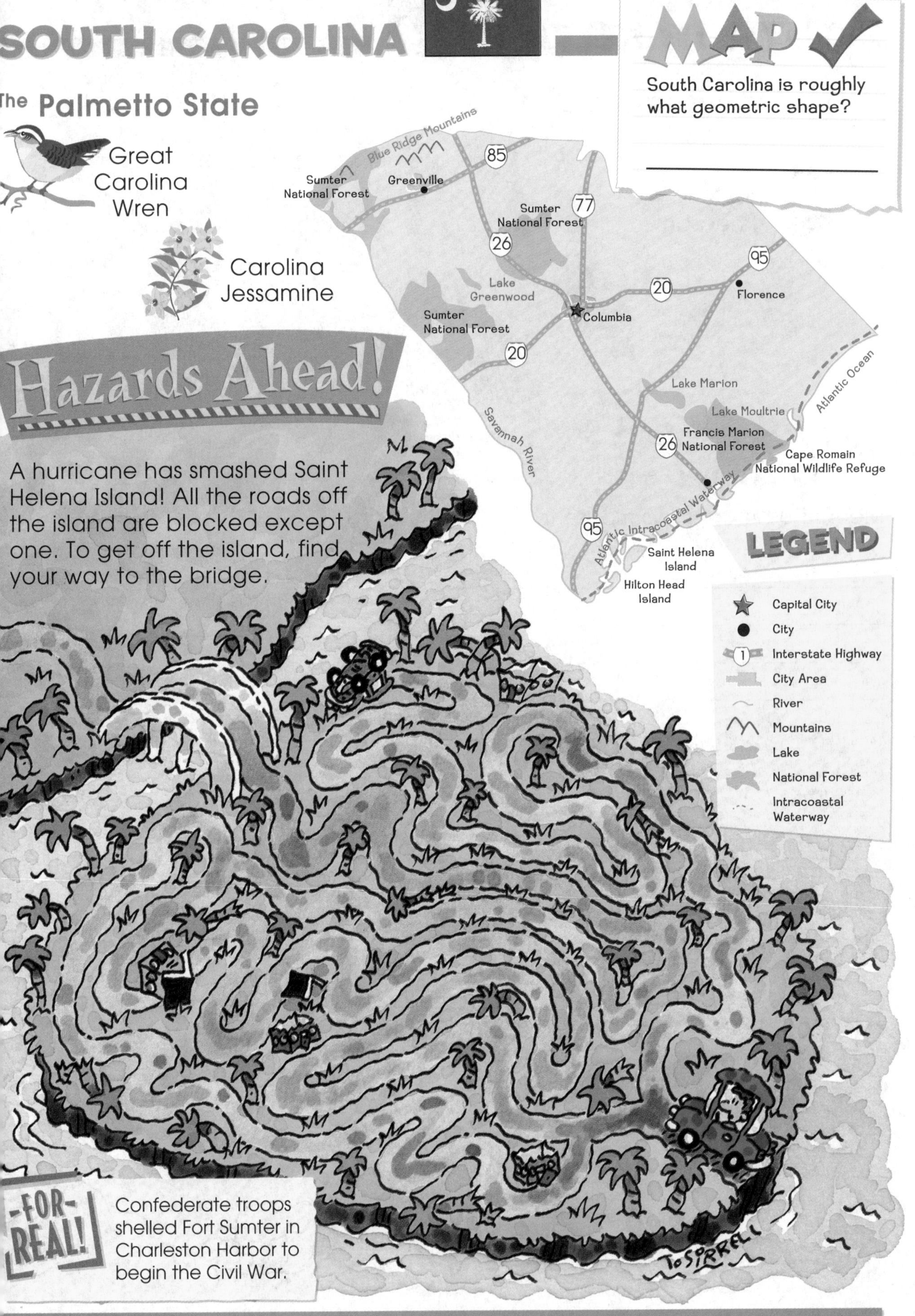

Hazards Ahead!

A hurricane has smashed Saint Helena Island! All the roads off the island are blocked except one. To get off the island, find your way to the bridge.

FOR REAL! Confederate troops shelled Fort Sumter in Charleston Harbor to begin the Civil War.

SOUTH DAKOTA

The Mount Rushmore State

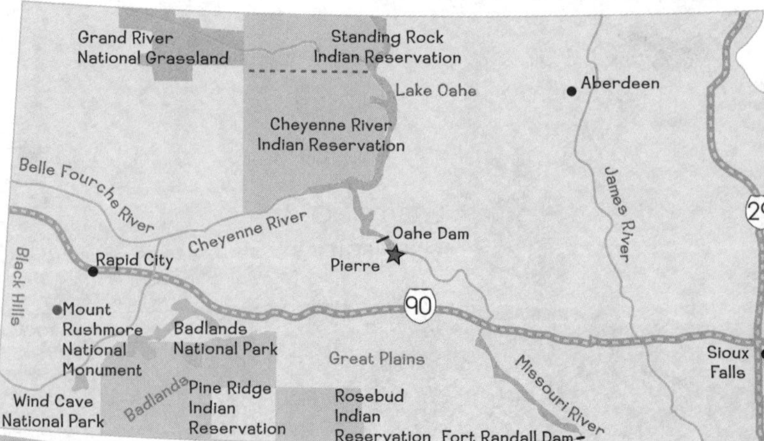

Great Stone Faces

Mount Rushmore pays tribute to which famous Americans?

____

____

____

____

How many Indian reservations are shown on this map? Which one is the smallest?

____

Whose likeness would you add to Mount Rushmore? Sketch that person's portrait.

-FOR-REAL! The geographic center of the U.S. (including Alaska and Hawaii) is in western South Dakota.

TENNESSEE

The Volunteer State

Mockingbird

Iris

Mississippi River
Memphis
40
Tennessee River
65
Nashville
Cumberland River
Cumberland Mountains
24
Lookout Mountain
40
Oak Ridge National Laboratory
Kingston
Tennessee River
75
Chattanooga
75
Cumberland Gap
Knoxville
Mountains
Smoky
Great
Clingmans Dome
Great Smoky Mountains National Park

LEGEND

- Capital City
- City
- Interstate Highway
- City Area
- River
- Mountains
- Lake
- National Park
- Military Area
- National Monument
- Indian Reservation

MAP ✓

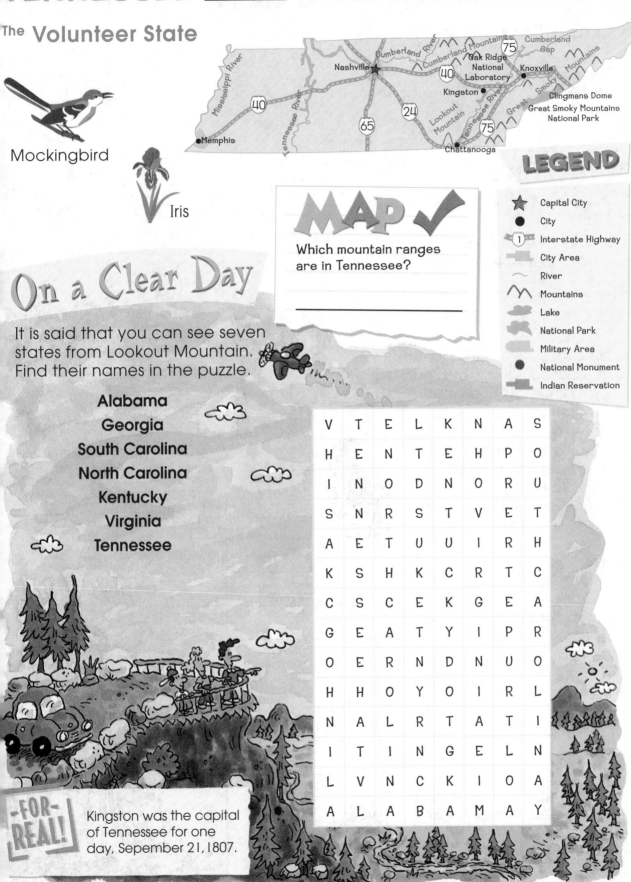

Which mountain ranges are in Tennessee?

____

On a Clear Day

It is said that you can see seven states from Lookout Mountain. Find their names in the puzzle.

Alabama
Georgia
South Carolina
North Carolina
Kentucky
Virginia
Tennessee

V	T	E	L	K	N	A	S
H	E	N	T	E	H	P	O
I	N	O	D	N	O	R	U
S	N	R	S	T	V	E	T
A	E	T	U	U	I	R	H
K	S	H	K	C	R	T	C
C	S	C	E	K	G	E	A
G	E	A	T	Y	I	P	R
O	E	R	N	D	N	U	O
H	H	O	Y	O	I	R	L
N	A	L	R	T	A	T	I
I	T	I	N	G	E	L	N
L	V	N	C	K	I	O	A
A	L	A	B	A	M	A	Y

-FOR- REAL! Kingston was the capital of Tennessee for one day, Sepember 21, 1807.

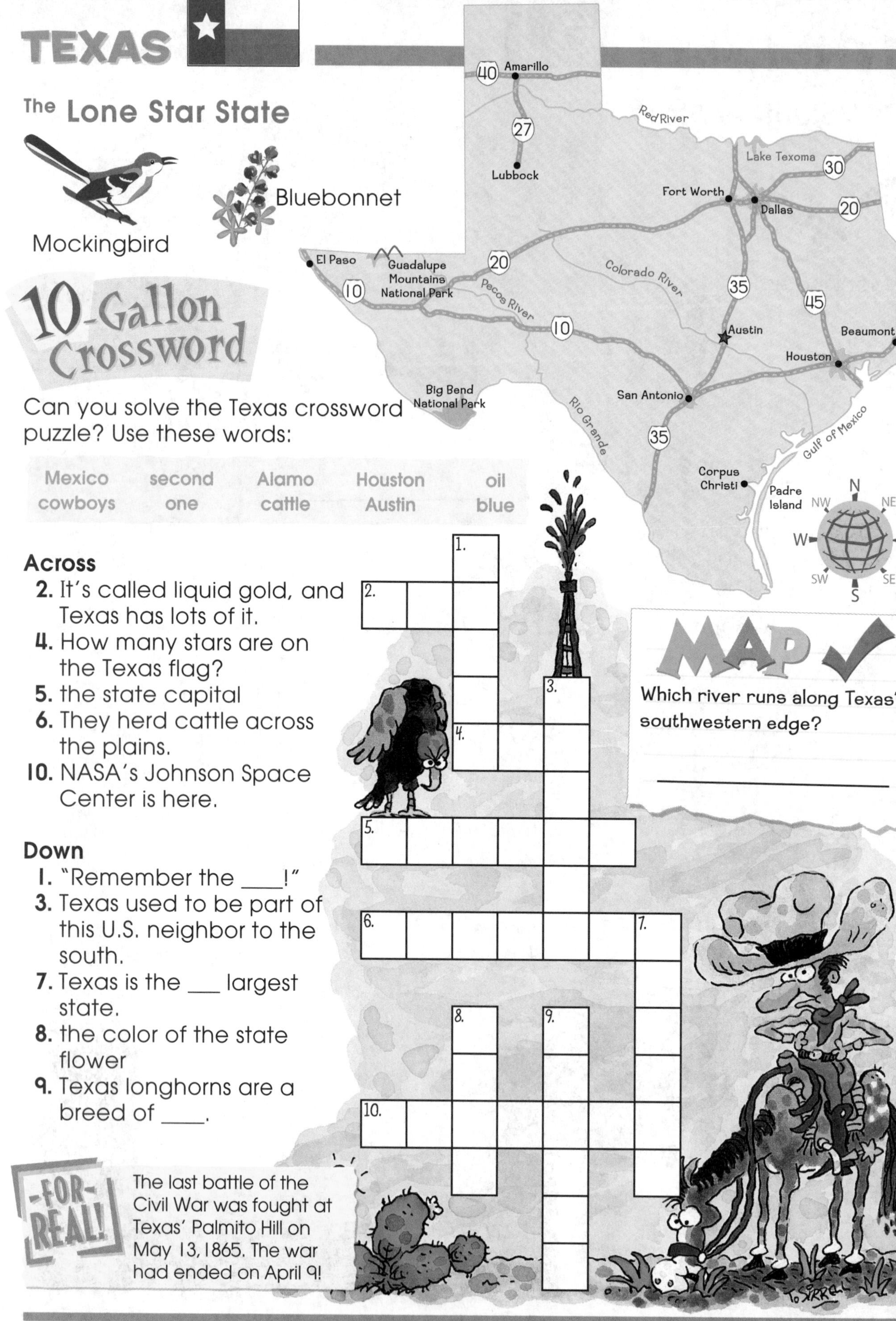

TEXAS

The Lone Star State

Mockingbird

Bluebonnet

10-Gallon Crossword

Can you solve the Texas crossword puzzle? Use these words:

Mexico	second	Alamo	Houston	oil
cowboys	one	cattle	Austin	blue

Across

2. It's called liquid gold, and Texas has lots of it.
4. How many stars are on the Texas flag?
5. the state capital
6. They herd cattle across the plains.
10. NASA's Johnson Space Center is here.

Down

1. "Remember the ____!"
3. Texas used to be part of this U.S. neighbor to the south.
7. Texas is the ___ largest state.
8. the color of the state flower
9. Texas longhorns are a breed of ____.

1. 2. 3. 4. 5. 6. 7. 8. 9. 10.

MAP ✓

Which river runs along Texas' southwestern edge?

____

FOR REAL!

The last battle of the Civil War was fought at Texas' Palmito Hill on May 13, 1865. The war had ended on April 9!

UTAH

The Beehive State

Seagull

Sego Lily

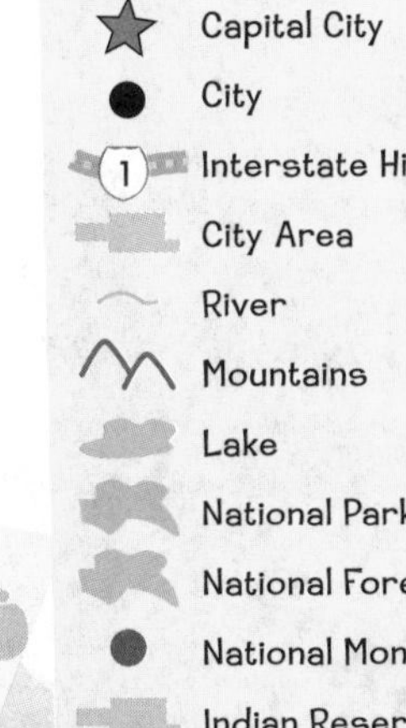

Great Salt Lake
84
Ogden
Wasatch Range
Great Salt Lake Desert
84
Wasatch-Cache National Forest
Rocky Mountains
80
Salt Lake City
Ashley National Forest
Great Basin
Provo
Uintah & Ouray Indian Reservation
Ashley National Forest
15
70
Arches National Park
Colorado River
Fishlake National Forest
Canyonlands National Park
15
Bryce Canyon National Park
Lake Powell
Natural Bridges Monument
Glen Canyon National Recreation Area
Zion National Park
Rainbow Bridge National Monument

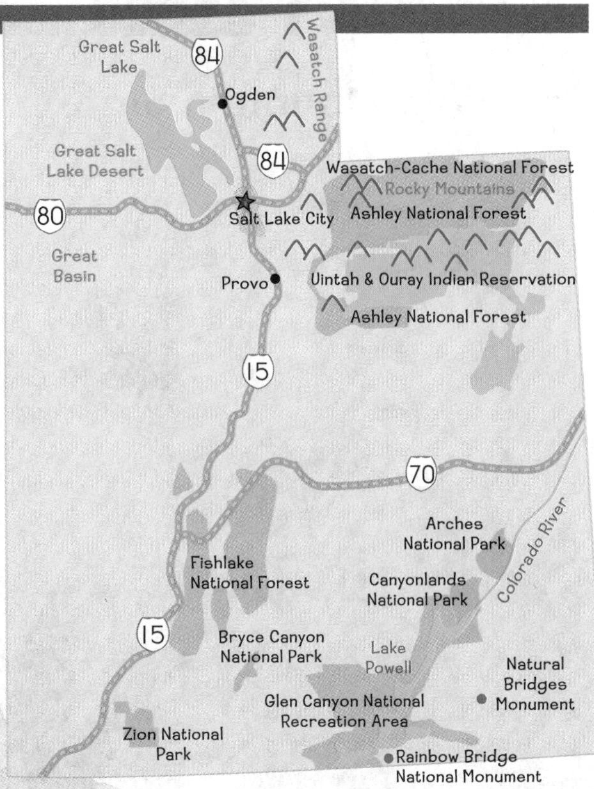

Critter Capture

You can see lots of interesting animals in Utah. Can you identify the ones below? Write the numbers in the boxes.

1. trout
2. badger
3. black bear
4. coyote
5. goose
6. moose
7. tortoise
8. pheasant
9. skunk
10. weasel
11. mule deer
12. mountain lion
13. rabbit
14. buffalo
15. pronghorn sheep

Which interstate highway goes just south of the Great Salt Lake?

____

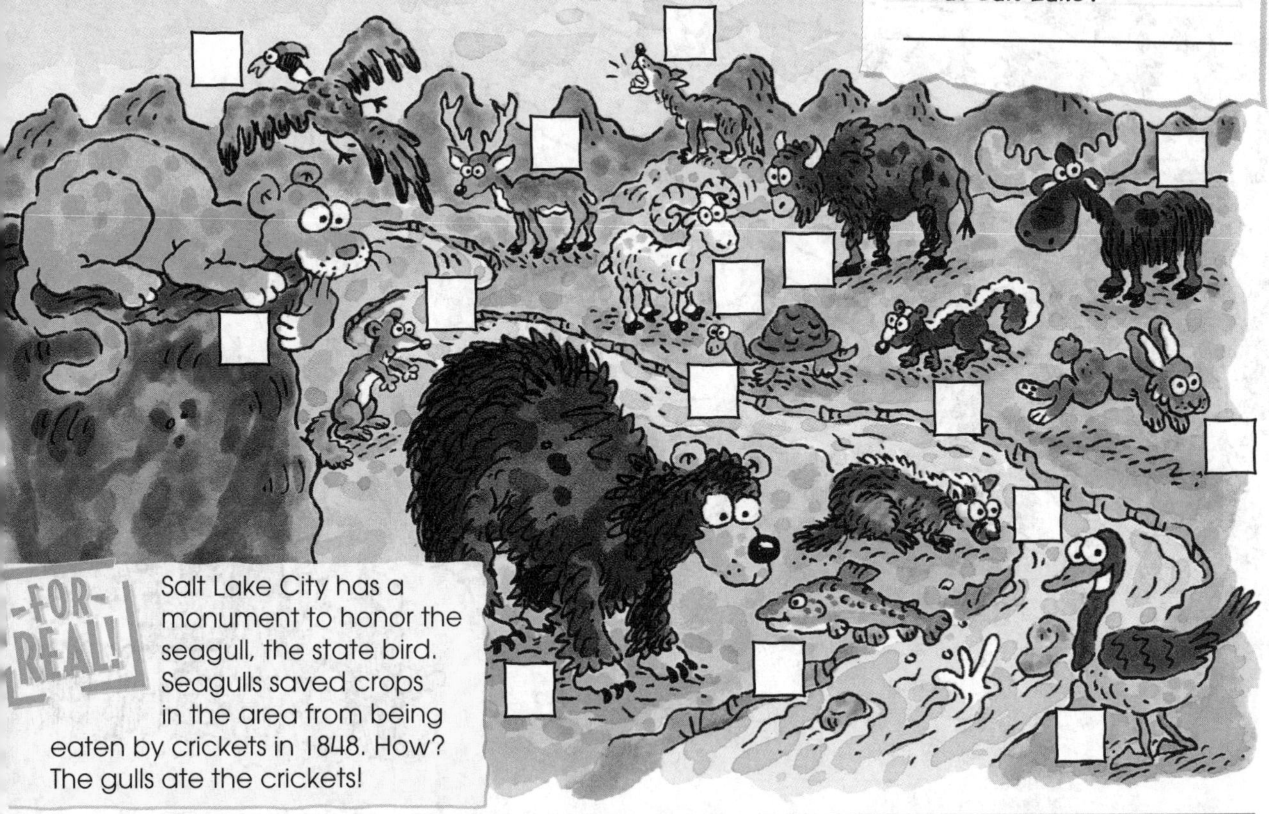

FOR REAL! Salt Lake City has a monument to honor the seagull, the state bird. Seagulls saved crops in the area from being eaten by crickets in 1848. How? The gulls ate the crickets!

VERMONT

The Green Mountain State

Hermit Thrush

Red Clover

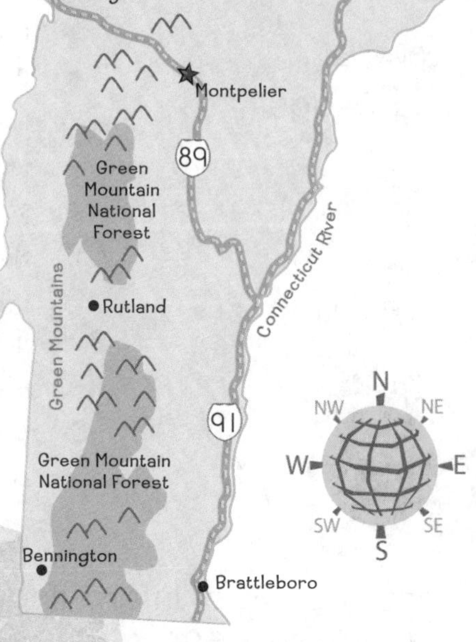

Downhill Racers

Vermont's Green Mountains are a wonderful place to ski! Help this skier choose the shortest path down the mountain.

On which side of the state is Burlington?

____

SKI LODGE

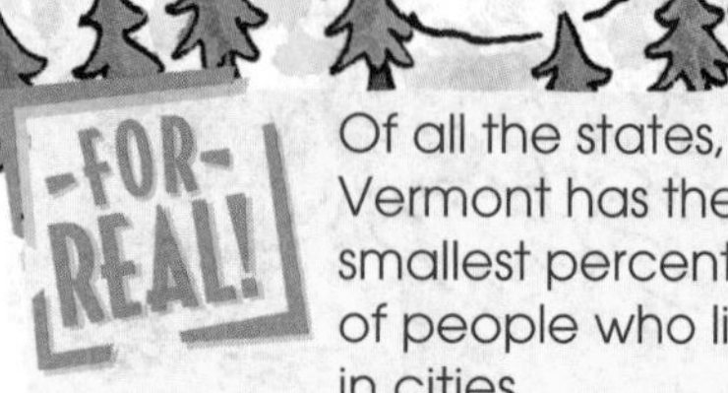

Of all the states, Vermont has the smallest percentage of people who live in cities.

VIRGINIA

The Old Dominion State

Flowering Dogwood

Cardinal

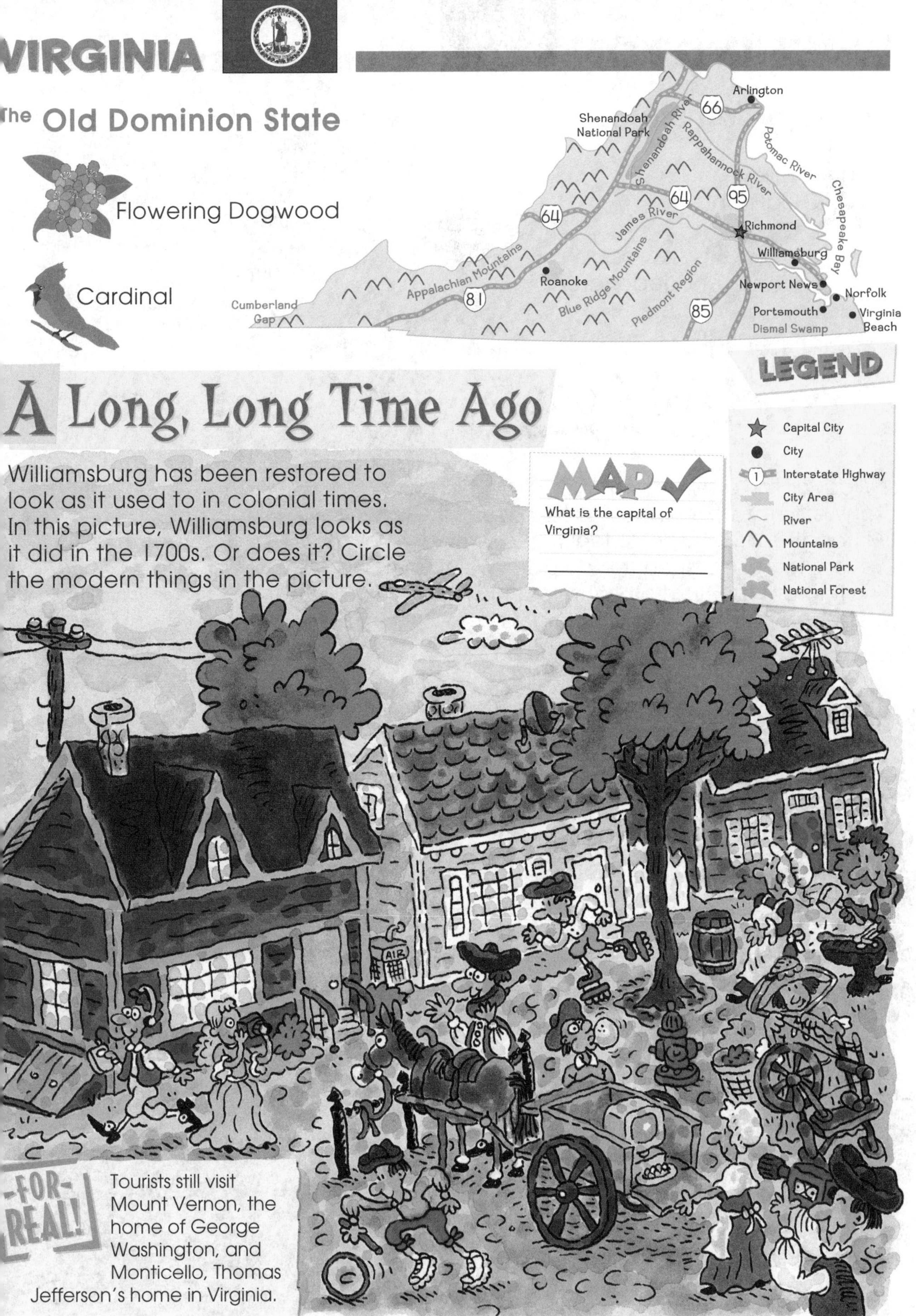

A Long, Long Time Ago

Williamsburg has been restored to look as it used to in colonial times. In this picture, Williamsburg looks as it did in the 1700s. Or does it? Circle the modern things in the picture.

MAP ✓

What is the capital of Virginia?

____

FOR REAL! Tourists still visit Mount Vernon, the home of George Washington, and Monticello, Thomas Jefferson's home in Virginia.

WASHINGTON

The Evergreen State

Willow Goldfinch

Coast Rhododendron

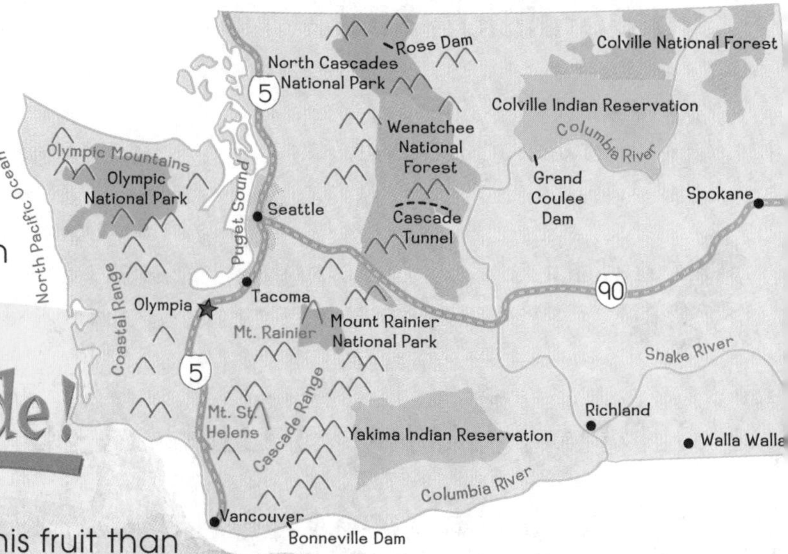

Ross Dam
Colville National Forest
North Cascades National Park
5
Colville Indian Reservation
Columbia River
Olympic Mountains
Olympic National Park
Wenatchee National Forest
North Pacific Ocean
Puget Sound
Seattle
Grand Coulee Dam
Spokane
Cascade Tunnel
Coastal Range
Tacoma
90
Olympia
Mt. Rainier
Mount Rainier National Park
Snake River
5
Cascade Range
Mt. St. Helens
Richland
Yakima Indian Reservation
Walla Walla
Columbia River
Vancouver
Bonneville Dam

Crack the Orchard Code!

Washington grows more of this fruit than any other state. It is also a top producer of another fruit. Start at the ▼ and write every fourth letter on the outside circle to find out the first fruit. Write every third letter on the inner circle to find out the second fruit.

Outside circle: V B C A R H M P E N S P T B O L E D L E C M X S

Inner circle: Y F C R T H L A E T S R X X R N Q I B N E L V S

____

____

MAP ✓

The Cascade Tunnel is located in which national forest?

____

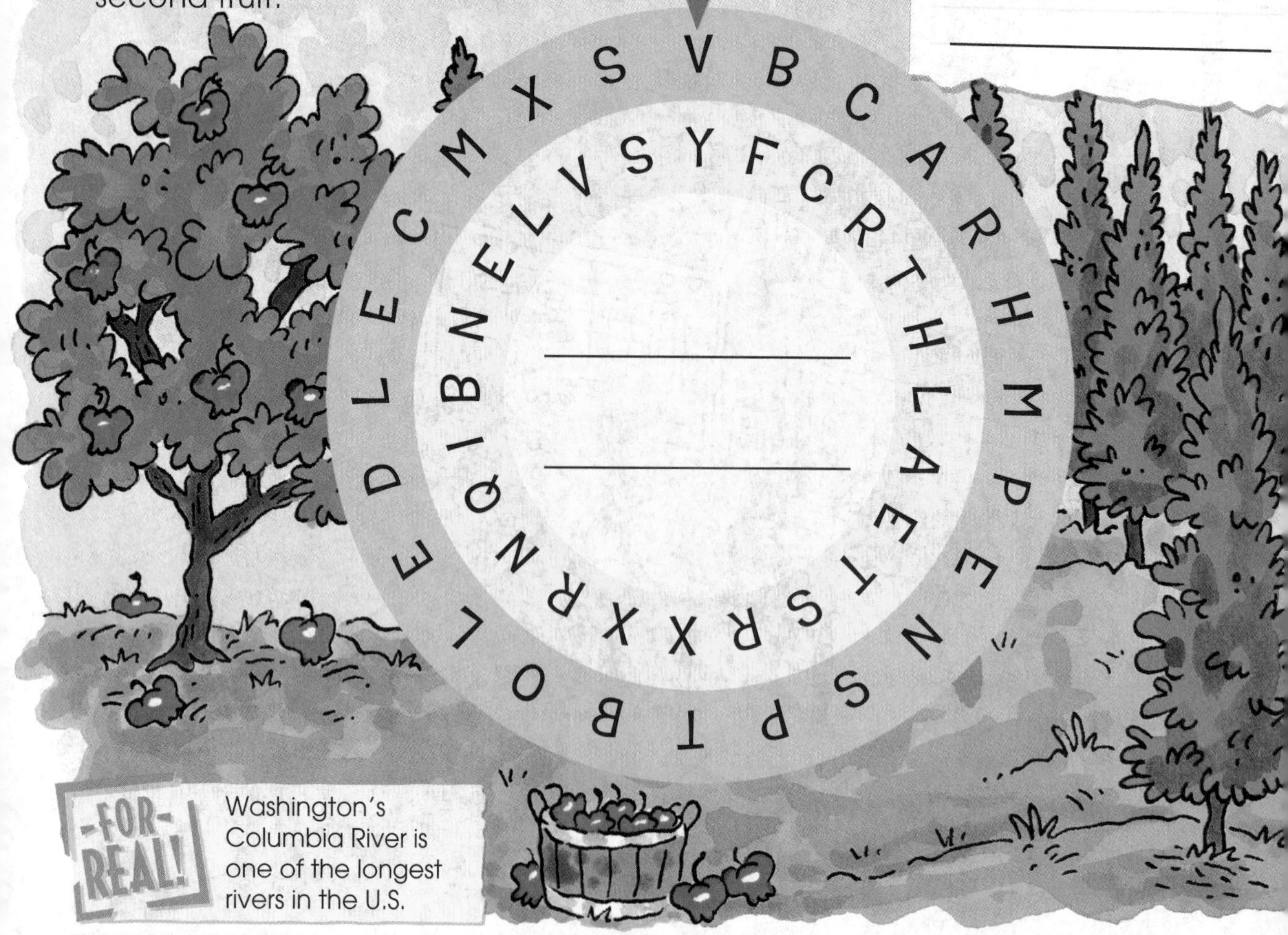

-FOR- REAL! Washington's Columbia River is one of the longest rivers in the U.S.

WEST VIRGINIA

The Mountain State

Cardinal

Rhododendron

Uphill & Down

Take a hike through the Mountain State. Draw yourself and some friends. Then color the rest of the picture.

MAP ✓

Which mountain range is further east?

____

-FOR- REAL! During the Civil War, the town of Romney changed hands between the Union and the Confederacy approximately 56 times!

WISCONSIN

The Badger State

Robin

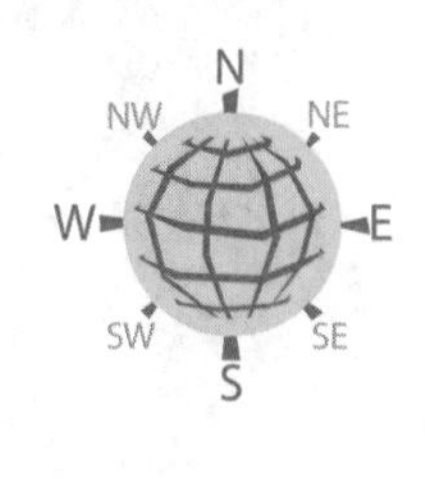

Wood Violet

Where's My Mooother?

Wisconsin is known as America's Dairyland for its huge herds of dairy cattle that make the state the leading milk producer. These calves have lost their mothers. Draw a line from each cow to her matching calf.

What is the name of the biggest lake in the state?

____

FOR REAL! On October 8, 1871, the same night as the Great Chicago Fire, the Peshtigo Forest Fire killed between 1,200 - 2,500 people in northeast Wisconsin.

WYOMING

The Equality State

Meadowlark

Indian Paintbrush

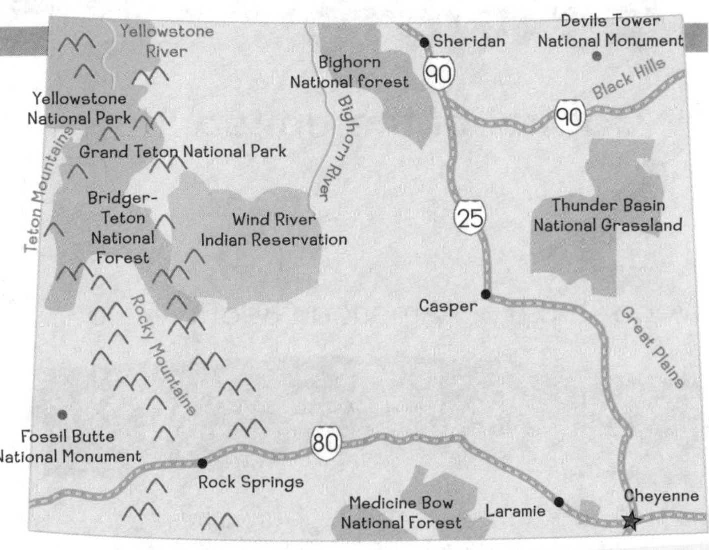

It's a Gusher!

Yellowstone Park is the oldest and biggest national park in the U.S. One of its many attractions is an enormous geyser that spouts steam and water hundreds of feet into the air. Letters that spell the name of this geyser are hidden in this picture. Find the letters and write the geyser's name.

____

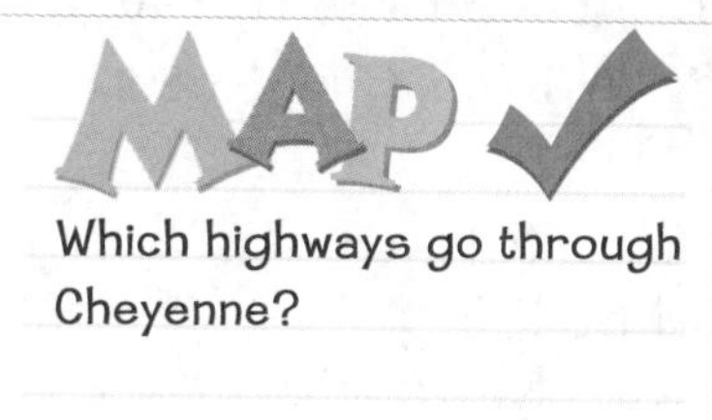

Which highways go through Cheyenne?

____

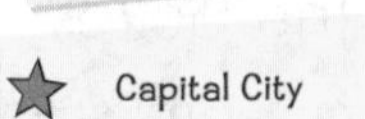

- Capital City
- City
- Interstate Highway
- City Area
- River
- Mountains
- Lake
- National Park
- National Forest
- National Monument
- Indian Reservation

FOR REAL! Wyoming has the fewest people of any state.

WASHINGTON, D.C.

The Capital of the United States

Wood Thrush

American Beauty Rose

Maryland
Rock Creek Park
16th Street
Rock Creek
Connecticut Ave.
Wisconsin Ave.
Massachusetts Ave.
Potomac River
Anacostia River
White House
Arlington
Washington Monument
National Mall
U.S. Capitol
Arlington National Cemetary
Independence Ave.
East Potomac Park
Pennsylvania Ave.
N NE E SE S SW W NW
Alexandria
Potomac River
Virginia

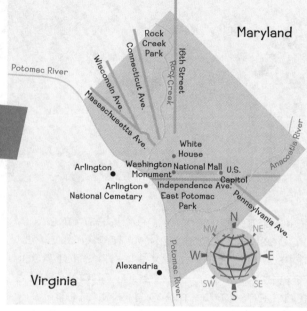

Sight for Sore Eyes

Here are some of the sights visitors see in Washington, D.C. How many can you identify? Write the letters in the boxes.

a. United States Capitol
b. Supreme Court Building
c. Vietnam Veterans Memorial
d. Air and Space Museum
e. White House
f. Jefferson Memorial
g. Lincoln Memorial
h. Original Smithsonian Institution
i. Reflecting Pool

Which river borders Washington, D.C.?

____

Washington, D.C. is the only U.S. city that is not part of a state. **D.C.** stands for District of Columbia.

OCTO PUZZLE

Introduction

Octo puzzles require a wide variety of techniques to solve. Many of the positional techniques used to solve Sudoku puzzles can be used with Octo puzzles. The basic addition and factoring techniques used to solve Kakuro puzzles are also helpful.

The real fun and challenge in solving Octo puzzles is combining several techniques (and sometimes inventing new ones) to place the numbers 1 through 8 uniquely into the Octo grid.

What's the Goal?

The goal of an Octo puzzle is to place the numbers 1 through 8 in each of the octagons such that the numbers are not repeated in any octagon, row, column, or diagonal. Major diagonals use each of the numbers 1 through 8. Minor diagonals use either four or six of the numbers 1 through 8 with no repeats.

The sums of the numbers in each minor diagonal are provided at the beginning and end of each minor diagonal. The sums of the four numbers that border each diamond are provided in each diamond. (The numbers that border the diamonds do not have to be unique.)

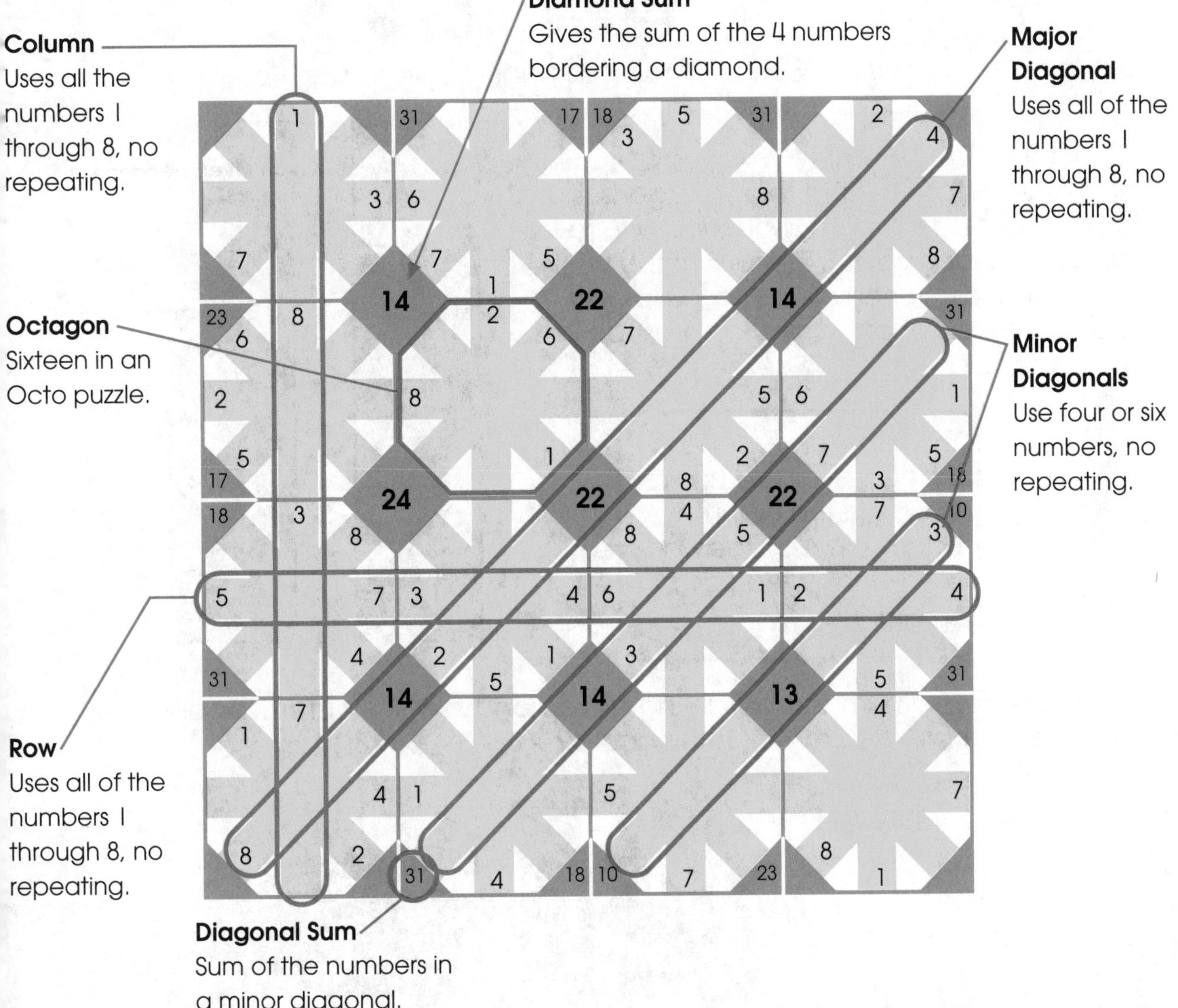

Diamond Sum
Gives the sum of the 4 numbers bordering a diamond.
Column
Uses all the numbers 1 through 8, no repeating.
Major Diagonal
Uses all of the numbers 1 through 8, no repeating.
Octagon
Sixteen in an Octo puzzle.
Minor Diagonals
Use four or six numbers, no repeating.
Row
Uses all of the numbers 1 through 8, no repeating.
Diagonal Sum
Sum of the numbers in a minor diagonal.

OCTO PUZZLE

Basic Solving Techniques

Your first strategy for solving an Octo puzzle is to look the numbers you can fill in quickly.

1. Look for a row, column or major diagonal where most of the numbers are already filled in.

This number must be a **1** or a **3** because **2**, **4**, **5**, **6**, **7**, and **8** are already used in the column. Since 1 is already used in the same octagon, this number must be a **3**.

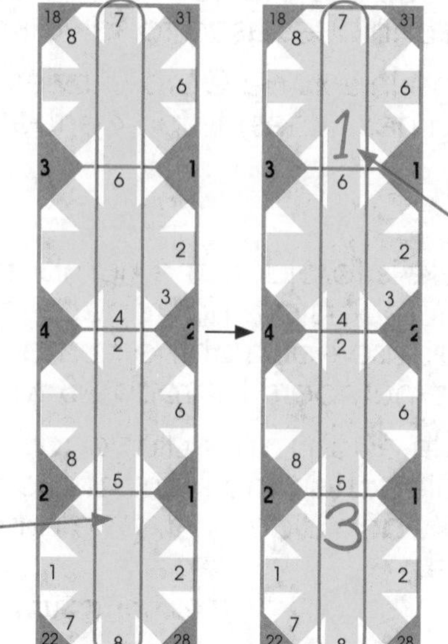

Now you can fill in this number **1** because it's the only unused number in the column.

Keep in mind this doesn't work with minor diagonals, since they don't include all eight numbers.

2. Look for a column where one number shows up in three of the four octagons, but not in the column. (This also works with rows and major diagonals.) This technique works with minor diagonals only when you are certain the number in question must be in that short diagonal.

This number must be a **3** because there has to be a **3** in the column and there's already a **3** in each of the other octagons.

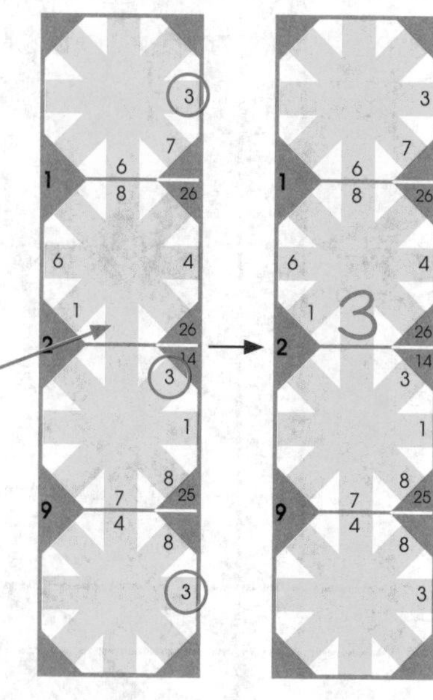

3. Three out of four numbers bordering a diamond sum will automatically give you the fourth number (in this case, **2** + **8** + **5** + **6** = 21).

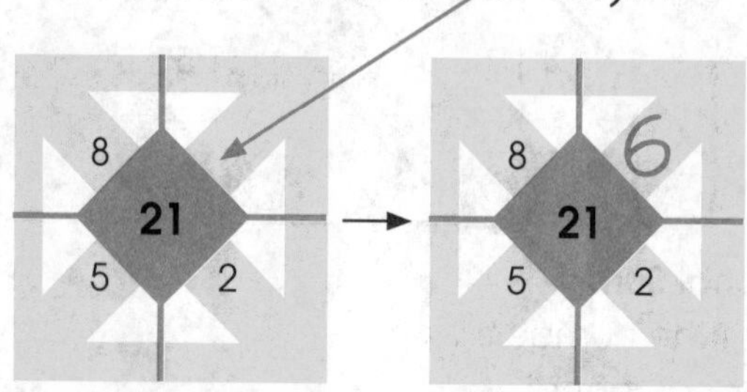

4. Often, having two of the four numbers around a diamond can be just as useful. In this case, you should test each number **1** through **8** and its "partner" to reduce the possibilities. In the following example, the numbers that go in the two circles must add up to **11** (so all four numbers will add up to the diamond sum, **17**):

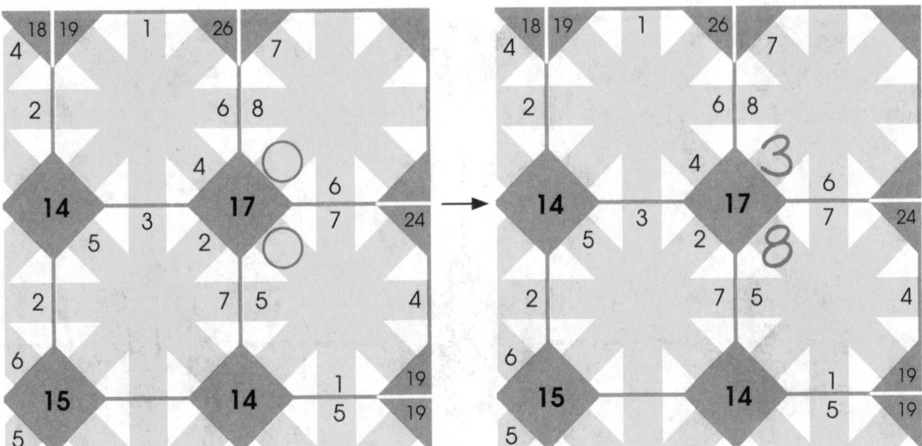

- The top circled number cannot be a **1** or a **2** because then the bottom number would have to be greater than **8** (**9** or **10**, respectively.)
- The top number cannot be a **5** because there is already a **5** in the same diagonal.
- The top number cannot be a **6**, **7**, or **8** because those numbers already exist in the same octagon.
- That leaves a **3** or a **4** for the top number. However, if the top number is a **4**, the bottom number would have to be a **7**—but it can't be because there is already a **7** in the same octagon.

So, the top number must be a **3** and the bottom number must be an **8**.

5. Look at the octagon where one number is already in all but one row, column, and diagonal (this technique is called "Triangulation".)

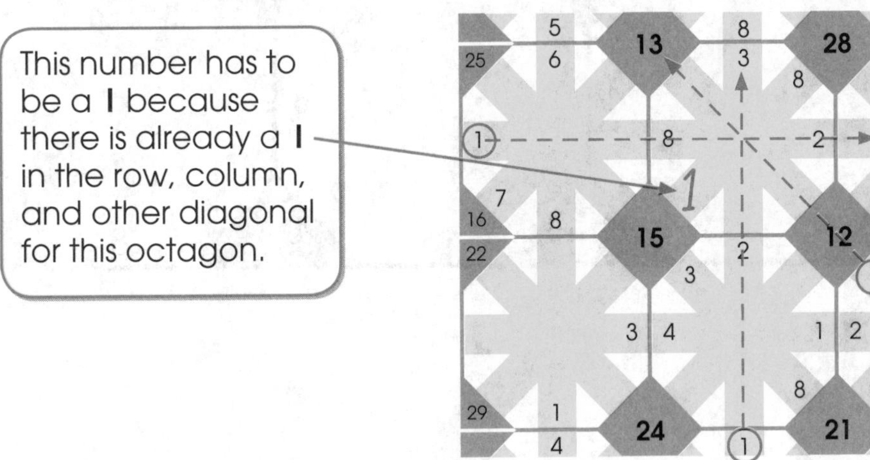

This number has to be a **1** because there is already a **1** in the row, column, and other diagonal for this octagon.

OCTO PUZZLE

Solve the puzzle.

6 31 7 15 14 6 30 5
2 1 2 5 7 2
3 7 2 5 1 8 6
4 6 4 1 8
5 **15** 3 **26** 7 **14** 3
25 7 2 1 7 25
6 2 8 4 5
8 4 7 3 2
6 5 5 6 3
15 1 **16** 1 **18** 2 **18** 14
22 2 8 15
1 5 2 3 4 3
4 6 7 1 8
7 5 7 1 5 6
30 8 4 4 2 31
25 **15** **15**
3 6 5 6
7 5 1 1
1 7 4 8 5
6 8 3 2 2 7
25 22 15 3 25 8

OCTO PUZZLE

Solve the puzzle.

2 27 7 12 18 4 26 3
4 6 7 8
7 8 5 2 6 3 1
6 3 1 5
1 2
16 **21** **13**
30 7 1 7 5 25
1 7 3
5 4 6 8 7
8 3 6 4 8
12 4 5 3 4 18
20 **15** **17**
16 2 6 1 19
2 7 1 3 5
8 4 3 5 1 2 7 6
1 7 8 2
26 5 6 7 8 27
19 **17** **19**
6 6
7 3 1 7 1 4
1 2 7 5 4 8
4 8 2 5 3 5
8 25 4 16 19 8 30

OCTO PUZZLE

Solve the puzzle.

4 25 1 21 24 5 23
1 7 3 3
5 3 8 6 4 2
8 6 5 7 7 6
3 6 8 8
18 **20** **24**
23 7 1 24
3 6 6 5 5
4 8 3 7 1 6
5 4 3 7
21 1 7 6 24
21 **18** **17**
18 3 3 3 22
4 7 8 6 8
5 3 7 1 2 8 4 6
6 5 4 5 2
23 6 1 25
21 **16** **18**
5 4 7 2
8 3
1 7 3 8 4 5
6 1 7 3 1 1
2 24 8 18 22 4 23 6

OCTO PUZZLE

Solve the puzzle.

OCTO PUZZLE

Solve the puzzle.

6 26 1 19 21 3 25 7
4 6 5 2
3 2 5 7 8 6 4 1
8 8 4 8
5 4
22 **20** **19**
25 3 5 2 1 29
2 5 6 3 6
6 3 7 5
2 5 4 8
19 6 21
21 **14** **24**
18 2 8 7 4 21
4 7 5 8 5
7 3 5 6 4 2
5 1 6 3 3
25 8 2 6 26
15 **15** **15**
1 4 2
2 5 5 4 7 3
6 8 1 7 3 4
2 1 1 6
4 29 6 18 21 8 25 8

OCTO PUZZLE

Solve the puzzle.

7 21 4 16 20 29 1
4 3 3 8
2 7 3 8
5 7 4 2 3
8 2 2 7
22 15 11
32 6 8 6 23
5 1 4 1
8 3 6 1 7 4
4 4 5 6
16 1 7 5 20
17 17 11
24 4 3 14
6 6 7 2 1
1 2 4 8 6
1 8 5 7 5 4
29 2 6 3 21
24 19 26
5 6 3 4
4 8 2 8 2
2 1 7 5 4 8 3 6
7 2 3
3 23 1 24 14 7 32 5

OCTO PUZZLE

Solve the puzzle.

OCTO PUZZLE

Solve the puzzle.

29 3 16 23 24 7
5 4 3 8 5
1 8 7 2 6 4
7 2 6 1 1 2
6 4 4 3
15 **13** **23**
24 7 2 6 2 31
2 6 3 7
3 8 7 2 4 6
8 5 3
16 1 1 4 23
21 **21** **20**
16 3 5 3 8 18
8 4 4
5 4 7 2
1 2 8 6
24 7 2 1 29
10 **22** **15**
2 8 5 5
6 4 3 7 1 2
7 1 6 8 2
8 1
31 16 18 8 24 6

OCTO PUZZLE

Solve the puzzle.

8 30 7 23 19 7 23 8
6 3 4
3 5 4 6 2
1 3 4
2
19 **17** **16**
27 2 1 28
6 3 7 2
7 3 4 2 6 1 8
4 5 8 2 7
23 1 4 3 19
26 **20** **19**
17 4 4 1 4 18
8 5 2 8 8
7 1 8 2 4 6 5 3
5 6 1 7
23 6 3 3 30
21 **15** **19**
8 5
7 1 4
2 3 6 5 7 8
1 6 2 3
5 28 5 17 18 6 27 7

OCTO PUZZLE

Solve the puzzle.

29 1 26 14 8 27 3
2 6 8 4
7 4 2 3 1 5 6 8
1 1 2
8 5 5
21 **14** **6**
30 3 7 26
5 4 1 1 6
2 7 1 6 5 3
7 5 8 3 8
26 1 6 4 2 14
19 **23** **24**
15 8 2 8 20
6 6
7 5 2 8 6 4
8 3 1 3
27 2 5 29
18 **9** **16**
7 2 6
2 6 3 1 8
1 8 6 4 7
1 6 5
5 26 4 15 20 3 30 4

OCTO PUZZLE

Solve the puzzle.

8 26 3 11 20 8 31 3
7 4 7
3 5 4 7 6 2 8 1
1 5
2 6
10 16 25
26 4 1 3 7 25
2 3 6 4
8 3 2 6 5
7 5 5 3
11 6 2 2 20
28 22 21
17 3 5 4 23
8 2 5
4 5 2 7 6 8 3
2 6 3 6 2
31 1 4 4 26
12 16 20
7 5
8 2 6 1
1 8 2 5 7 6
4 3 8 4
5 25 7 17 23 6 26

OCTO PUZZLE

Solve the puzzle.

25 5 3 26 20 3 2 29 3 5 4

6 3 2 4 8 1

1 8 23 7 17 7 19

25 6 7 3 8 4 6 1 27

2 1 6 7 4 8 3

7 3 1 7

26 4 25 17 5 10 4 20

19 8 2 4 8 3 4 2 7 20 5

2 8 7 5 6

29 7 7 3 4 25

5 19 5 13 15

3 1 7 3 4

8 4 3 2 7 6

5 1 5 5 7

2 27 6 19 20 4 25 8

OCTO PUZZLE

Solve the puzzle.

7 33 1 22 16 8 30 2
8 3 1
6 7 1 4 8
8 5 6 4 5
2 3
19 **21** **19**
23 6 29
3 8 5
6 5 7 8 4 1 2 3
7 1 4 3 5 1
22 8 7 6 16
21 **10** **23**
13 1 2 5 3 19
2 8 8 7
4 6 3 1 8
4 1 7 2
30 5 7 4 33
17 **16** **21**
1 7 6
2 1 7 5 6 4 3
8 5 2 2
6 29 8 13 19 2 23 8

OCTO PUZZLE

Solve the puzzle.

5 30 5 16 15 3 30 3
2 6 3 1 7 4
3 4 7 5 2
7 5
7 6
22 19 13
28 1 5 7 31
4 4 4 6
3 6 2 1 7 4
5 7 3 8
16 2 7 6 2 15
16 16 25
17 6 2 4 8 14
4 5 8 8
8 3 6 5 4
5 5 3 3 7
30 3 1 30
20 17 18
1 3
3 5 1 4 7 6 8 2
7 4 1
8 31 8 17 14 8 28 4

OCTO PUZZLE

Solve the puzzle.

25 1 17 22 3 30 4
8 5 2 1
1 7 6 2 4 5
2 6 2
6 7 7
19 23 19
23 8 1 28
6 5 3 4 2
8 1 4 6 5 3
3 7 3 1 4
17 4 8 6 22
23 10 15
11 6 2 2 23
1 7 5 4
7 4 1 3 8 6 5
5 7
30 2 6 25
23 18 22
3
8 6 8 8
2 5 7 4 1
4 6 2 6
1 28 4 11 23 4 23 5

OCTO PUZZLE

Solve the puzzle.

1 27 5 18 17 4 29 1
3 5 3
8 6 7 2
6 7 2 3 2 7
8
22 **17** **23**
29 8 3 33
7 5 3
6 3 5 7 1
1 6 7
18 5 2 2 4 17
12 **10** **23**
17 6 8 3 12
6 3 2 1 3 8 5
8 4 5 6
1 7 4 4
29 7 8 6 27
19 **24** **16**
2
2 7 5 8 4
8 2 6 1
1 4 7 5 3
33 17 12 29
6 1 3 6

OCTO PUZZLE

Solve the puzzle.

31 3 15 18 2 30 5
1 5 1 3
8 6 2 4 1
6 4 1 7
7 4 6
19 **18** **18**
23 4 5 27
8 7 4 6 7
7 8 3 5
3 5 8
15 3 4 2 18
11 **19** **18**
21 8 1 6 18
2 1 5 7
4 1 7 2 3 5
3 4
30 8 6 7 31
21 **17** **13**
7
5 8 7
2 4 8 1 5
4 4 2 3
6 27 1 21 18 5 23 8

OCTO PUZZLE

Solve the puzzle.

23 7 19 18 2 27
5 8
1 2 5 8 7 4
5 6 2
8 8 1 5
19 **13** **15**
27 8 6 26
6 1 1
8 7 2 3 5
3 8 6 3
19 4 18
17 **22** **19**
17 5 2 22
4 8
6 8 7 3 2 5 1
2 5 1 5 7
27 6 2 23
16 **18** **21**
6 3 4 4
6 5 3
8 7 3 2
7 5 8 2
3 26 1 17 22 27 8

OCTO PUZZLE

Solve the puzzle.

OCTO PUZZLE

Solve the puzzle.

4 30 5 12 13 2 30 6
3 4 8
6 1 3 5 7 4
5
7 7
20 23 14
29 6 27
2 8 6
7 4 3 6 8
2 4 1 5
12 3 3 4 13
22 13 16
19 1 2 6 8 18
6 8 8 7
4 3 1 8 5 6
5 1
30 5 1 30
14 15 14
5
5 1 4 8
7 8 5 2 1
1 7
6 27 1 19 18 5 29 3

OCTO PUZZLE

Solve the puzzle.

28 8 15 14 8 28 5
3 2
5 6 2 8 3
6 3 4 4 7
4 1 2
23 **25** **19**
29 7 2 4 29
8 2
4 2 7 3
1 3 3 1
15 2 6 6 7 14
20 **13** **23**
20 5 3 5 1 17
8 6 1
1 5 4 8
2 1 6 4
28 7 3 6 28
17 **10** **18**
3 7
5 7 2 4
4 8
6 29 1 20 17 7 29 8

OCTO PUZZLE

Solve the puzzle.

OCTO PUZZLE

Solve the puzzle.

5 26 1 16 16 7 27 4
4 6 5
8 6 4 3
1 8 7
18 19 15
24 3 4 8 1 32
5 8
5 8 1 4 2
2 4 1
16 6 5 7 16
9 21 20
20 4 1 23
3 6 7 1
7 1 5 3 4
3 8 3
27 1 7 6 8 26
20 10 20
5 5
3 1 2
5 7 3 8
4 5
8 32 3 20 23 4 24

OCTO PUZZLE

Solve the puzzle.

5 27 17 20 22
8 1 1
2 8 7 3
7 5 7 4
4 1 6
27 **20** **20**
21 7 5 7 33
8 3
5 3 6 1 8 2
2 5 8
17 8 20
9 **18** **23**
22 2 7 19
8
4 2 3 1
7 3 6 8 2
22 27
5 8 5
15 **21** **15**
8 6 6 1
1 4 5
7 3 2 1 8 6
4 3 4
33 22 19 21
6 1

ANSWER KEY

Page 1

downsize, countdown, downhill, sundown, downpour, touchdown, downtown, downstairs (Order may vary.)

Page 2

Q S A N J O S E W Z T S O K
P H I L A D E L P H I A D V
S Z N Q C D F C Q O K N K S
A F D T K N E K V U R D J A
N P I W S S V T G S K I Q N
F J A Q O P B C R T X E L A
R Q N K N T H G H O Q G J N
A Y A M V N V O D N I O P T
N C P R I N E X E A J T N O
C U O S L M Q W W N L P J N
I N L L L B W K Y J I L C I
S Q I H E Z B C F O R X A O
C W S C H I C A G O R J M S
O L O S A N G E L E S K W O

Page 3

Page 4

Where can a burger get a good night's sleep?

In a bed of lettuce!

Page 5

Page 6

fireworks, fireplace, fireside, campfire, firefly, firefighter, fireproof, firewood, backfire (Order may vary.)

Page 7

Across
1. mosquito
3. cockroach
5. vampire
6. flea
9. gypsy moth

Down
2. scorpion
4. housefly
7. termite
8. rat

Page 8

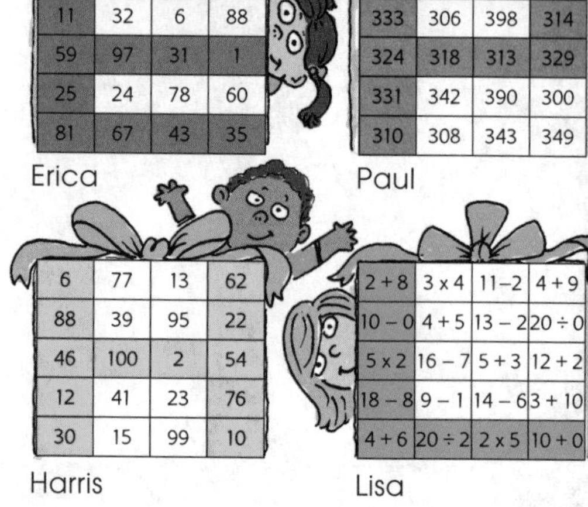

91	3	17	47
11	32	6	88
59	97	31	1
25	24	78	60
81	67	43	35

Erica

319	312	340	328
333	306	398	314
324	318	313	329
331	342	390	300
310	308	343	349

Paul

6	77	13	62
88	39	95	22
46	100	2	54
12	41	23	76
30	15	99	10

Harris

2 + 8	3 x 4	11 – 2	4 + 9
10 – 0	4 + 5	13 – 2	20 ÷ 0
5 x 2	16 – 7	5 + 3	12 + 2
18 – 8	9 – 1	14 – 6	3 + 10
4 + 6	20 ÷ 2	2 x 5	10 + 0

Lisa

Page 9

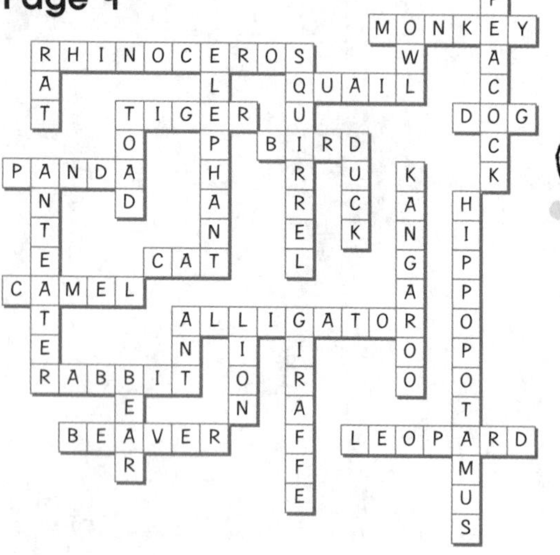

Page 10

false
true
false
false
false
true
true

Page 11

Page 12

Ⓛ

Page 13

What is the only coat that goes on wet? A coat of paint!

Page 14

(Variations to this path are possible.)

Page 15

4
3
6
2
1
5
She had mittens!
mice cream

Page 16

Across	Down
3. Christmas	**1.** Thanksgiving
5. Memorial	**2.** Labor
6. Valentine's	**3.** New Year

Page 17

P R S T R A W B E R R Y P O
N E A P O L I T A N R O V N
P C P W C H E R R Y H D S Q
I J K P F G X Z J P S A U B
S J C C E N A V W M H J B U
T T O Q N R L A K O Q C D T
A N F H J L M N L O C H P T
C Q F L N B X I O S J O J E
H W E K D V J L N E K C Z R
I G E L T O K L H T B O Q P
O F X V Y Q K A G R V L P E
N Q J K Z W H G Q A K A G C
H C O C O N U T G C J T W A
Z D F T B P K J P K H E L N
B L U E M O O N W S Q K G M

Page 18

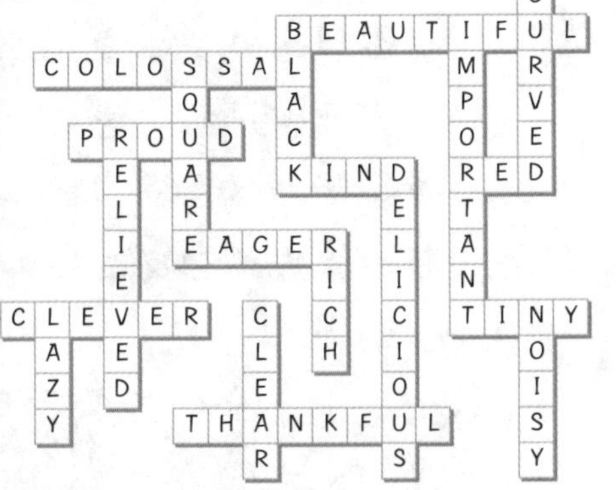

Page 19

C, B, D
(Order may vary.)

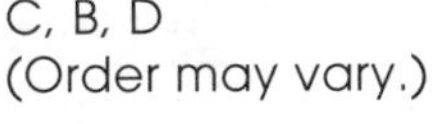

Page 20

1. 7	**5.** 6	**1.** 6	**5.** 7
2. 4	**6.** 10	**2.** 9	**6.** 4
3. 2	**7.** 9	**3.** 5	**7.** 2
4. 3	**8.** 5	**4.** 8	**8.** 1

The 1 pin is left standing.

The 3 pin is left standing.

Page 21

Add "light." Add "out."
Add "man." Add "land."
Add "cat." Add "book."
Add "down." Add "house."

Page 22

How did the founding fathers decide on our country's flag?

They took a flag poll.

Page 23

chip sip
clip skip
drip slip
flip snip
hip strip
jip tip
lip trip
nip wip
rip zip
ship

(Answers may vary.)

Page 24

Brian	Logan	Ellsworth	William
Brenda	**Karina**	**Lindsey**	**Morgan**
9	10	11	8
Margie	**Susan**	**Joe**	**Hannah**

Page 25

4'5"	4'7"	4'2"
Rachel	**Nick**	**Sam**

Chocolate Cake

Page 26

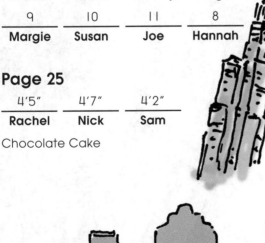

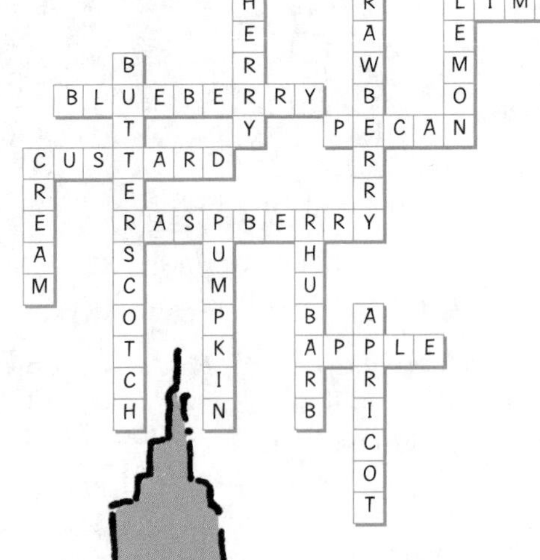

Page 27

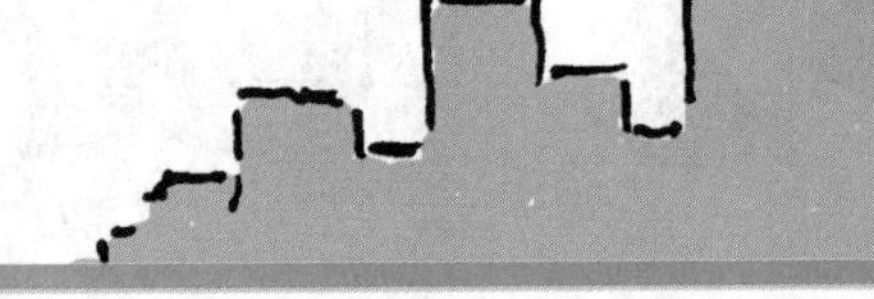

ANSWER KEY

Page 28

<
>
=
<
<
=
>
<
>
<
<

Page 29

true
false
true
true
false
true
true

Page 30

6:10 6:25 6:45 7:10
9:00 10:10 11:20 12:30
12:50 2:15 3:40 5:05

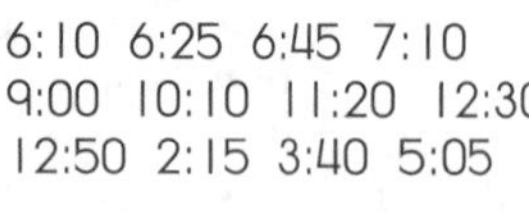

Page 31

Page 32

Across
4. Lake Michigan
6. fifty
7. Wyoming
8. California
10. Rhode Island
11. Lake Superior

Down
1. Pacific
2. Alaska
3. Mississippi
5. New York
9. Atlantic

Page 33

seed
drain
pair
day
spot
pool
patch
lake

Page 34

(Items circled may vary.)

Page 35

Across
2. Go
3. Trivial Pursuit®
4. Candy Land®
5. Chess
7. Clue®
8. Chutes and Ladders®

Down
1. Monopoly®
4. Checkers
6. Scrabble®

Page 36

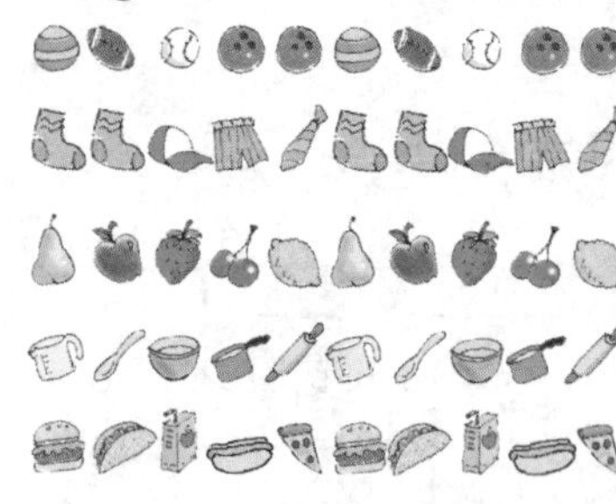

Page 41

Page 37

88 keys
11, 0, 8,
1, 24,
9, 4.5,
20, 8.5,
2
true

Page 38

(Items circled may vary.)

Page 39

a cub tub
a June tune
a damp lamp
a funny bunny
a sick chick
a loud crowd
a lucky ducky

Page 40

C
46
36
151

Page 42

What did one flag say to the other flag?

Nothing, it just waved!

Page 43

Across
2. annual
5. young
6. glad
9. tight
10. elder
12. plain
13. easy
14. female

Down
1. dry
2. angry
3. naughty
4. rushed
7. strange
8. bent
11. every

Page 44

ANSWER KEY

Page 71

Why did the gardener bury her money?
Because she wanted the soil to be rich.

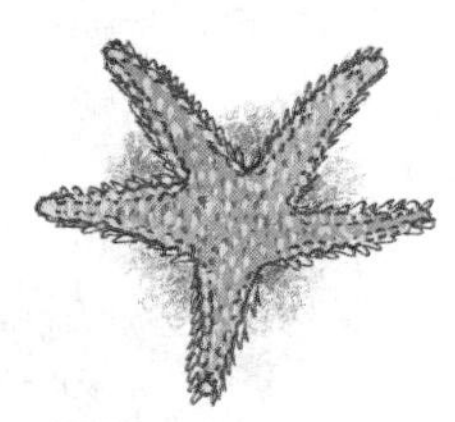

Page 72

1.			s	t	a	r	f	i	s	h
2.		s	e	a	w	e	e	d		
3.	w	h	a	l	e					

4.	s	h	a	r	k		
5.	d	o	l	p	h	i	n
6.	c	r	a	b			
7.		s	q	u	i	d	
8.	s	e	a	l			

sea horse

Page 73

1. end
2. chick
3. light
4. last
5. shine
6. weed
7. a
8. u

Tickle it, and see which end laughs!

Page 74-75

Results will vary.

Page 76-77

Results will vary.

Page 78-83

Stories will vary.

Page 84

Code 1:
Are we there yet?

Code 2:
I can't wait to swim in the ocean!

Page 85

Results will vary.

Page 86

Q	L	D	W	S	E	B	I	S	O	N
S	B	O	D	O	L	P	H	I	N	H
F	U	G	H	A	E	F	F	D	H	O
W	W	T	I	F	P	G	O	W	J	R
A	H	G	F	R	H	L	C	X	H	S
L	Q	A	D	B	A	T	L	S	F	E
R	B	N	L	H	N	F	L	A	F	M
U	L	V	W	E	T	Y	F	D	M	A
S	R	C	D	M	O	O	S	E	H	A

Page 88

G	X	B	O	C	C	I	E	R	K	V	L
F	Y	E	C	R	O	Q	U	E	T	O	M
B	K	M	W	F	O	O	T	B	A	L	L
A	S	G	N	D	P	A	X	C	B	L	D
S	M	O	X	A	G	H	O	C	K	E	Y
E	W	L	C	R	S	R	B	Z	Q	Y	T
B	F	F	D	C	O	T	L	X	S	B	A
A	H	T	S	H	E	U	I	L	X	A	B
L	D	N	V	E	V	R	U	C	M	L	O
L	K	S	K	R	G	P	O	B	S	L	C
E	N	J	H	Y	T	E	N	N	I	S	Q

Bowling because you can hear a pin drop.

Page 87

C	R	W	U	J	G	F	S	D	X	Q
E	A	S	P	A	R	A	G	U	S	S
L	D	U	D	O	D	F	H	V	E	H
E	C	D	L	E	T	T	U	C	E	S
R	A	S	P	I	N	A	C	H	H	Y
Y	R	J	E	G	F	G	T	S	K	N
S	R	K	A	J	W	L	A	O	D	Q
G	O	B	E	A	N	V	O	K	S	H
H	T	E	K	F	T	M	Z	W	W	K
Q	B	R	O	C	C	O	L	I	E	T
Y	A	M	Q	B	W	D	R	K	M	R

		a	s	p	a	r	a	g	u	s
				l	e	t	t	u	c	e
	p	e	a							
s	p	i	n	a	c	h				
			t							
	y	a	m							
		g								
	c	a	r	r	o	t				
	b	r	o	c	c	o	l	i		
		d								
	c	e	l	e	r	y				
b	e	a	n							

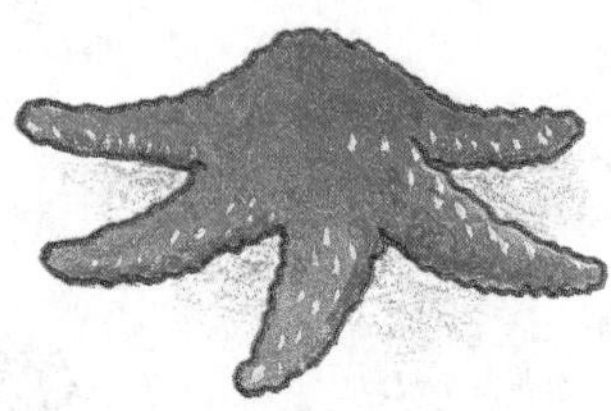

ANSWER KEY

Page 89

Page 90

S P A R R O W
A P L X H K N
G O R N G B M W
H D B G W B L U E J A Y E
O A U G N A C O K E X T A U
N C W S M A B Y V Z H O S T R I C H
O W L A M K X S M P D P O G D E S W D A T
W P S Q U A I L E M O P A N I O N
L K Z O E G N N Z L E G F U P A
J D G T E O G F D C U G E T O
O I O P U B F K L Q A H H F
H R Q N N I E I E L D P V E A M
C R M S S N N Q N R O B I N R C T O
E A W A Z S R B O C S D Y V K O U L C X L
P A R R O T E T O X H W U Z B A N E X D H K E J F O
B E N D R O A D R U N N E R A K I N G F I S H E R L
S L V I D P D W S T
F C I F N T N S P
D U C K A V L T
U P A X L E
B Z N O
A C

Page 91

1. warmer
2. hollow
3. food
4. rocket
5. air sacs
6. tail feathers

Page 92

Across
4. curved
6. parallelogram
8. edge
9. sphere
11. trapezoid
12. line
13. angle

Down
1. symmetry
2. perimeter
3. hexagon
5. congruent
7. area
9. solid
10. face

Page 93

Across
5. umbrella
6. postcard
9. holiday
10. pool
11. car
12. airplane
14. tourist
15. suitcase

Down
1. souvenir
2. boat
3. kennel
4. map
7. camping
8. vacation
13. hotel
14. train

Page 94

Across
3. avalanche
5. tornado
7. earthquake
8. hurricane

Down
1. cyclones
2. blizzard
4. flood
5. tsunami
6. typhoons

Page 95

Across
3. horse
4. cow
5. pigs
7. goat
9. rabbit

Down
1. sheep
2. chicken
6. goose
8. turkey

Page 96

Across
4. light
5. file
7. pound
8. ball

Down
1. rattle
2. plant
3. kind
6. hand
7. play

Page 97

Across
1. pickup
2. tank
4. van
5. dump
7. concrete

Down
1. platform
3. garbage
6. panel

Page 98-99

Across
2. Jack and Jill
4. cow
5. Peter
7. London
9. mouse
10. Humpty Dumpty

Down
1. spider
2. Jack
3. Little Bo Peep
6. three
8. old woman
9. Mary

Page 100

Across
2. spinnerets
6. poison
8. insect
9. bones

Down
1. silk
3. eight
4. two
5. food
7. webs

Page 101

Across
1. bee
4. horsefly
6. termite
7. mayfly
8. ant
9. dragonfly

Down
1. butterfly
2. mosquito
3. firefly
5. ladybug

Page 102

Across
1. roots
3. wood
5. evergreen
7. food
8. botanists
9. soil and water

Down
2. seed
4. deciduous
6. grow

Page 103

Across
2. lungs
5. temperature
7. dinosaur
8. land

Down
1. plates
3. backbone
4. reptiles
6. shell

Page 104

Across
4. whisper
5. scream
7. joke
8. chat

Down
1. discuss
2. speak
3. brag
6. report

ANSWER KEY

Page 105

Across
3. kelp forests
6. sea horse
8. roots
9. coral reefs

Down
1. waves
2. stonefish
4. tidal pools
5. polyps
7. tides

Page 106

Across
2. rain forests
4. salt water
8. ocean
10. wetlands

Down
1. grasslands
3. desert
5. tundra
6. forest
7. ponds
9. swamps

Page 107

Across
1. grow
2. mammals
4. capybaras
5. diseases
6. rodents
8. herbivores

Down
1. gnaw
2. mice
3. scientists
7. fur

Page 108-109

Across
1. giraffe
5. bat
6. elk
7. horse
9. cat
10. zebra
11. wolf
13. hippo

Down
1. goat
2. rabbit
3. elephant
4. whale
8. raccoon
9. cheetah
12. fox

Page 110-111

Across
2. elephants
5. acrobats
8. trapeze
9. horses
10. jugglers
11. roustabouts
13. Big Top

Down
1. band
3. parade
4. rings
6. costumes
7. clowns
8. tigers
12. tricks

Page 112

Across
3. table tennis
5. softball
6. bowling
9. football

Down
1. volleyball
2. basketball
3. tennis
4. squash
6. baseball
7. golf
8. soccer

Page 113

Across
3. fat
5. polar bear
7. skin
9. rubbery
10. front

Down
1. walrus
2. fur
4. hoofs
6. hibernate
8. zero

Page 114

Across
2. salt
3. steer
5. mammals
7. blowhole
8. seals

Down
1. water
3. surface
4. walrus
6. blue

Page 115

Across
4. oil
5. hummingbirds
8. toes

Down
1. frogs
2. down
3. straight
6. molt
7. cones

Page 116-117

Across
3. Gutenberg
5. Lister
6. Edison
7. Kellogg

Down
1. Wright
2. Benz and Daimler
3. Graham Bell
4. Franklin

Page 118-119

Across
4. February
6. July
7. November
8. December

Down
1. May
2. September
3. January
5. October

Page 120

Across
1. players
7. racket
9. love
10. doubles
11. sets
12. net

Down
1. point
2. ace
3. singles
4. duece
5. service
6. ball
8. court

Page 121

Across
- b. quotient
- d. fraction
- g. denominator
- h. divisor
- i. product
- j. sets
- k. factors

Down
- a. sum
- c. numerator
- e. remainder
- f. difference
- g. dividend

Page 122-123

Across
2. greyhound
6. retriever
7. setter
8. Afghan
10. boxer
11. dalmation

Down
1. husky
2. Great Dane
3. dachshund
4. pointer
5. beagle
9. poodle

Page 124-125

Across
2. subway
4. taxicab
5. motorcycle
7. bicycle
8. truck

Down
1. automobile
2. streetcar
3. bus
6. train

ANSWER KEY

Page 126

Across
1. passengers
3. control tower
6. gates
7. tickets
8. hangars
10. baggage

Down
1. pilot
2. security guards
4. runways
5. terminal
9. fuel

Page 127

Across
5. square
6. rectangle
7. cone
8. cylinder

Down
1. circle
2. sphere
3. triangle
4. cube

Page 128-129

Across
3. honeycomb
6. flowers
8. insects

Down
1. drones
2. worker
3. honeybees
4. hives
5. queen's
7. sting

Page 130

Across
2. pitcher
6. diamond
7. bat
8. five
9. umpire
11. base
13. outfield
14. glove

Down
1. strike
3. home
4. run
5. catcher
8. fly ball
10. inning
12. Series
13. outs

Page 131

Across
2. carnivore
4. water cycle
6. habitat
7. ecology
8. herbivore
9. omnivores
10. botany

Down
1. parasite
3. meteorology
5. oxygen

Page 132

Across
1. eyes
2. muscles
4. heart
5. lungs
7. brain

Down
1. ears
3. skeleton
6. skin
7. blood

Page 136

Across
2. pronouns
5. nouns
6. interjections
7. adverbs

Down
1. conjunctions
2. prepositions
3. adjectives
4. verbs

Page 134-135

Across
2. printing press
3. television
4. satellite
5. computer
6. map
7. wheel
8. camera
9. airplane

Down
1. microscope
2. plow
3. telephone
5. clock

Page 133

Across
2. sunspots
5. galaxy
6. light & heat
8. life
9. Milky Way

Down
1. core
2. solar flares
3. star
4. gas
7. energy

Page 137

Across
1. cinematographer
2. screenwriter
3. producer
5. documentaries
8. art director
9. Oscar

Down
1. costume designer
4. director
6. animation
7. actors

Page 138-139

Across
1. Wilson
2. G.W. Bush
5. Lincoln
8. Carter
9. Reagan
10. Nixon
13. Jefferson
14. Ford

Down
1. Washington
3. Clinton
4. F.D. Roosevelt
6. Truman
7. T. Roosevelt
11. Obama
12. Kennedy
14. Fillmore

Page 140

Across
1. glaciers
4. high-altitude
5. Wyoming
7. magma
9. Congress

Down
2. Louisiana Purchase
3. petrified
6. geyser
8. rocks

Page 141

Across
1. voting machines
3. candidate
4. districts
6. registration
8. suffrage

Down
1. Voting Rights Act
2. election
3. campaign
5. women
7. ballot

ANSWER KEY

Page 142-143

Across
- **2.** Mars
- **3.** Moon
- **4.** Uranus
- **6.** Saturn
- **8.** Jupiter
- **9.** Pluto
- **10.** Earth

Down
- **1.** Venus
- **2.** Mercury
- **5.** Sun
- **7.** Neptune

Page 144

Across
- **1.** stadium
- **3.** school
- **4.** castle
- **7.** hospital

Down
- **1.** skyscraper
- **2.** museum
- **5.** hotel
- **6.** house

Page 145

Across
- **1.** Amazon
- **3.** petroleum
- **4.** Brazil
- **5.** Andes
- **7.** Colombia
- **8.** rainforests

Down
- **1.** Angel Falls
- **2.** Pampa
- **6.** Ecuador

Page 146-147

Across
- **3.** minerals
- **4.** diamond
- **6.** microscope
- **8.** sedimentary

Down
- **1.** igneous
- **2.** hardness
- **3.** metamorphic
- **5.** fossils
- **7.** magma

Page 148

Children should circle a sphere (balloon), cylinder (present), cone (party hat), cube (present), rectangular prism (present), and a pyramid (present).

Figure	Number of Faces	Number of Edges	Number of Corners
cube	6	12	8
cylinder	2	0	0
cone	1	0	0
sphere	0	0	0
rectangular prism	6	12	8
square pyramid	5	8	5

Page 149

1. 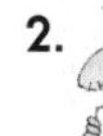

2. 

3. 

4. 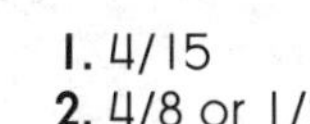

5.

6.

Page 150

- **1.** 4/15
- **2.** 4/8 or 1/2
- **3.** 3/8
- **4.** 7/11
- **5.** 2/4 or 1/2
- **6.** 4/5
- **7.** 2/5
- **8.** 5/7

Page 151

1=A 2=B 3=C 4=D 5=E 6=F 7=G 8=H 9=I 10=J
11=K 12=L 13=M 14=N 15=O 16=P 17=Q 18=R 19=S 20=T
21=U 22=V 23=W 24=X 25=Y 26=Z

equation	2 x 2 =	5 x 3 =	9 - 2 =				
number	4	15	7				
letter	D	O	G				animal
equation	4 - 1 =	8 + 7 =	4 x 4 =	20 - 4 =	5)25 =	6 x 3 =	
number	3	15	16	16	5	18	
letter	C	O	P	P	E	R	mineral
equation	12 + 7 =	2 x 7 =	1 - 0 =	5 + 6 =	10 ÷ 2 =		
number	19	14	1	11	5		
letter	S	N	A	K	E		animal
equation	5 + 10 =	7 x 2 =	18 ÷ 2 =	8 + 7 =	15 - 1 =		
number	15	14	9	15	14		
letter	O	N	I	O	N		vegetable
equation	9 - 6 =	3 + 2 =	4 x 3 =	25 ÷ 5 =	24 - 6 =	5 x 5 =	
number	3	5	12	5	18	25	
letter	C	E	L	E	R	Y	vegetable
equation	6 x 3 =	7 x 3 =	10)20 =	32 - 7 =			
number	18	21	2	25			
letter	R	U	B	Y			mineral

Page 152

Forest: Zombie, Troll, Wolfman, Griffin
Beach: Big Foot, Dragon, Cyclops, Satyr

The Cyclops ate the most pizza.

Page 153

- **1.** +
- **2.** ÷
- **3.** -; 0
- **4.** x
- **5.** + or x
- **6.** ÷; 4
- **7.** +; 11

ANSWER KEY

Page 154

1	3	14	6	90	4	102
66	17	11	29	58	88	30
64	32	12	67	54	20	18
100	78	53	91	40	36	24
8	34	9	16	82	98	48
22	46	71	56	14	50	6
68	80	77	87	109	97	98
72	100	2	44	62	11	106
86	38	26	60	28	35	82
42	84	94	52	50	91	111

Page 155

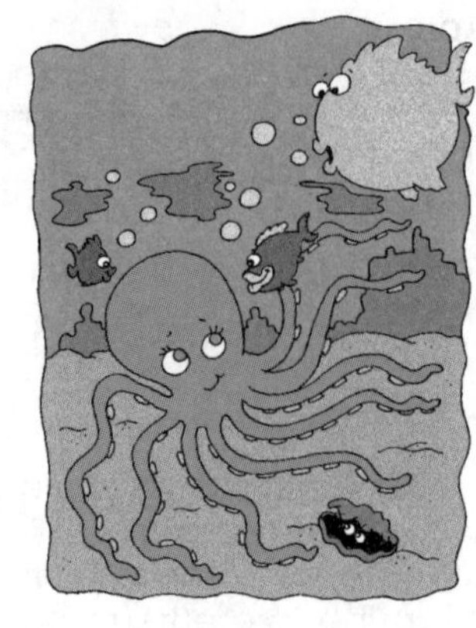

Page 156

1. 4
2. 4/12 or 1/3
3. 9
4. 18
5. 2
6. 3,9
7. 4/20 or 1/5
8. 1/5
9. 20%

Page 157

♩; 2,2,4,1,1,1,1

♪; 2, 1, 1, 2, 2, 1, 1,1,1/2,1/2

o; 1/2, 2, 1/2, 1, 4, 4

𝅗𝅥; 2, 2, 1, 1, 1, 1, 2, 2

Page 158

1. x
2. -
3. ÷
4. +
5. ÷ ÷
6. + -
7. x ÷
8. + ÷
9. x -
10. + =

Page 159

1. early
2. late
3. early
4. 10:37
5. 11:36
6. 12:08
7. 11:56
8. 12:18

Page 160

1. magnet; 4,000 + 500 + 60 + 7
2. laser; 1,999
3. magnet; 2,000+1
4. laser; 100,220
5. magnet; 900,000 + 4,000 + 300 + 10 +4
6. laser; 10,506
7. laser; 712,712
8. magnet; 3,000,000 + 300,000 + 30,000 + 3,000 + 300 + 30 + 3
9. magnet; 10,000 + 3,000 + 20 + 6
10. magnet; 4,000,000 + 800,000 + 70,000 + 5,000 + 600 + 90

Page 161

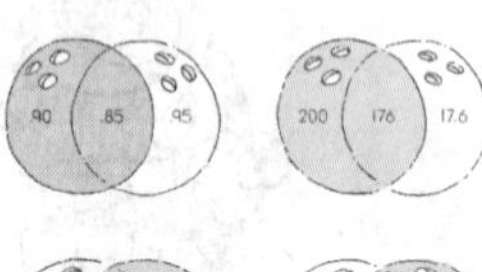

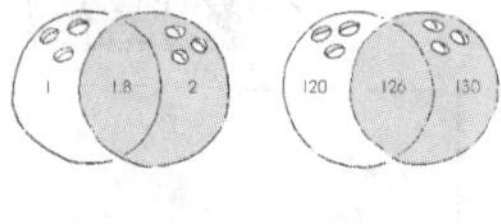

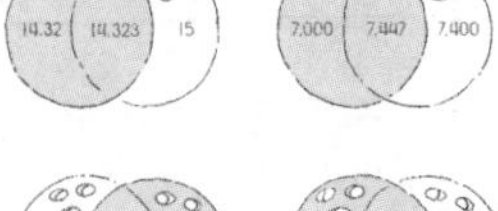

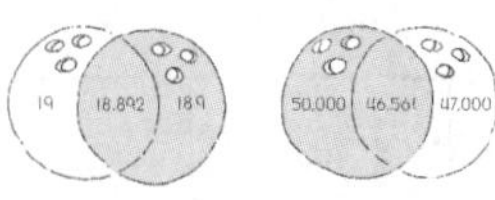

Page 162

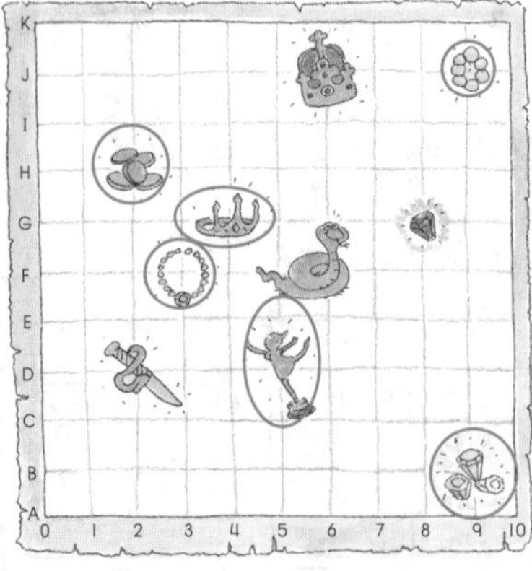

Page 163

These sentences are true:

3. Pitzi likes candy bars less than others do.
7. Penny ate the same number of candy bars as the number of times she lifted barbells.
12. Onion is the least favorite pie.

Page 164

Reading vertically, every column in the first pyramid adds up to 25.

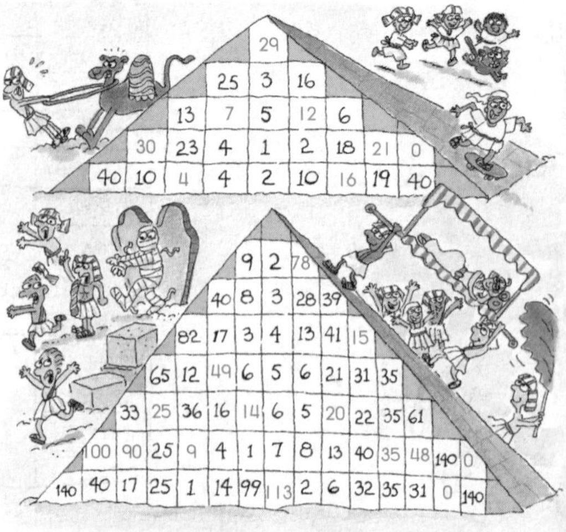

ANSWER KEY

Page 165

Pauline can buy the bookends, basket, comic book, pencils, calculator, or magnets.

She can buy the bookends, calculator, or magnets with exact change.

Page 166

1. 8
2. 2
3. 12

Page 167

1. turn **2.** flip **3.** slide
4. flip **5.** turn **6.** turn
7. slide **8.** flip **9.** slide

Page 168

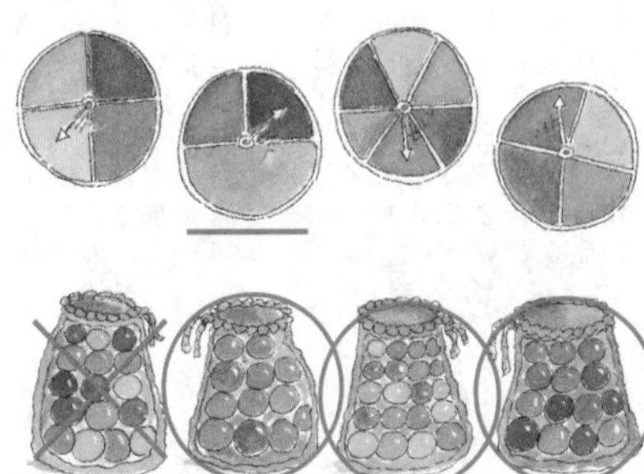

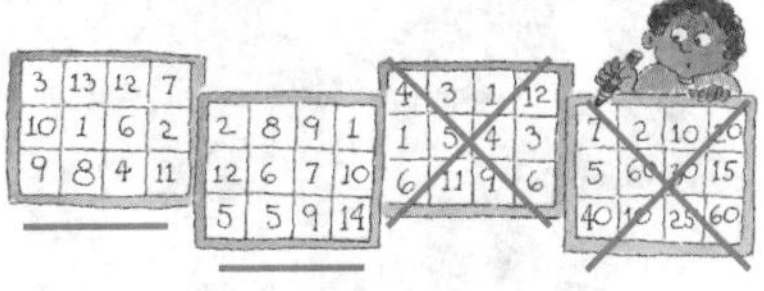

Page 169

1. liter
2. hour
3. yard
4. day
5. pound or pint
6. meter
7. dollars
8. mile

The dog that tells the best time is a watchdog.

Page 170

1. $2.19
2. 55.0 mph
3. 8.25 years
4. $1,000.00
5. 102.7 FM
6. 9.9
7. 8.50" x 11"
8. 67.3°F
9. 2.54
10. 58.8 mph

Page 171

1. 3	0	2. 1		3. 5	4. 7	6	5. 7
8		6. 1	7. 8	1	8		4
0		8. 1	4	7	6		2
9. 5	10. 8	1	2	4			3
	9				11. 7	7	6

Page 172

Estimates will vary.

You could have multiplied 10 dots per row by five to get 50 and then estimated the number of dots missing and subtracted.

You could have multiplied 4 hearts per row by 10 rows to get 40 and subtracted the missing hearts.

Page 173

The first T-shirt in the third row is different.

Page 174

DKAS
CGJBGLNU
XMFWSXICTYS
DLBKIJOFRSDCD
WEGYNSFHLAMVA
PFCLVBATVDFSTT
MGKSQEUBGPLFBUJ
UDMDOLPHINREWC
SYDROCXIHMSXRHD
JWALRUSJTAKTMJO
PJWRBSKMONKEYXRAKI
XFLAKCEBNHTRLIHSPYL
RMSDOGLIVSKUNKMEEO
YANSVFJDMGOATHSCN
HCLN ODJ
PCU REP
YQOY UEB
RTO HR
ASGN YPW

Page 175

A. monkey
B. raccoon
C. dolphin
D. elephant
E. giraffe
F. bat
G. walrus
H. deer

Page 176

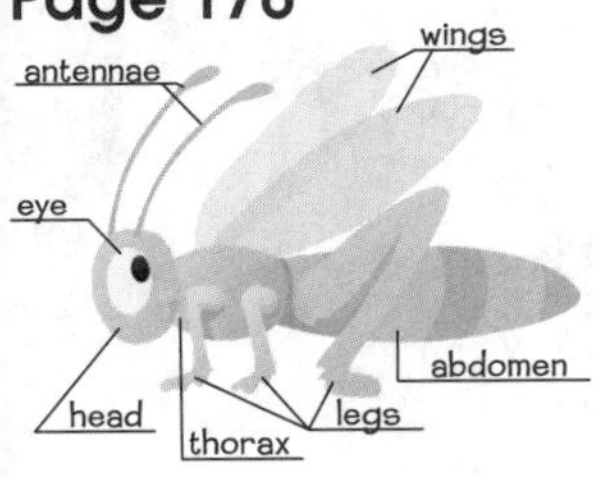

Page 177

BCAM
FTMVIFIY
BCUYLGOUCQCJHY
FDRCJGYDSWASPDBN
LONIVLRTEBQTDIFUFT
PEYMCBHAEHVSUYASTJB
GANTKXKSDTERFIFYTTNM
SBJHFEVFSTYFGHYTHEJKB
TLCKMTYNHXRBILGKORVDE
VHDCOCKROACHUFDUJFNYE
NISRTTGKPWFVHGJGKLFAKT
WGHNHIFWPLYCKMLATYPRHE
PMBDIBUIETJSMMAMDMIBU
NFCEBLSDRAGONFLYNYWKC
IYTERMITEDEFEOUFGTI
PBJTXTHPFVSTHTPLHY
MNSLHODILBIFBHJY
OYDELKATYDIDRR
STFHRIFSK

ANSWER KEY

Page 178

```
      A T B G C W K
I G U A N A V G X U B H I C V
V E V S F H S W C O E U L C S W R T C
D I L T A I K D K D N A S C H L D N O S A H
E M D E K L E S N I E F G I R K I F T A H E S
F A L S A L A M A N D E R F J B O E R Y K J H
G Q K I G I W H G K H G M O G T R S T O G E K
H R T H Z G D E Y H G E K T G Y O T K E G X
A U R J A N G R K W M V K B X I A B T Y
N S A J C T R J C R O C O D I L E J D U S J I
K W K T F G O K D Y P L D S T U H O K W R K H B
B L F A M L R Y A Q F L H E O N L M L E T L F J T
M T O R T O I S E J K Y N L W M E S F M L A M M R
S U Y A B U J K         N M O T W N G E N F D
O O Q O W A               I R H T H K I O H
```

Page 179

1. green tree frog
2. frilled lizard
3. tuatara
4. tailed frog
5. eft
6. rattlesnake

Page 180

```
H A
V E
B K R M P
L I M O E
U N W J N
E G S H G
L J F T Q U
H A I S C I
W P Y S C V N
N U T H A T C
V W O S E A G U
P H O L D R J W K
C D G O M D T B X K
D R O A D R U N N E R
W O O B F P F C O I B
K C P N B H P E I K L K
S J F A M I Y V C K G
J R T A N R N P I K C R E K D I
Q S G         D J O S T R I C H D W T E H D U O S
W U D L S D Q C Y S P A R R O W N A T I C R F V B L N T
A H U M M I N G B I R D I S M Z N L N Y R B U H U O
C V I H S N D T P G O L D F I N C H A J A Q O W L I
W P E L I C A N         C K         F J M E L I J
```

Page 181

Page 182

```
D A T S G T A
U Q L R F K E L P H
W J S H R I M P A J K I
V F H H O N J M B W K D O
A         E S V K A N C S M P E B O
F C       F H H L C K L A T E Q E F L
D A R A B G D S E A H O R S E J O A D T P
O M H A S Q U I D R H R M Q P U K P F J H
B T Y B I V H J K S A I L F I S H U A I
J B A R N A C L E P L A N K T O N J S N
C G K J K S O G M E Q S T A R F I S H V
L O H A       S T L T E Q H O N Q U I
S M D           S E A A N E M O N E
T
```

Page 183

Page 184

Page 185

```
T W
O L R           H M O T
H Y E C A P Y B A R A
E M A R M O S E T N A R
T L L G O U Y U R D N S Y
V A E F O P R L T R G I J
G O J P P A R R O T I U E W
H N K S I H U I H U L T R L
T O U C A N R A C L N L A I K
F S C O R P I O N J L O N S
K R L C X M I C G T F A I B
E L E O P A R D P O K L R
H V B T A M A R I N M M
N J R Y H C U S C U S
G A       G R
```

Page 186

```
T B O H
C C O I C
R T Y R A N N O S A U R U S N D
S Y U E E A J E X T I N C T R J E K
X F A T H P O Y F P F O S S I L G S
F Q R T P X F Y T R I C E R A T O P S
M V L O S A F R W S I A T L O T J X T I
P A L E O N T O L O G Y L P S L R Q N
B R A C H I O S A U R U S E T Y U
D E V U A B R S H J Y I N C T K O
L S T E G O S A U R U S B I       R
G A L L O S A U R U S M
N I U Y O E N R H Y R
H A D R O S A U R W
V S O N
J R
```

Page 187

```
N W A I C
M C D N J H B
S K E H M L E S O
D O C S L X W R P Y N
E L S W A O T R F V I
S I G T P B N Y K G O
R V D T R M I V N R J T
E O N I A C H L H T H U
B I R C G W A T P W K I T V P G I
M P O I J B O J L P L C G O K M O L H P G
D A T E R C E F G U K E N V R Q F L I E N B
W Y P N T L P N R H I M L M J B A N A N A C Y
L M A H G Y I M U R T E M U O R T N R K C D I
I G Y C W O N K F J Y U N B P N H W G U H K N
M U A Y X R E W T G I P R G R A P E F E H O I
E G P K U T A P L R A S P B E R R Y H N L D
E A P P L E P X H O V B T O V P F G M I
Y R G R T R P G R A P E F R U I T I
W C H B L U E B E R R Y W A T O G
E T J E Z W K A J F T V H
R E T S A F R U
```

ANSWER KEY

Page 188

```
TNA VAMT DTN
ARREM NTLQJ BASY
BPWOSCXCITEHKDSTLO
DGOEAVOCADOFEBFPIFMD
KBRVPREHBGVJRKEAKBJH
FOMXCBPJYBLOFASJREGEYK
SXVISACEHAXCNBRNAFEXEM
YTDCRKFULRGHAKIPWGCHZYT
LAIEINTCLHEIGDVOIUATUKP
DKMLTGMUFIJNTGRTNSFRCAJ
SHPEAMKMVUFCDYDANRJCCSM
OINRFBLBTGDLTILTDCHOHZL
XCMYECJEMUPSOHXOBIMRIUH
XARNWRTBWGNFGSNNAN
ORCIGNOBEANKIHIO
PRDHYIJWRMN
WVOHIMPBZH
LSHTRKV
XMO
```

Page 189

```
LTA RMA
ABRSHADIUSA S
CNARAINFORESTC
DDWMOHFNEDOKTCWHD
NSEOEEWSCVGREUAEO
GYTUODTFABRFEFMPUF
CGWLNGDRGCTDNDSYJMGE
DEPFTRALIHCSDEVTHSNL
CIFIACORALREEFWRECBAP
NUOSISJORNBHSRUYIRWMYJ
VDGNWUKSYDXEENTMUKAOP
POLARICESMPLRBIAPBELMI
TFMMXAGHLDWHTLCMWLCYMP
GBASNCSTNSFTYNOSWAMPCN
LNMARSHLANDORFBNITDI
HLCULIPLRPDNNDPRA
GATA W
TUNDRAR
AGSDOU
IHRT
NCSA
KATW
HWS
```

Page 191

```
TE GHS APLE DTS
AEMDVQMRPIDXSCRWREYFDJBPCMVPG
HPJSFDNVYBOWIERDOSQDSEONHCWSC
JFPDSUBLETTEKICOLTERRMOTLLND
ECLRECLARKXAYONCPGCEINRYOEE
TBFEIKAWIVGJKHNFKLNLSEBSUBW
MDWTSTFRFEBSGWEGSEYHOYQTGOG
TRUKETHSNEHMDRCPWTENWHAHI
ONSTSEKIORLEIFWPIRTJIYLLW
VPKHKMDMJNEYLTMBSIXONHRIT
PYSNBRIDGERWEHLRWHITMAN
```

Page 192

```
AU TAHE
GOYWHVJ IRZUAPE
CCKICKAPOOCUWAIPTAIROQUOISYC
CPWPROEUTKIUFSHUKWPNVCJVDODA
HAXTCHEYENNEWHVUPAWUHAOALE
XKWDHRBSIUAIPPAOXUIFIUFVJN
GIQTEZLBEWVUCWGWHKWOPTYGOA
UHUROONOYAMEHRPNWCFPCOLH
TCROWINQZJOAINONEZPERCEI
LIVKPRTXEOTPSJELEECWYNO
OKEHNIPKWYANIXOBHKAEWN
SEMINOLEDCOLOCBUALCL
ZOCIMWOPHPKWUTEOPU
IUOAHIEYANNXEXI
OKFXRJCKIPO
```

Page 195

```
S
AB
LR
NBID
OA TUETV GM
UWQFNRICQKA
SNUTATSIHYT
WTNSVAHRTAH
ML AOWUWCSND
XUBEHSA VIJTAONCH EO
NEWFOUNDLANDANDL AVNQATIO
VNOVASCOTIADUOHNFLABRADORMR
PRINCEEDWARDISLANDLABSYW
UWSKRTCHEOABRITISHCOLRQSAS
ZUASASKATCHEWANWUANOEHRB UMBIA
ETIAFBSITQARTEPISTTBDP
NKDUMANITOBASACAQEH
NEWBRUNSWICKNQRUC
ATCYKFOSJBYSTI
NORTHWESTLEKIO
DF A AG
Y
U
K
O
N
```

Page 197

```
BCYH
LEWUNIPNLMD
DAMUNDSENROACYLWAEC
RWQKDCARTIERODARRL
OTDUSYWRNSKVLREQTK
CNSFOLIEMTFTULTULI
OHGGIHSGDSOGHLKEGW
LSIYRTINPMTYMEBTSF
URULGIWBNASRTNRTII
MEAJLIVINGSTONEEV
BAKCHAMPLAINRNHKD
UBGLLIRQORTGBBGO
SVMEAGFYUYHRTLN
CORTALCB FND
TWDHF L DOU
HUDSONIMUHLEAHCPUAIPLHK
HYERIKSONCQWTNNACFQOUD
NFKAHIARDUIUMPHBRFLH
KTDSKMHKNISDSXRSOTOA
PONCEDELEONTUMFKTI
```

Page 199

```
ECUADORVA
FRODBGCSP
APYLMOUUAC
LRZDOLGYRL
KTGREMULAKY
VRLUHECTBZGNI
ZBGNEAFBGNHYIURAK
ISYRHUNJRZVTHNAEHL
DCTIUNOYDEAVBNIFYCIU
ECHNFLRCDIUZLEHZNDLJ
BOLIVIAVIKSRIUVNLKAMK
JYALYANCHNLCLIEAGUAY
GWFRENCHGUIANAVNLUMD
HPGSUZVAFNDNMSYMIAN
UHCEODKEZIRLDOEVTUR
PDPURUGUAYPHSZHPYPT
EYCUBIUYZQHANYCBTAZE
```

Page 200

```
CB
AEC
SD UT RCR
EE CE YI BN LY ISP
HP NA AK FH IP BFH
QGJ DU SG L F IW BNL OIL
UHTIMBERBA ER JA SGLACIERUW
OUAMINERALS MUSHERSRYA
YWM UTKOUJL
HMOUNTAINSTNKM
KAYAKYGYAGNENTVORPD
JEMINANCHORAGEMHA
VSKHLGRYTFRJ
ETDSTWRN
VABIHPMJ
DEHLRQOUUB
GORSUISNR
VOLCANOES
LIFHKUBAT
CMUIEITUK
VAVKRTIS
NOAG
```

ANSWER KEY

Page 201

N C E U A
Y H T S Y P W H J V B
C G I R U Y L P C N W S C N M K T
N K J Y O E L A G R A N D C A N Y O N S C
S C T M R W A L R D C E R A E N Y K E O H G U
F Y O S E M I T E B L H F K D S D L A F N E
I W N G I A L S V F G S O G L D W A E D R T W E G L
H X G O S D Y N I A L H B V W H E B O L Y M P I C Y M O H
L N L O I E V E R G L A D E S A E T O B I H
S C A N Y O N L A N D S A G T I K Y D E
H A N C E S A C U K C H O R H O N L K X
E G I V H F G L A U S N V Y N L
E N E A M V E A C A V R E
R Y N L E A G W L H J N
V M A R N U S L O K
A P C N V A T E Y G
D Y U S D R O Y S
E C V R O E O D
S N H G X A N R
T O A C H D H O
B A D L A N D S
G Y V O I S S V
V L R W A N B A
E N O M I

Page 203

A R A
B V P D T N
C T G R P T Y U C
T H D U N A S M P D
R C P W S A K L I R I X
R A E F H D D L A T B K E
I A S D T M R E A P C H S E H
A U R C H I O D A Y L Q H L L S O
B W N P A Y O R U A I I U W I W S P I
H R O E I D N Y E O T L N D P S A X K E M
S R I U R K E R I T N N V O I R E T N E Y A
E T R X Y A D T I E I O D R X E A N L R K U K
D V N C H S K R R W M A R H R L T O I N I
S I E R R A N E V A D A C E U G A C B A N
L O N D I G R E A T S M O K Y N O K H L N
V A I O K D P L H E G P G Y N O I
C H Y A U C D A A
G E R T T

Page 205

A T B E R N G
L I B N O R T H Y T L A
I L A R C T I C E K D R A C F O
C E B R T N A T L A N T I C S I C H
R H M E D I T E R R A N E A N F M P I N
G Y G R R C I G A I I R W A D R I A T I C
C A N I L H B E N E B T R I C Y H C N D B H
E E N I T P A I B E B A L T I C I F I C O
B G G H R N R H R D E T H N E F R T G
K D A O T C I E I E Y A U D I I K N
L W T F B D Y N L A T N I L C I K
R M A N T A R C T I C B A P M T
E B F C N T R I S G N N F A
D H C O C O C H I E O
P I F O P A C F P
A N R K N I A
L B L A C K R
C Y A T L S
I C L F A

Page 207

G Y T A
E V O I N A I B
L L J B H W O J M S
D P A I N T E D O T
G Y S D E S R E J E
B V A T A C A M A T H F
G M B L Y H G Y T W A C
S H J H O I W N A M H K H M
I P A Z I P V J K R I R V Y J B I
J T A R C V A L W A U B L A D P M J
U A H M K W S K T C N L V U I L U K A B
I V L A U S T R A L I A N E N L Y I T I L
M S K M R W N I G T V H M S H E C M A H
P N W Y N T V G O H I A E I G Y J N D N
T A R A B I A N I L R T O B E A I O
N A T C P A I L Y I P A B V K S P
J K A R A K U M Y S G A P T
H N T L E
S W H S
T Y

Page 209

L H N S W Z I W O T I
C E Z V A L L E Y Y O
I N N P F U T N K P A
V K S S I R L A M I S S I S S I P P I C O L I
H O E M K O R M U L A M F Y P M Y K C T U N M
A D L N I N N I D T V S N N M I S S O U R I G
O A Y G T R I O G R A N D E N A Z O N I O L R
Y N N U A I U P T A E M P I H W Y E G D N E E
G U V K L V I T W A T U A P Z T G H O N Y C N
H B K N K E T R S R G I H Z T L I V B G H G C
C E C O L R D Z I R E V O Y O Y A N G T Z E S
T Y F B N B C H D T N Y I N A N H T U R I N T

Page 210

Clockwise from top:
tornado, tsunami,
flood, earthquake

Page 211

Clockwise from top:
volcano, blizzard,
rockslide

E A L O N O K Y U U A Q M A
B Y R O H U R R I C A N E T Y A I S U N A I N
C L C Y O N D C S V T Z V A B L I Z Z A R D M T R C
T F E D O I G I L N W R L C D V S M K X F R C Y H Y
S D O A Y O S T M E T E O R O L O G I S T R N P K E
U N R F R A G C W N Y F R C Z I D L H U N F T H F C
G G T I A T D T P G P U Q V K M T G C O I N G O A G
B L O A R S H O Y H N H I C H S Y F I A U H Y O H N
I I R U I U I Q R O N U V Z I F L O O D N X F N I
L Z N B C N C R U R O L O G Z E T I R S T O L E K
K Z A K Q A V A L A N C H E K A K C D O R G O I T
L Y D L N M W N L O K H N A Q L R Y L E M K D L
Q M O U E I U R R W C E M L K U O N T
N U N T S N S T B L I
U O E O K
S N I

ANSWER KEY

Page 214

 North

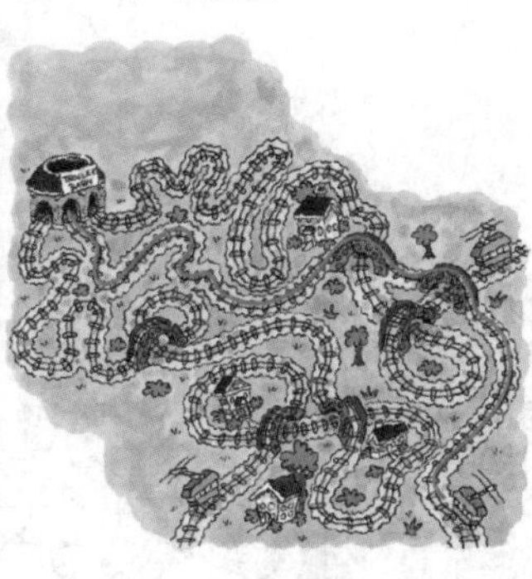

Page 215

MAP ✓ Barrow

inland water

Page 216

MAP ✓ Interstate 40

A	K	S	A	K	B	C	R	O
C	B	S	A	G	U	A	R	O
P	E	O	S	A	T	N	T	K
I	A	N	B	L	T	Y	Y	D
N	R	P	I	C	E	O	L	E
N	C	K	E	S	A	N	L	E
A	Y	H	C	V	I	T	O	R
C	R	P	O	A	M	E	S	A
L	M	Y	N	L	T	R	U	P
E	P	E	L	L	L	R	K	M
Y	C	L	S	E	Y	A	S	L
C	I	K	N	Y	U	C	C	A
H	S	P	B	K	I	E	L	H
B	A	N	T	E	L	O	P	E

Page 217

MAP ✓ The Mississippi River

35 diamonds (including the ace of diamonds)

Page 218

MAP ✓ The Sierra Nevada Mountains

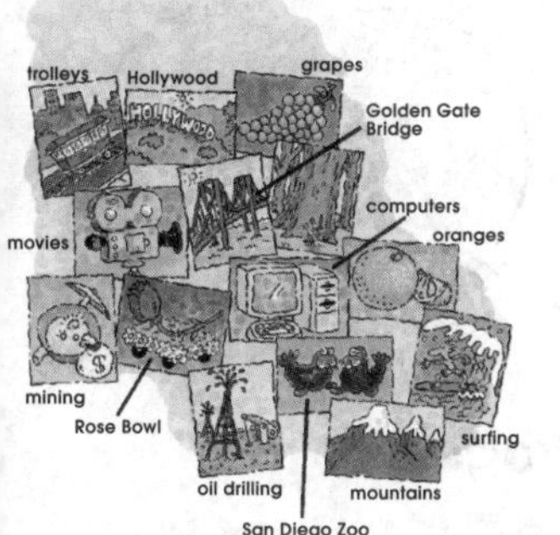

Page 219

MAP ✓ 14,110 ft

Mile High City

Page 220

MAP ✓ Interstates 84 and 91

Page 221

MAP ✓ Delaware Bay

29 chickens

Page 222

MAP ✓ Tallahassee

B	A	J	H	E	K	B	A	D	A
S	W	G	M	Y	R	T	L	E	S
M	I	A	F	D	I	F	W	E	C
A	L	L	I	G	A	T	O	R	S
N	L	G	S	P	E	L	N	R	A
G	O	B	H	E	N	Z	C	H	W
R	W	F	A	L	K	R	C	M	G
O	S	U	N	I	B	A	Y	S	R
V	A	G	Y	C	T	T	P	K	A
E	D	H	W	A	H	N	R	B	S
S	N	P	A	N	T	H	E	R	S
D	Y	K	I	S	B	A	S	N	Y
H	L	S	N	A	K	E	S	R	A

Page 223

MAP ✓ The Okefenokee Swamp

Page 224

MAP ✓ 8

ANSWER KEY

Page 225

MAP ✓ Boise

Page 226

MAP ✓ South

Across
5. Illinois
7. sixteenth
8. lawyer
9. assassinated
10. seceded

Down
1. Republican
2. Honest Abe
3. Kentucky
4. Civil War
6. Mary Todd

Page 227

MAP ✓ Interstates 70, 74, and 65

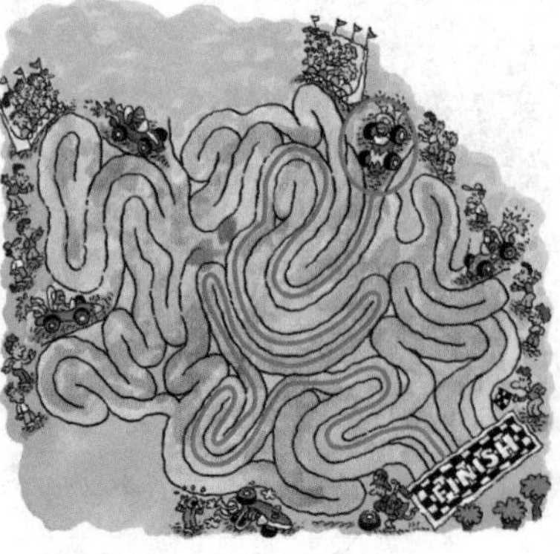

Page 228

MAP ✓ West: Missouri River
East: Mississippi River

Page 229

MAP ✓ Fort Riley

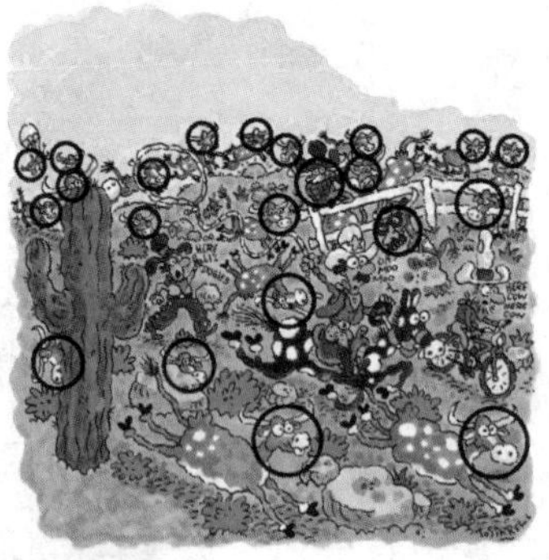

Page 230

MAP ✓ Interstate 64

Man O' War

Page 231

MAP ✓ The Mississippi and Red Rivers

Page 232

MAP ✓ The north

C	P	I	N	E	B	H	D	R	H
E	H	M	A	P	A	F	B	S	K
B	E	E	C	H	S	A	I	P	E
K	L	I	M	A	S	B	R	R	E
O	C	H	E	L	W	E	C	U	B
M	A	P	L	E	O	S	H	C	F
C	B	K	U	K	O	C	P	E	R
L	S	I	P	C	D	W	K	M	U
D	P	U	N	B	I	R	N	H	M

Page 233

MAP ✓ The Chesapeake Bay

Page 234

MAP ✓ 2

► POST OFFICES

► WORLD SERIES

Page 235

MAP ✓ Lakes Michigan, Erie, Huron, and Superior

Across
3. Motor City
5. eagle
6. fruit
8. Lansing
9. two

Down
1. wolverine
2. four
4. cereal
7. tourists

ANSWER KEY

Page 236

MAP ✓ Superior National Forest

Page 237

MAP ✓ Jackson

great water

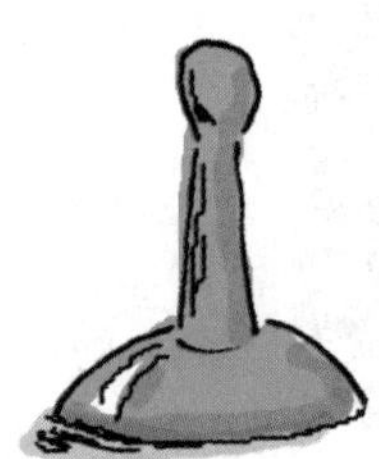

Page 238

MAP ✓ Kansas City

Page 239

MAP ✓ 7

Across
3. mountains
5. Canada
6. fourth
8. Billings
9. silver
10. cattle

Down
1. Glacier
2. gold
3. Sky
5. coal
7. Helena

Page 240

MAP ✓ The east side

C O Y O T E S H U P
C S D U C K S R N I
O L O P C B A C L K
T R A E H U P E H E
T A N R O I S D A S
O B R C K E O A C G
N B A H E S O R K P
W I C G C M P S B H
O T C U H B O U E E
O S O D E I P T R A
D R O O R E P L R S
S N N W R S I Y I A
Y M S P I N E S E N
B A D G E R S O S T
N K Y O S K U N K S

Page 241

MAP ✓ Nellis Air Force Range; The south

1. LAKE MEADE
2. CACTUS
3. SILVER
4. LAS VEGAS
5. HOOVER DAM
6. FORESTS
7. RENO
8. MINES

RAINFALL

Page 242

MAP ✓ The Merrimack River

ALAN B. SHEPARD, JR.

Page 243

MAP ✓ Southwest

C P U M P K I N S H W P A
A O C R A N B E R R I E S
B T S S G S Q U A S H A N
B A E K R P B I L N P C A
A T O M A T O E S B K H P
G O T E P L E T T U C E B
E E S W E E T C O R N S E
S S Q F S N U L W E A N A
B L U E B E R R I E S P N
S W E E T P O T A T O E S

Page 244

MAP ✓ Interstate 25

PUEBLOS

ANSWER KEY

Page 245

MAP ✓ Lakes Erie and Ontario

Possible words include:

blue	state	later	tease	yeast
beast	forest	tray	better	treat

Page 246

MAP ✓ North

Page 247

MAP ✓ 3

THE BADLANDS

Page 248

MAP ✓ Youngstown

Warren G. Harding—P
Neil A. Armstrong—A
William McKinley—P
William Howard Taft—P
Ulysses S. Grant—P
John H. Glenn, Jr.—A
Orville Wright—I
Thomas A. Edison—I
James A. Garfield—P
Rutherford B. Hayes—P
Wilbur Wright—I
Benjamin Harrison—P

Page 249

MAP ✓ The Wichita Mountains

Page 250

MAP ✓ Interstate 5

Page 251

MAP ✓ The Delaware River

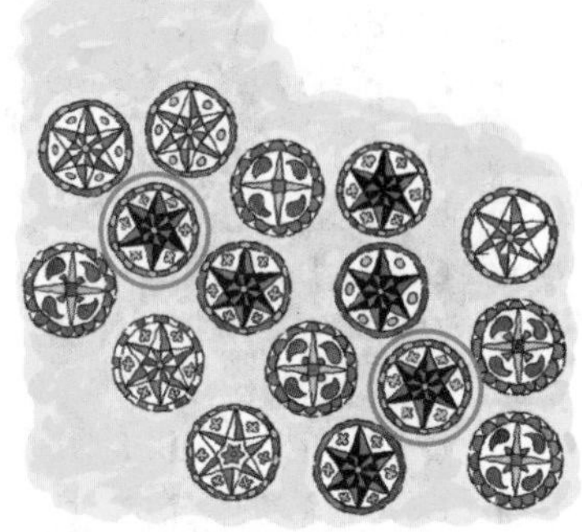

Page 252

MAP ✓ The Scituate Reservoir

Page 253

MAP ✓ A triangle

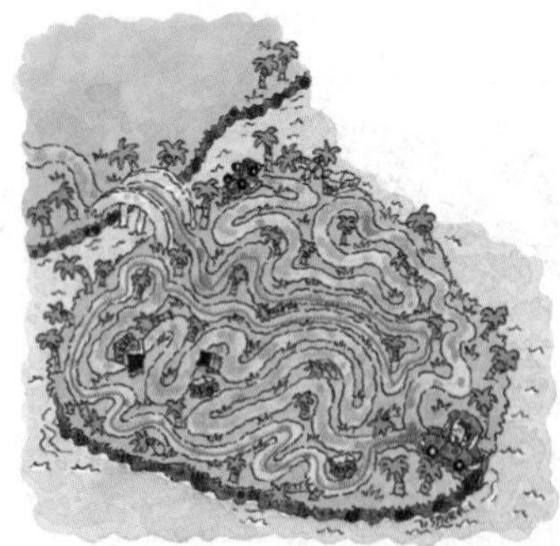

Page 254

MAP ✓ four; Rosebud Indian Reservation

George Washington, Thomas Jefferson, Theodore Roosevelt, and Abraham Lincoln

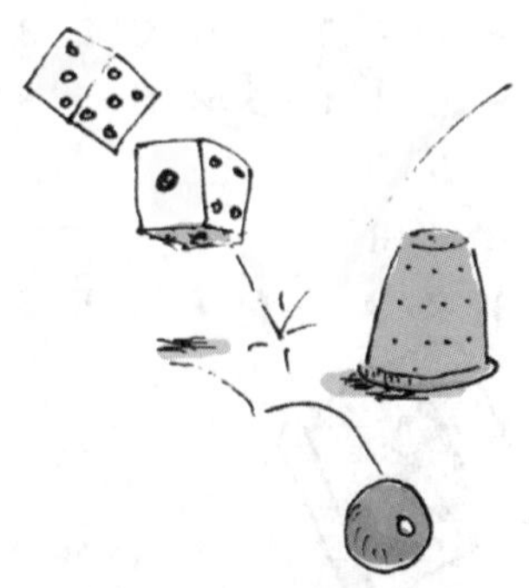

Page 255

MAP ✓ The Great Smoky Mountains and the Cumberland Mountains

V	T	E	L	K	N	A	S
H	E	N	T	E	H	P	O
I	N	O	D	N	O	R	U
S	N	R	S	T	V	E	T
A	E	T	U	U	I	R	H
K	S	H	K	C	R	T	C
C	S	C	E	K	G	E	A
G	E	A	T	Y	I	P	R
O	E	R	N	D	N	U	O
H	H	O	Y	O	I	R	L
N	A	L	R	T	A	T	I
I	T	I	N	G	E	L	N
L	V	N	C	K	I	O	A
A	L	A	B	A	M	A	Y

ANSWER KEY

Page 256

MAP ✓ The Rio Grande

Across	Down
2. oil	1. Alamo
4. one	3. Mexico
5. Austin	7. second
6. cowboys	8. blue
10. Houston	9. cattle

Page 257

MAP ✓ Interstate 80

Page 258

MAP ✓ The west side

Page 259

MAP ✓ Richmond

Page 260

MAP ✓ The Wenatchee National Forest

APPLES; CHERRIES

Page 261

MAP ✓ The Appalachian Mountains

Page 262

MAP ✓ Lake Winnebago

Page 263

MAP ✓ Interstates 80 and 25

OLD FAITHFUL

Page 264

MAP ✓ The Potomac River

Page 268

Page 269

Page 270

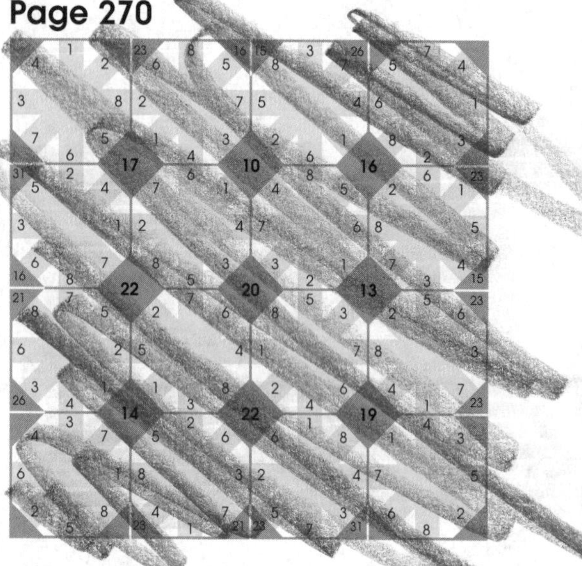

Page 271

Page 272

Page 273

ANSWER KEY

Page 274

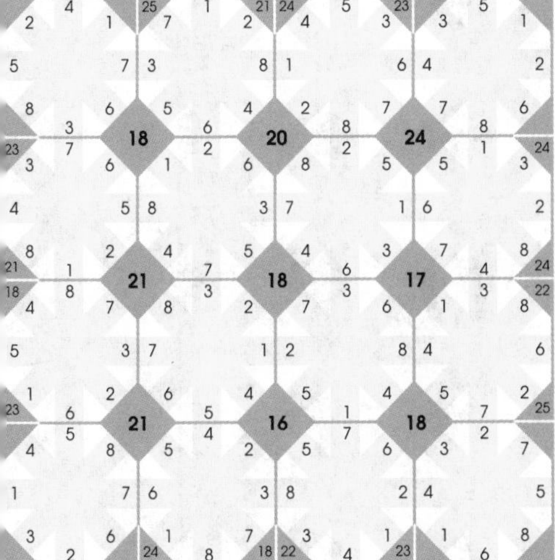

Page 275

Page 276

Page 277

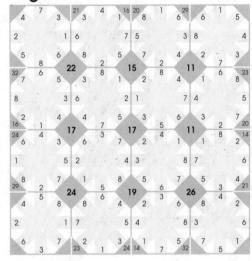

Page 278

Page 279

ANSWER KEY

Page 280

Page 281

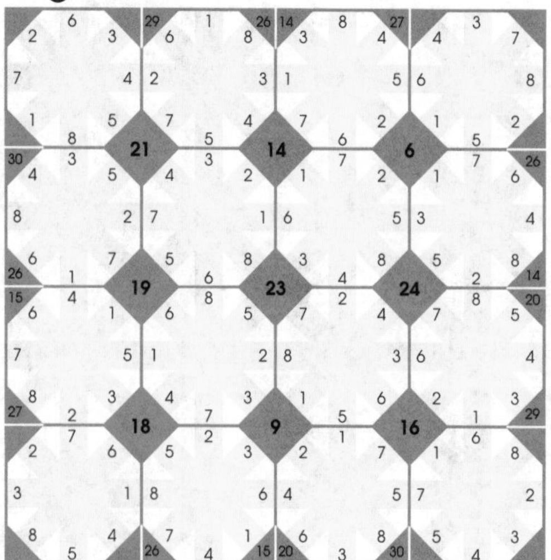

Page 282

Page 283

Page 284

Page 285

Page 286

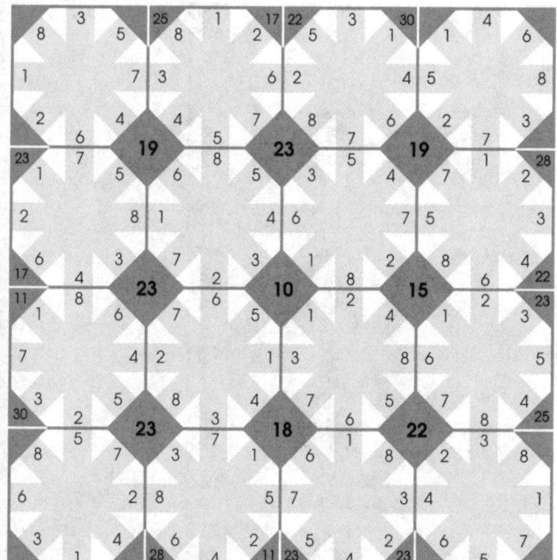

Page 287

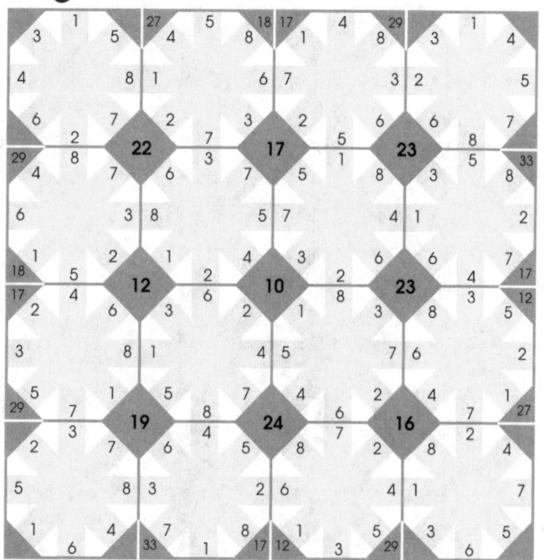

Page 288

Page 289

Page 290

Page 291

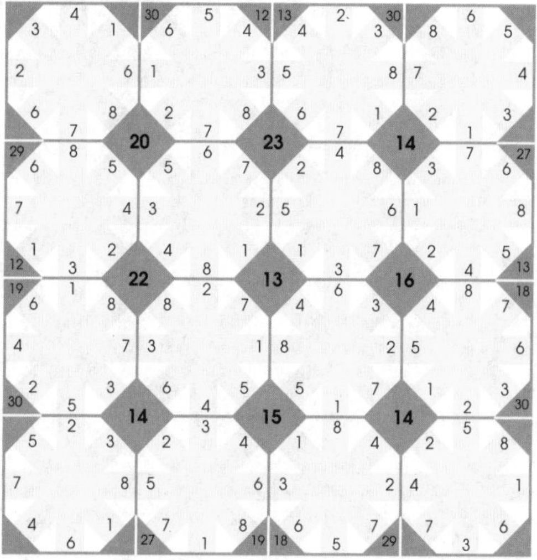

ANSWER KEY

Page 292

Page 293

Page 294

Page 295